THE
JOHANNINE
WORLD

SUNY Series in Religious Studies
Harold Coward, Editor

THE JOHANNINE WORLD,

Reflections on the Theology of the Fourth Gospel and Contemporary Society

DAVID J. HAWKIN

State University
of New York
Press

Published by
State University of New York Press, Albany

© 1996 State University of New York

Production by Susan Geraghty
Marketing by Theresa Abad Swierzowski

Printed in the United States of America

For information, address State University of New York
Press, State University Plaza, Albany, N.Y., 12246

Library of Congress Cataloging-in-Publication Data

Hawkin, David J.
    The Johannine world : reflections on the theology of the Fourth
Gospel and contemporary society / by David J. Hawkin.
        p.   cm. — (SUNY series in religious studies)
    Includes bibliographical references and index.
    ISBN 0-7914-3065-0 (alk. paper). — ISBN 0-7914-3066-9 (pbk. : alk
paper)
    1. Bible. N.T. John—Theology. 2. Church and the world-
-Biblical teaching. I. Title. II. Series.
    BS2615.5.H38 1996
    226.5'06—dc20   95-46390
                                                                 CIP

10 9 8 7 6 5 4 3 2 1

To Kathleen Clarkson and Katharine Temple
amicae in perpetuum

CONTENTS

ACKNOWLEDGEMENTS

I am grateful to the editors of *Laval Théologique et Philosophique, The Evangelical Quarterly*, and *The Epworth Review* for permission to use material I have already published in their journals. Material from "The Function of the Beloved Disciple Motif" and "Johannine Theology and the Johannine Redaction," *Laval Théologique et Philosophique* 33 (1977), pp. 135–150 and 36 (1988), pp. 89–98, appears in chapter two. Material from "Orthodoxy and Heresy in John 10:1–27 and 15:1–17," *The Evangelical Quarterly* 47 (1975), pp. 208–213 also appears in chapter two. Extracts from chapter four appear in *The Epworth Review* 21 (1994), pp. 85–92.

Some of the material in chapter three was previously published in *Christ and Modernity: Christian Self-Understanding in a Technological Age* (Canadian Corporation for the Study of Religion and Wilfrid Laurier University Press, 1985), pp. 85–93. I am grateful to the Canadian Corporation for the Study of Religion and Wilfrid Laurier University Press for permission to use this material.

Material from chapter two has appeared in a course manual for Religious Studies 3251, which was prepared for the School of General and Continuing Studies at Memorial University of Newfoundland.

Unless otherwise stated, all English quotations of the Bible are from the Revised Standard Version.

ABBREVIATIONS

AB	The Anchor Bible
ATR	Anglican Theological Review
Bib	Biblica
Bib Theol	Biblical Theology
Bib TheolBull	Biblical Theology Bulletin
BJRL	Bulletin of the John Rylands Library (Manchester)
BZ	Biblische Zeitschrift
CBQ	Catholic Biblical Quaterly
CH	Corpus Hermeticum
CUP	Cambridge University Press
ET	English Translation
ExT	Expository Times
EvTh	Evangelische Theologie (Munich)
FRLANT	Forschungen zur Religion und Literatur des Alten und Neuen Testaments
HTR	Havard Theological Review
IQS	The Qumran Manual of Discipline
Interp	Interpretation (Richmond, Virginia)
JBL	Journal of Biblical Literature
JSOT	Journal for the Study of the Old Testament
JSP	Journal for the Study of Pseudepigrapha
JTS	Journal of Theological Studies
Lexicon	Walter Bauer, *A Greek-English Lexicon of the New Testament*. Trans. William F. Arndt and F. Wilbur Gingrich, 2nd. ed. 1958. (Chicago and London: University of Chicago Press.)
LondQuartHolR	London Quarterly Holborn Review
NovT	Novum Testamentum
NRT	Nouvelle Revue Théologique
NTA	New Testament Abstracts
NTS	New Testament Studies (Cambridge)

OUP	Oxford University Press
RB	Revue Biblique
RGG	Die Religion in Geschichte und Gegenwart
RivBib	Rivista Biblica (Brescia)
RSV	Revised Standard Version
SBT	Studies in Biblical Theology (London: SCM)
ScJTh	Scottish Journal of Theology
SNT	Supplements to Novum Testamentum (Leiden: Brill)
TWNT	Theologisches Wörterbuch zum Neuen Testament
VT	Vetus Testamentum
ZKT	Zeitschrift für Katholische Theologie
ZNW	Zeitschrift für die Neutestamentliche Wissenschaft
ZTK	Zeitschrift für Theologie und Kirche

INTRODUCTION:
THE JOHANNINE ENIGMA

No New Testament book has proved to be a greater enigma for commentators than the Fourth Gospel. It began its course as a Gospel shrouded in obscurity and mystery, its Gnostic flavor leading many to regard it with suspicion. Irenaeus's emphasis on its orthodoxy, and his claim that it was written by none other than John the Apostle, legitimized it within the church at large, where it came to occupy a central position as the "spiritual gospel." And so it remained for many centuries, until more recent scholarship reopened the debate about its origins and its unique theology. It has now come to be seen as inadequate to claim that the "spiritual" nature of the Fourth Gospel explains the differences between it and the synoptics—or, indeed, between it and the rest of the New Testament. Many have, in fact, come to see the Fourth Gospel as sectarian in origin and as having a dissonant theology. For some who believe in mainstream Christian theology, this is very threatening, but for others it is liberating.

This book is an attempt to correct, or at least to modify, some of the recent trends in modern Johannine scholarship. In much of the recent discussion the self-understanding of the Johannine community has been either inadequately understood or simply ignored. The common assertion that the Johannine community was sectarian, for example, does not bear up under scrutiny. Rather, a close examination of the Fourth Gospel reveals that the community self-consciously defined itself as within the broad stream of the Christian tradition. This is not to say that the theology of the Johannine community as found in the Fourth Gospel is not unique. It is certainly unique. Within its pages the Fourth Gospel has a radical critique of ideology quite unlike anything else in the New Testament. The enigma of the Fourth Gospel lies not in its alleged sectarian nature, nor in its supposed Gnostic universe of discourse. On the one hand such themes and motifs as "truth," "paraclete," and "beloved disciple" are orchestrated to secure acceptance within the church at large for the Gospel's unique and radical theology, while on the other hand, by its sustained theology of revelation, it offers an unrelenting critique of all ideology. Thus the Fourth Gospel argues for its own acceptance within the church at large while rejecting the values of the world at large.

The argument of the following pages is cumulative. It begins with a discussion of the general context for understanding the Johannine enigma. This involves a discussion of the nature of early Christianity as well as an examination of some of the political interpretations of Christianity such as those found in liberation theology. The main body of the book is in chapter two, which focuses specifically on the text of the Fourth Gospel and some of its motifs and thematic complexes. We especially focus on the motif of the Beloved Disciple, which we argue is quite central to under-standing the Fourth Gospel's argument for acceptance within the church at large. We then move to a discussion of the modern world. The argument is that before we can understand the rele-vance of the Fourth Gospel for us today, we need to appreciate the nature of the world in which we live. Chapter three discusses the nature of the modern world and the predominant ideology that underlies it. Once we see clearly the nature of this ideology we will see that it is quite inimical to the Johannine world of dis-course. The argument thus has an interdisciplinary scope. It encom-passes both the fields of biblical studies and modern political and philosophical thought and seeks to relate the two. The conclusion attempts to achieve this by bringing together the two main foci of the book: the argument the Fourth Gospel makes for its own acceptance within the church at large and its rejection of the ide-ology of the world at large. *Pro christo et ecclesia. Contra mundum et fautores.*

CHAPTER 1

Understanding the Context of the Johannine Enigma

1. THE STUDY OF EARLY CHRISTIANITY

To understand the full dimensions of the Johannine enigma we must set our inquiry within the larger context of the study of early Christianity. By doing so we will see that the questions raised by the study of early Christianity are intricately related to the questions raised by the study of the Johannine enigma. We therefore begin with an examination of the nature of early Christianity. What was early Christianity like? What did the early Christians believe? How do we know what they believed? What particular difficulties does the inquirer encounter when asking questions about early Christianity?

A close examination reveals that there is considerable disagreement relating to these questions, many of which are grounded in different suppositions about the method and scope of historical inquiry. Such disagreements—and their significance—are well illustrated in the debate over orthodoxy and heresy in earliest Christianity. In this discussion the Fourth Gospel has come to occupy a central place.

In the history of Christian thought, "orthodoxy" is conceived of as right belief, belief that corresponds to and is grounded in Divine Revelation. It thus is seen in contrast to "heresy," i.e., false or defective belief. In this conception orthodoxy and heresy constitute a binomial; moreover, each is used to define the other. Nevertheless, orthodoxy logically precedes heresy, for one cannot have heretical belief without a norm against which to judge it defective or false. As such, orthodoxy usually reaches formal definition with the appearance of heresy.

This point has relevance to the premises of what is called the Eusebian view of history, for, according to this position, orthodoxy historically predates heresy. This Eusebian or "classical" view saw the pattern of early Christian development as unbelief, right belief, and deviations into wrong belief. That is to say, unbelievers are first converted into orthodox Christian believers, and only later are there deviations from the norm with the rise of heresies. The pure Christian doctrine was revealed by Christ to his apostles, who were commissioned to take this unadulterated gospel to the portions of the world allotted to them. It was not until the apostles had died that the Church experienced its first heresy.

The Thesis of Walter Bauer

It is this interpretation of early Christianity's growth that Walter Bauer challenged in his book *Rechtgläubigkeit und Ketzerei im ältesten Christentum*, translated into English as *Orthodoxy and Heresy in Earliest Christianity*.[1] After being neglected for many years, this book became the focal point of an important debate. The discussion which so belatedly ensued in the wake of Bauer's work focused attention on the problem of orthodoxy and heresy not only in early Christianity, but by implication in modern theology.

Bauer's view was sponsored by Bultmann and accepted by many Bultmannians, including Bultmann's most famous student, Ernst Käsemann. Käsemann wrote an article in which he asked: "Does the New Testament canon establish the unity of the Church?" His answer showed Bauer's influence—the New Testament canon rather established the "plurality of confessions."[2]

Bauer's pioneering study is important because of the crucial issues it raises. He has given renewed impetus to viewing Christian origins from the standpoint of diversity. Specifically, Bauer's work raises the following problems: Can the terms "orthodoxy" and "heresy" be applied correctly to earliest Christianity? Is "orthodoxy" to be seen as no more than that which gained acceptance by the church at large? Does Bauer's work contradict the claim of the Church to be in direct historical continuity with the apostles? Again, Bauer uses the terms "orthodoxy" and "heresy" without reference to the claims of the "orthodox" and "heretical" parties themselves; that is, he does not judge the claims or condemnations of either party. Eusebius used the terms "orthodoxy" and "heresy" with the claim that the assertions of the "orthodox" are true and those of the "heretics" false. Is there an alternative way of using these terms?

Such churchmen as Eusebius viewed history providentially. They believed that the view that won out is true because of the work of the Holy Spirit. Bauer insisted on a "scientific" approach to history. Are these two views mutually exclusive? Has the orthodoxy/heresy debate reached an impasse at this point?

Now that we have discussed some of the questions raised by Bauer's work, we can examine in some detail his thesis.

In the introduction to the book, Bauer gives a programmatic sketch of intention, where he outlines his approach, in the spirit of the dictum *audiatur et altera pars* (Let the other side be heard). Hence, in his discussion of orthodoxy and heresy, he consciously avoids allowing his judgement to be swayed by one party:

> That party which perhaps as much through favourable circumstances as by its own merit eventually was thrust into the foreground, and which possibly has at its disposal today the more powerful, and thus the more prevalent voice, only because the chorus of the others has been muted.[3]

Bauer asserts that orthodoxy and heresy will be decided not by the church, but, ultimately, by history.[4]

The ecclesiastical position has four main suppositions: First, Jesus "revealed the pure doctrine to his apostles, partly before his death, and partly in the forty days before his ascension."[5] Second, after Jesus' death the apostles took the unadulterated gospel to the portions of the world allotted to them. Third, after the death of the apostles false doctrine crept in at the instigation of Satan. The pattern of development in earliest Christianity is thus envisaged as running unbelief, right belief, deviations into wrong belief. Bauer is disconcerted by the fact that there is scarcely "the faintest notion anywhere that unbelief might be changed directly into what the church calls false belief."[6] Fourth, there is the supposition that right belief is invincible.

It is these suppositions that Bauer intends to examine. As a historian he refuses to employ the correlatives "true" and "untrue," "good" and "bad." He is not easily convinced of the moral inferiority usually attributed to the heretics, nor does he believe it to be self-evident that heresies are a deviation from the genuine.

Having thus announced his intention, Bauer applies himself to his task. He begins with an examination of the region of Edessa in the post-apostolic age. Was there in the second century in Mesopotamia a large body of ecclesiastically organized Christians? After a lengthy and somewhat intricate discussion of the evidence, Bauer concludes that this is not the case. The orthodox arrive so late on the scene that they cannot even claim for themselves the title of Christians, for such a designation does not distinguish them from the Marcionites.

Next Bauer turns his attention to Egypt. He notes the almost total silence with regard to Christianity in Egypt and Alexandria in the first two centuries. This makes him very suspicious, for Christianity obviously came to Egypt very early. Why do we know so little of Christian origins in that country? Because the situation there was somewhat of an embarrassment for later orthodoxy—"even into the third century, no separation between orthodoxy and heresy was accomplished in Egypt and the two types of Christianity were not yet clearly differentiated from each other."[7]

As for Ignatius of Antioch, he is less concerned with depicting the actual situation than with portraying an ideal. Although it is true that the majority of Christians in the churches of Asia Minor at Ephesus, Magnesia, Tralles, and Philadelphia held to a form of Christianity that Ignatius could condone, we must beware of extending this judgment to cover the whole of Asia Minor, or merely only its western part. For "the surviving clues concerning Antioch, Philippi, and Polycarp's Smyrna should at least urge us to be cautious, if not frighten us away from such a generalization."[8]

Ignatius knows of "difficulties" in Ephesus. Moreover, we can infer from I Timothy—with its opposition to a Jewish type of gnosticism—that there existed

> a gnostic Jewish Christianity large and powerful enough to evoke opposition, so that one could not simply classify the Jewish Christianity of this region as being on the side of ecclesiastical orthodoxy without further examination. Thus Jewish Christianity would be divided, just as gentile Christianity was divided, into orthodox and heretical types.[9]

For Bauer, that which triumphs as "orthodox" is the Christianity of Rome. Why did Roman Christianity come to dominate the whole of Christendom? Bauer finds a number of reasons, not the least of which is the affluence of the Roman church:

> If we ask to what degree donations of money should be of importance in the warfare of the spirits, our imagination would have no difficulty in suggesting all kinds of ways. . . . The encomium of Eusebius teaches us that Rome viewed it as an altogether legitimate practice in religious controversies to tip the scales with golden weights.[10]

Apart from material advantage, the Roman church was endowed with "a shrewdness, energy and communal unity" engendered by the experiences of persecution. The Roman church was essentially unanimous in the faith and in the standards of Christian living; after it had rid itself of the Marcionites it was never endangered by serious heresy. By the end of the second century, being meticulously organized and methodically governed by the monarchical bishop, the Roman church was ready to flex its muscles and extend its power.

Not unexpectedly, Bauer is somewhat cynical about the Roman church's claim of direct continuity to Peter. He finds specific ecclesiastical requirement more operative here than historical memory. Bauer notes that although Peter was linked originally with Paul at Rome, he is later singled out and elevated above the apostle to the gentiles because he alone provides the close tie to Jesus which guarantees the purity of church teaching.[11]

In his treatment of the use of literature in the conflict Bauer focuses on the work of Eusebius. (After all, it is Eusebius who wished to show that the general rejection of false belief could be found in the very earliest Christian literature.) Eusebius does not fare well under Bauer's scrutiny. He is simply inaccurate in depicting an abundance of orthodox literature extant in the first centuries.

Bauer adduces evidence of much chicanery in the use of literature. Opponents' views were distorted, their characters maligned, and their documents tampered with and falsified. Once the orthodox party gained the upper hand, they suppressed (where possible) all heretical literature. Hence we cannot hope to gain a true picture of the circumstances prevalent in the first few centuries by considering its literature at face value.

Bauer sums up his position thus:

> The form of Christian belief and life which was successful was
> that supported by the strongest organization—that form which
> was the most uniform and best suited for mass consumption—in
> spite of the fact that, in my judgement, for a long time after the
> close of the post-apostolic age the sum total of consciously ortho-
> dox and anti-heretical Christians was numerically inferior to
> that of the "heretics."[12]

Furthermore:

> It appears no less self-evident that the Roman government finally
> came to recognize that the Christianity ecclesiastically organized
> from Rome was flesh of its flesh, came to unite with it, and
> thereby actually enabled it to achieve ultimate victory over unbe-
> lievers and heretics.[13]

With respect to the New Testament itself, the conclusions of
Bauer are no less far-reaching. The Gospel of John began its
course as a heretical Gospel.[14] As for Paul, he scarcely knew a
heretic, and he had "calm confidence" that the Christian religion
would eliminate from itself what was alien to it. At this juncture,
Bauer deftly inverts the argument and roundly declares that Paul
is the only heresiarch known in apostolic times. The Judaizers,
who were the main critics of Paul, were to be judged more harshly
by history:

> The arrow quickly flew back at the archer. Because of their
> inability to relate to a development that took place on hellenized
> gentile soil, the Judaists soon became a heresy, rejected with con-
> viction by the gentile Christians. . . . Thus the Judaists became an
> instructive example of how even one who preserves the old posi-
> tion can become a "heretic" if the development moves suffi-
> ciently far beyond him.[15]

Bauer concludes his book thus:

> It is indeed a curious quirk of history that western Rome was des-
> tined to begin to exert the determined influence upon a religion
> which had its cradle in the Orient, so as to give it that form in
> which it was to achieve world-wide recognition. But as an other-
> worldly religion that despises and inflexibly orders life in accord
> with a superhuman standard that has descended from heaven, or
> as a complicated mystery cult for religious and intellectual con-

noisseurs, or as a tide of fanatical enthusiasm that swells today and ebbs tomorrow, Christianity never could have achieved such a recognition.[16]

To summarize. First, Bauer maintained that one should not retroject the categories of orthodoxy and heresy into a description of earliest Christianity. Second, those later called heretics were the first Christians in many areas. Third, what we now term orthodox was in fact imposed by the Roman Church.

The Reply of H. E. W. Turner

It was the Anglican scholar H. E. W. Turner who made the first detailed response to Bauer in his book, *The Pattern of Christian Truth: A Study in the Relations between Orthodoxy and Heresy in the Early Church*.[17] Turner first describes the classical theory of orthodoxy and heresy. Before true doctrine there is no heresy. Such a rigid view, however, is criticized by the heretics themselves. Marcion, far from looking on himself as an innovator, called himself a conservative. The Gnostic tradition, though secret, was every bit as genuine to its participants as the official orthodoxy. Meanwhile, both parties, heretic and orthodox, defended their respective positions and their "Christian" lineage with relevant scriptural references.[18]

All things considered, says Turner, the classical view of orthodoxy is too static to fit the realities and is therefore deservedly challenged. To describe heresy as a deviation from a fixed norm is simply inadequate. Similarly, it is wrong to reduce the Apostolic Fathers to a doctrinal common denominator or to use a single theological rubric to interpret the New Testament.

Having questioned the classical view of orthodoxy, Turner looks briefly at three modern views, those of R. Bultmann, A. Harnack, and M. Werner. These, too, question the notion of a fixed norm, and point out the diversity and fluidity of early Christian thought. Furthermore, they suggest that the "orthodoxy" that did win out was simply not at one with earliest Christianity.

Neither of the extreme positions on the orthodoxy/heresy question is to Turner's liking. He finds the classical view of a fixed and static norm too simple a reading of a rather more complex theological development. But at the same time he considers the moderns' argument, which stresses diversity, to be too open-ended and believes that it implies too high a degree of flexibility. Thus, he proposes to mediate between these extremes:

> The development of Christian theology as a whole (and not merely in the Patristic period) may be perhaps better interpreted as the interaction of fixed and flexible elements, both of which are equally necessary for the determination of Christian truth in the setting of a particular age.[19]

The key here is to discern what those fixed elements are. To begin, argues Turner, there are the tradition's "religious facts themselves, without which there would be no grounds for its existence."[20] Here we quote Turner at length, as this point seems to have been misunderstood by some later writers:

> Belief in God as a Sovereign Father of a creation which is his handiwork forms an essential part of the basic realities of the Christian Church. His being may at times be described in terms more appropriate to the static and transcendent Absolute of Greek metaphysics, His Fatherhood too closely approximated to mere causation, His Providence defined in terms drawn from the Hellenic concept of Pronoia. The religious fact still underlies the changing categories under which it is expressed. The fact of Christ as the Historical Redeemer serves to differentiate even the most metaphysical of Christian thinkers from the Greek "flight from history." The Christian estimate of history was already a stone of stumbling to Celsus, and here Origen, despite his fundamental sympathy with much of the Greek spirit and the priority which his theory of exegesis was to assign to the mystical over the historical, remains inflexible. If there was a tradition in Christology which saw the Divine Logos in the Incarnate Lord and scarcely had eyes for anything else, the Church as a whole never lost her grip upon the concept of the incarnation as an act of Divine Irruption into human history.[21]

This is crucial: "The Church's grasp on the religious facts was prior to any attempt to work them into a coherent whole."[22] *Lex orandi* is what Turner calls the idea of "the relatively full and fixed experimental grasp of what was involved in being a Christian."[23] For example, centuries before the fixing of the Nicene orthodoxy, Christians lived a faith strongly influenced by the concept of the Trinity.

Other fixed elements in the Christian tradition involved the Creed, Biblical Revelation, and the Rule of Faith. For example, from the New Testament *kerygma* through the *credenda* summaries to the early creeds proper there is a clear line of development. Although the creeds are the start of a new phase, this phase, too, is the extension "of a process which takes its origins from the formalized oral tradition of the Apostolic Church itself."[24]

One of the key "differences in Christian idiom," in Turner's view, is contained in the tradition's flexible elements. While many analysts distinguish sharply between the metaphysical and eschatological interpretations of Christianity, he argues that the "Christian deposit of faith is not wedded irrevocably to either idiom":

> The selection of a distinctive theological idiom, whether it be eschatology, ontology, or even in more recent times existentialism, illustrates one possible element of flexibility in Christian thinking.[25]

Turner also sees the individual styles and personalities of the various theologians as a source of Christian doctrinal flexibility.

The essence of Turner's argument is that Bauer draws too sharp a line between orthodoxy and heresy. The developments he describes are better accounted for in terms of a "penumbra" or merging area between these two. Furthermore, his concept of orthodoxy is too narrow, ignoring much of its variety and depth. Orthodoxy, says Turner, "resembles not so much a stream as a sea, not a single melodic theme but a rich and varied harmony, not a single closed system but a rich manifold of thought and life."[26]

The following passage sums up Turner's dissatisfaction with Bauer's position:

> His fatal weakness appears to be a persistent tendency to oversimplify problems, combined with the ruthless treatment of such evidence as fails to support his case. It is very doubtful whether all sources of trouble in the early Church can be reduced to a set of variations on a single theme. Nor is it likely that orthodoxy itself evolved in a uniform pattern, though at different speeds in the main centres of the universal Church. The formula "splinter movement, external inspiration or assistance, domination of the whole Church by its orthodox elements, tributes of gratitude to

those who assisted in its development" represents too neat a generalization to fit the facts. History seldom unfolds itself in so
orderly a fashion.[27]

In his wider discussion of the topic, Turner discusses how the
major heresies depart from or challenge the Christian norm. In
Turner's view, gnosticism, a product of outside (non-Christian)
elements, dilutes it;[28] Marcionism cuts several important elements
off the core tradition;[29] Montanism distorts it;[30] and Arianism is an
empty version of Christian theology.[31] Turner dismisses as mere
"archaisms" those heresies that cling only to the past with no
regard for meaningful dialogue with the present.

On the positive side, Turner's aim is to have us see that heresy
is less a questioning of the total tradition than it is a concern that
major elements within the tradition be properly interrelated. Christian common sense intuitively rejects heresy.[32] But the outcome of
this kind of development should be measured not only by the
coherence principle, "the logical articulation of the Christian faith
into a systematic whole," but also "by the further principle of correspondence with the Biblical facts themselves."[33]

Although debate over the issue of orthodoxy and heresy in
early Christianity continues, Bauer and Turner remain central to
the discussion. The trend of the subsequent debate has been to
retroject the orthodoxy/heresy question into the New Testament.
The participants in this venture have tended to take their point of
departure from Bauer rather than from Turner. We will now turn to
a discussion of why the differences in approach between Bauer
and Turner are so significant for the study of early Christianity
and the New Testament.

Understanding Early Christianity

Bauer's approach to the study of early Christianity is illustrative of the
old adage, "The question determines the answer." Bauer's questions—
being reductionist and limited—do not enable him to come up with
an understanding of early Christianity which does justice to its complexity and mystery. H. E. W. Turner, on the other hand, asks questions that are more insightful and fruitful. We will briefly examine
some of the major issues at stake in the discussion about orthodoxy
and heresy and we will determine the fruitfulness of Turner's insights.

The Semantic Problem   It is tempting, when one reads Bauer, to think of the whole problem of orthodoxy and heresy as merely semantic. But is it really a question of semantics? Is it simply a question of how one defines orthodoxy and heresy?

Certainly this is one of the confusing issues underlying the discussion: How should orthodoxy and heresy be defined? Bauer said that in using these terms he was referring to what one "customarily and usually understands them to mean." But in fact, as the ensuing debate showed quite clearly, there is no "customary and usual understanding" of the terms. Moreover, Bauer himself averred that he would not use "dogmatically conditioned" definitions of orthodoxy (derived from church councils) because they enshrine value judgements, and he believed value judgements were not the business of the historian. Most historians, however, would disagree with Bauer here. History is not "value free," if what we mean by that phrase is that the historian refrains from making value judgements. Historical inquiry aims at settling matters of fact, but this cannot possibly exclude value judgements from the matters of fact to be settled. History does not say who was orthodox and who was heretical. It does, however, have something to say about who *claimed* to be orthodox and who charged whom with heresy. Such claims are part and parcel of the historian's data. Value judgements do have a role in the work of the historian. They should not, of course, substitute for evidence. They guide the choice of historical questions without presuming to answer them. As Bernard Lonergan puts it:

> History is not value-free in the sense that the historian refrains from value-judgements. . . . The historian ascertains matters of fact, not by ignoring data, by failing to understand, by omitting judgements of value, but by doing all of these for the purpose of settling matters of fact.[34]

Any definition of orthodoxy and heresy must therefore take account of the thinking of the early Christians themselves, for the early Christian's world of meaning belongs indispensably to the data of which the historian must take account. Definitions of orthodoxy and heresy should, moreover, be both specific enough to meet real issues and flexible enough to apply to different times and places.

This is where Bauer fails as a historian. He does not take development into account. He fails to see that Christianity is an ongoing process. By later standards some of the beliefs of early Christianity were "heretical" but they were not seen to be so at the time. What was believed matters as much as *when* it was believed.

H. E. W. Turner's "Fixed" and "Flexible" Elements   Turner approaches the study of early Christianity in a different way. He sees that the self-understanding of early Christianity reveals an interaction between what he calls "fixed" and "flexible" elements. Only by grasping this point does the unity *and* diversity of early Christianity become intelligible. Both Eusebius and Bauer are mistaken in their view of early Christianity. Christianity was not uniform and monolithic at the beginning, as Eusebius claimed; but neither was it completely variegated and diverse, as Bauer claimed.

This debate about Christian origins is not merely some abstruse and solely academic argument—it has theological implications. Many see Christianity as a syncretistic phenomenon. But Turner argues that there is a unity to Christianity. A first-century Christian in Alexandria may not have had the same beliefs as a fifth-century Christian in Rome. They lived in different eras, spoke different languages, and thought differently. But despite differences in style, idiom, and historical context, Turner would argue that their Christian faith has a basic structural similarity in subject matter and content. Turner, in other words, argues for a dynamic unity to Christianity.

The *Lex Orandi* and Development   Turner, it will be recalled, gave the name *lex orandi* to the "relatively full and fixed experimental grasp of what was involved in being a Christian."[35] What is meant by this requires more elucidation, for it is quite central to the idea of development in early Christianity.

Religion precedes theology, explains Ninian Smart in *Philosophers and Religious Truth*: "The apprehension in experience of the Holy is the primary datum in religion, and theological ideas are secondary to it."[36] That is to say, people live a faith before they try to conceptualize it; for example, trinitarian religion preceded trinitarian theology. The triune baptismal formula of Matthew 28:19 is universally cited in the practice of the early Church. Even the Arians accepted the text. The doctrine of the trinity was primarily an extension and exploration into the baptismal formula. That is to say, the early Christians began with the practice of baptism, during which they uttered the phrase "In the name of the Father, and of the Son, and of the Holy Spirit," and only later did they begin to think through the full implications of what they were saying. It was in pondering these implications that the early Christians came up with the doctrine of the trinity. They did not begin with the doctrine; they began with the practice (the *lex orandi*).

Lex orandi, then, covers the instinctively adopted devotional and liturgical attitude within the early Church. It indicates that there is a close connection between spirituality and theology. The Russian Orthodox Church uses the term *sobornost* ("together-ness") to describe this reality—the idea that devotion and worship form the bedrock on which theological speculation is built.

For missionary and apologetic reasons the early Church found it necessary to articulate the faith in a reasoned and structured way. The degree and precision of such articulation was dictated by historical circumstances. The Church was subject not only to attack from without, but also to disruption and differences within. Celsus treats Gnostics as Christians, and sixty years later we find Origen vigorously refuting this. Orthodoxy had evidently become much more selective in that sixty-year span. There is nothing odd about this; it merely indicates that certain tendencies within Christianity were seen as gradually leading to positions that were irreconcilable with the basis of the faith. Historically it is difficult to see how it could happen otherwise. It is wrong to think that the Church had a blueprint from the beginning which was the touchstone of correct Christian belief. Heresy was not a known in the sense of trans-gressing a fixed theological law.

In the beginning the Church was a collection of people bound together by the common belief that Jesus was the Christ, the bringer of salvation. The exact implications of such belief had to be worked out in the course of time as the need arose. The history of the early Church is thus a history of doctrinal explorations; it was not immediately obvious that certain avenues were culs-de-sac. Yet although the journey down a certain avenue may have begun, once the life and reflection of the Church revealed that route to be a dead end, it was abandoned and others were explored. Those who continued along that road eventually reached the point of no return, and the Church had to disown them as it carried its search for truth down other avenues.

The first major problem that the Church faced in erecting its "intellectual scaffolding" around the faith was the reconciliation of its trinitarian religion (given in the *lex orandi*) with the monotheism of the faith from which it had sprung (Judaism). This occupied the mind of the Church until the Council of Nicea (A.D. 325). The relation of the Father to the Son was the first item of reflection, as this was so central in preaching and teaching. Once this was settled the precise nature and position of the Holy Spirit within the Godhead was formulated—as is evidenced by the quite rapid development of the doctrine of the Holy Spirit in the period A.D. 327–381.

The formulation of Christian doctrine was the result of the interplay of various ways of thinking within the Church. The characteristics of the Church militated against extremism. The various great traditions of the Church tended mutually to correct each other. The Western tradition, with its love of the concrete and the balanced, was a good foil for the Eastern tradition, with its love of the mystical and speculative. Turner's notion that the development of early Christianity is best seen as an interaction between fixed and flexible elements accords with this picture. It is of course wrong to envisage this development as having fixed and narrow limits. As Turner puts it:

> The customary limitations imposed by human sin, human error, and human blindness can be observed even here. Christian theology is not exempt from the law of oscillation which applies to all branches of human thought. Premature syntheses required subsequent modification and the dangers of distortion and accretion were not slow in making their presence felt.[37]

Diverse usages reflect diverse realities. There really are evolutions and devolutions, and not every sequence is a development. If the progression of orthodoxy did not proceed along the "straight and narrow" in quite the way envisaged by the classical approach, neither is it true to say that it often wandered off the road completely. To be sure, the development of early Christian doctrine is characterized by oscillations, but the quest for balance was always there, with the givenness of the New Testament data as the fulcrum. The development of Christian thought begins with the faith data; from this givenness certain inferences are drawn as historical circumstances dictate. These inferences at a later stage, after they have been explored and tested, become the postulates for theologizing.

We thus see how development helps us to understand better the ongoing process of Christian history. We also see how the notion of *lex orandi* helps us to understand more clearly the direction of this development. *Lex orandi* illustrates how early Christian development was governed by experience, the experience of the early Christians themselves. Moreover, the development is dynamic—it is, in Turner's words, the interaction between fixed and flexible elements. It is not confined within fixed and narrow limits, but neither is it so open-ended as to be capricious. Christianity is not a syncretism, it has a dynamic unity. In this sense Christian development can be said to be mysterious, as Ben Meyer observes:

> Development, unlike organic growth, unlike logical deduction, takes place in the sphere of spirit, subjectivity, freedom, meaning and history. It is unpredictable. Its authenticity is not discerned equally by all, nor all at once. It is taken in piecemeal, by a learning process, and is satisfactorily grasped after the fact.[38]

Bauer and Turner, then, represent quite different perspectives on early Christianity. At the deepest level they take different approaches not just to the historical task, but in perceiving Christianity itself. Is it meaningful to speak of *Das Wesen des Christentums*? Does Christianity have an "essence" or a unique identity? Or is it a syncretism, an ongoing multiplicity of interpretations with family resemblances? This is a central issue. Before considering this further, however, we must focus more clearly on the questions that arise from such a discussion within the context of politics, community, and faith.

2. POLITICS, COMMUNITY, AND FAITH

Edward Norman and the Politicization of Christianity

It is now several years since Edward Norman gave his Reith Lectures, *Christianity and the World Order*. In these lectures, Norman attacked liberation theology and indeed, all forms of "political Christianity." Christianity, he said, was concerned with "the relation of the soul to eternity."[39] It did not have, and should not have, any political agenda. Reaction to Norman was swift. This new "Norman Wisdom" was attacked,[40] sometimes vehemently, by those who thought that turning Christianity into a privatized and spiritualized phenomenon was to misunderstand its true nature and meaning. For his part, Norman seemed rather to enjoy the notoriety that his views brought him. But he was nevertheless quite serious in his insistence that Christianity should not be politicized. In making this asseveration, he claimed to be standing squarely within the Christian tradition. But if he claimed that his case was supported by a historical examination of Christianity, so did his opponents. The fact that both Norman and his opponents appealed to Christian history and tradition shows the complexity and ambiguity that can arise in discussions about Christianity and politics. Throughout the history of the Christian tradition there have been those who have emphasized that Christianity is unworldly and spiritual, and there have been others who have stressed its radical, worldly nature.

In the New Testament itself there is the famous passage in Romans 13 where Paul urges his readers to be subject to the ruling authorities who were "ordained by God" (Rom 13:2). The monastic movements of the second and third centuries encouraged Christians to withdraw from the world. Augustine in the fourth century distinguished between the "City of God" and the "City of Man."[41] Augustine's differentiation was to dominate Christian thought for many centuries, but there still remained those who thought that the establishment of the Kingdom of God on earth was the primary goal of the Christian life. Radical teachers arose periodically, urging Christians to bring about this objective by rejecting the present political order. Perhaps the most radical of them all was Thomas Muentzer, who was so outraged by the contrast between the way the peasants were treated and the way that he, as a Christian, thought they should be treated, that he urged them to use force to overthrow their oppressors. The result was the Peasants War of 1524–25, in which more than 100,000 peasants were killed as the uprising was brutally repressed. It was in reaction to people like Muentzer and their stress on Christian involvement with the world that Luther sharpened Augustine's distinction between this world and the world "above":

There are two kingdoms, one the kingdom of God, the other the kingdom of this world. . . . God's kingdom is a kingdom of grace and mercy . . . but the kingdom of the world is a kingdom of wrath and severity. . . . Now he who would confuse these two . . . would put wrath into God's kingdom and mercy into the world's kingdom, and that is the same as putting the devil in heaven and God in hell.[42]

It is against this background—where we see that the discussion about Christian involvement in the world goes back to the very beginnings of Christianity—that we should examine Norman's attack on liberation theology. Liberation theology as such may be a fairly recent phenomenon dating back to the late 1960s, but the issues on which it focuses and the questions it asks are not new.

The movement began in Latin America where the deplorable conditions in which many people live give an extremely sharp focus to the question of how Christians are to relate to ruling authorities who either tacitly or overtly allow the existence of such squalor. It increasingly became an issue for many Catholic priests who saw firsthand what it means to be poor in a third world country:

Five hundred million persons [are] starving; one billion six hundred million persons whose life expectation is less than sixty years . . . one billion persons living in absolute poverty; one billion five hundred million persons with no access to the most basic medical care; five hundred million with no work or only occasional work and per capita income of less than $150 a year; eight hundred and fourteen million who are illiterate; [and] two billion people with no regular, dependable water supply.[43]

In the face of such appalling squalor and deprivation many have called for "liberation." The English word is a poor translation of the Portuguese "*liberacao*" better rendered "libera(c)tion." The Boff brothers—both priests—have articulated the call for libera(c)tion as a commitment "to the life, cause, and struggle of millions of these debased and marginalized human beings, a commitment to ending this historical-social iniquity."[44] Through the eyes of their faith, Christians view these oppressed as "crucified persons." They hear Jesus crying, "As you did it to the least of these my brethren, you did it to me" (Mt 25:46). Liberation theologians further claim that the only way the poor will be helped is through political change. Therefore they believe the Christian has a duty to be involved in the world and committed to political change. It is important to note that liberation theologians generally do not talk about political reform, which works within (and implictly accepts) present political and institutional structures, but rather speak of something more radical, which emphasizes grass-roots self-help: "The oppressed come together, come to understand their situation through the process of conscientization, discover the causes of their oppression, organize themselves into movements, and act in a coordinated fashion."[45]

In coming together, the oppressed must seek to claim what is rightfully theirs: "better wages, working conditions, health care, education, [and] housing."[46] The ultimate goal is a society in which there is a "better and more just balance among social classes."[47]

Norman attacks liberation theology and movements like it because, he claims, it is a politicization of Christianity. "By politicization of religion is meant the internal transformation of faith itself, so that it comes to be defined in terms of political values—it becomes essentially concerned with social morality rather than with the ethereal qualities of immortality."[48]

This is a fundamental point for Norman—Christianity is not about liberation, nor, indeed, politics at all, but is about "the relation of the soul to eternity."[49] In making such a statement, Norman is betraying his Platonic leanings. Whereas liberation theologians put emphasis on history, and especially upon the historical Jesus, Norman stresses that the kingdom is "not of this world." The two positions provide a useful counterpoise to each other and reflect a fundamental tension in Christianity that is found in its very origins—the tension between the world views of Greek philosophy and Jewish religion. This is something to which we shall return in the conclusion.

Not only is it illuminating to see Norman's attack on liberation in the more general context of the tension between the Judaic and Greek constituents of Christianity, but it is also illuminating to see it in the light of the orthodoxy/heresy debate. Bauer, Turner, and Koester were essentially concerned with whether Christianity had an essence, and if it has, how it should be defined. Koester, it will be recalled, basically saw Christianity as having no essence or substantial identity. Christianity was, rather, an ongoing multiplicity of interpretations. It therefore adapts itself to the indigenous cultures rather like a chameleon adapts itself to its environment; it changes until it is no longer perceived as foreign. Turner, on the other hand, while acknowledging that Christianity had "flexible" elements, argued that there were fixed elements that gave Christianity a distinctive identity. The ongoing quest of Christian theology was to attempt to preserve that identity while at the same time expressing it through the media of various cultures.

Norman never alludes to the orthodoxy/heresy debate and shows no knowledge of it, but he is essentially grappling with the same question. He argues that in the Western world Christianity has become identified with liberal ideals. Liberalism is, as we shall argue later, the all-pervasive ideology of the western world, and the very ideology that enables technology to flourish. Seldom are the ideals of liberalism questioned. But Norman points out that it is just one of the many political ideologies, which come and go. To identify liberalism with Christianity, or as a "distillation of Christian wisdom," is, to say the least, "a short-term view."[50]

The concrete results of the church's holus-bolus swallowing of liberal ideals is that it is almost solely concerned with questions of justice and the political question of how material wealth may be distributed in a just society. Norman has no objection to church discussion or indeed involvement in such matters. What he objects to is the displacement of concern with Christian doctrine and belief by the concern with "the material problems of humanity."[51] Plans for social and political action do not in themselves constitute the central definition of Christianity. Christianity is losing its authenticity or, in the terms of the orthodoxy-heresy debate, its essence: "It is losing sight of its own rootedness in a spiritual tradition; its mind is progressively secularized; its expectations are prompted by worldly changes; and its moral idealism has forfeited transcendence."[52]

Norman finds an irony in the decline of Christianity in the West. It has not, he believes, declined because of attacks by its enemies, but because it has surrendered its unique views of its own spiritual nature. It has given up being a religion and has become (just another) social and political movement.

Norman pauses at this point in his attack to acknowledge that in the third world Christianity has a spiritual basis. He then goes on to claim that this is changing rapidly because of the influence of Western "bourgeois elites." These are the people who are imposing their version of a liberalized Christianity upon the poor of the third world. In short, Norman believes that the third world has been seduced by the first into politicizing its Christianity. But, asserts Norman, when Christians are counselled to love their neighbors, they are not being asked to engineer social change and are certainly not being asked to countenance Marxism. The disguising of Christianity as Marxism in the third world is sadly ironic, for while Christians may embrace Marxism, Marxists only wish to eliminate Christianity and will do so if they ever achieve their end—a communist society.

Norman, then, does not balk at attacking liberation theology as Marxist. Nor does he balk at attacking liberal notions of "human rights." It is common now for Christian theologians to speak as though human rights are part of the very fabric of Christian belief. Not so, says Norman. The very notion of human rights is political, not religious. What are considered human rights change from age to age. They are hardly, therefore, eternal truths. But it is (to use a phrase which Norman does not himself use) "politically correct" to support human rights, and so many theologians have adjusted the "traditional understandings of religious doctrine" to make acceptable political views embody "the spirit of the Gospels."[53] All that such an identification does is produce new heresies and create "massive internal divisions." The liberal doctrine of human rights becomes the standard for judging Christian belief, rather than the creeds.[54]

Norman's whole attack is predicated on the view that in Christianity we have a repository of eternal truths. These eternal truths must not be identified with contemporary cultural or political values. To do so is to fail to see that Christianity has as its central affirmation the view that there is a unique authority originating outside of historical circumstances.[55] It is to identify the "ultimate purposes of God with the shifting values of contemporary society":

> The orthodoxies of thought within western liberalism now rise and decline with remarkable rapidity, dragging the perpetual reinterpretation of the content of Christianity along with them. Today's solemn declaration of the "true" purpose of Christ's teaching is tomorrow's reviled illustration of false "prophecy."[56]

Norman does not say that Christians should not try to promote justice and lessen suffering. Rather, what he is saying is that political ideals as enshrined in, for example, liberalism, should not be identified with the essence of Christianity. Christianity is not about political action, but about the condition of the inward soul of man.[57] It is concerned with the imperfections of human nature, not the "rationalized imperfections of human society."[58] Christ himself was not a social reformer but someone who "directed others to turn away from the preoccupations of human society."[59] The kingdom that Jesus proclaimed was not of this world but eternal and otherworldly. Jesus would not have condoned a movement which in his name endorsed "a real and actual kingdom of righteousness, set up on earth, by armed guerrillas and Marxist intellectuals."[60]

For Norman, then, the political life and the religious life should be separated. Our life on this earth should be seen as a preparation for the next, not as an end in itself. Our earthly life provides us with the discipline which best enables us to order our lives so that we might "discern the shadow of eternity cast over time; it is the education of the soul."[61] Christianity is personal and private, not social and political. Christians are to reject the world's priorities and recognize the relativity of human values.

Norman is not without his critics. Indeed, his book caused a veritable storm of controversy. One of the sharpest and most acerbic responses to Norman comes from John Shepherd.[62] It is useful to look at Shepherd's response as it does include most of the criticisms made of Norman's position.

Shepherd begins by arguing that it is inaccurate to refer to Christianity as outside the boundaries of history and culture. Jesus himself was time- and culture-bound. Jesus' eschatological message was conditioned by his religious and cultural environment. Jesus accepted many of the cultural assumptions of his day, just as liberation theologians do.

Shepherd agrees that humanist or liberal values are not the essence of Christianity, but believes that if "Christianity does absorb the values and idealism of its surrounding culture, this is not necessarily a bad thing, even if they are secular and humanist."[63] Moreover, Shepherd claims that it is not essentially Christian to argue that society is imperfect and cannot be perfected. Of course,

Christianity has the doctrine of original sin, but "belief in original sin is not a justification for limiting one's commitment to the love commandment."[64] Moreover, there is within Christianity an important strand of belief which stresses humanity's potential "not only in modern theologies like Teilhard or Tillich, but also in mainstream Thomist tradition drawing in Aquinas, back to the teachings of the Fathers about the divinization of man."[65]

Christians have an obligation, claims Shepherd, to try to construct a social ethic that is consistent with biblical teaching. The essence of Jesus' teaching is love for neighbor, rooted in love for God. Some political systems harmonize with this ideal better than others. Christians have to choose. If Christians find that their views coincide with those of humanists, it does not mean that they are wrong but rather that humanists are right.

Granted that Shepherd's criticisms have to be taken seriously, it would be both unwise and unfair to discard altogether what Norman says. Norman's essential argument that political ideology should not be seen as an essential part of Christian faith has to be considered very carefully. The question he raises is at the heart of the orthodoxy/heresy debate: Does Christianity have a substantial identity? And if it has, how is that essence to be defined and successfully communicated to different ages and cultures? Do liberation theologians and others through their political interpretation of Christianity not only reinterpret it but transform its essence? In order to consider this question further we must turn to a more careful consideration of the root assumptions of liberation theology, especially focusing on how they relate to history and eschatology.

The Shadow of Albert Schweitzer, a Political Christ, and Liberation Theology

In his book *The Quest of the Historical Jesus*,[66] Albert Schweitzer not only summarized in a brilliant and exemplary way the quest up to the turn of the century, but also put forward his own reconstruction of the life of Jesus. Schweitzer, it will be recalled, argued that Jesus was an apocalyptic figure consumed with the task of bringing about the end of the world and inaugurating the Kingdom of God. He had expected the End to come at harvest time, and when it failed to arrive he embarked upon the heroic task of bringing it about by his own death and suffering. It was for this purpose that he went to Jerusalem and provoked his own crucifixion. But his crucifixion did not bring the end, and Jesus died a broken man with failure heavy on his shoulders.

And that, religiously speaking, would seem to be that. As a historical figure Jesus of Nazareth may be of interest, but how could such a figure say anything to the religious sensibilities of subsequent ages? Schweitzer had made Jesus an eschatological figure comprehensible in his own age but foreign to any other. Schweitzer himself spoke of the "spirit" of Jesus traversing the ages and speaking ever anew to peoples of all times and places. But for many other Christians Schweitzer's "strange and enigmatic" Jesus was simply too foreign to their own experience to command faith.

Historical Jesus research subsequent to Schweitzer recognized the "hermeneutical gulf" opened up by his work. What does this Jesus have to do with a world dominated by technology and gargantuan political and social structures? What possible relevance could his message have for ordinary people concerned about food, clothing, and housing? Much of the quest after Schweitzer was therefore concerned with what have been called "salvage operations." That which in the teaching of Jesus is out of step with modern cultural assumptions is either ignored or simply discarded, while what is in keeping with them is cautiously salvaged. A more radical approach is to dispense with the importance of the historical Jesus altogether. Hence Bultmann is content with the "that" of Jesus only, and focuses upon the theological presentations of Christ in Paul and John as being the normative core of Christianity. The reaction to this solution started some time ago when Ernst Käsemann called for a "new quest" of the historical Jesus, but it has gathered pace to the extent where now Bultmann's position has been almost completely repudiated. There has been an increasing emphasis on the centrality of the historical Jesus of Nazareth for Christian faith. This position is usually associated with the liberation theologians of South America, but it also has proponents such as Paul Hollenbach and Christopher Rowland, who belong to more traditional academic circles in the West.

What Hollenbach, Rowland, and others have effected seems at first glance to be yet another salvage operation. Their starting point is essentially the Marxist critique of society. Evil is to be found not only in the hearts of individuals, but in political and social structures. Therefore the message of Jesus, if it is to be relevant, must address this issue. Thus, Paul Hollenbach says that the "ideological presuppositions" of those engaged in the historical Jesus quest must be reexamined in order to "overcome the mythological presentation of a Christ who not only appears to contradict Jesus of Nazareth but also permits the Church to stand silent before or opposed to contemporary movements that embody the kingdom Jesus preached."[67] These movements include attempts to redistribute wealth and reform oppressive political structures. Christopher Rowland argues in his book *Radical Christianity* that Jesus' whole life was a repudiation of the rich and the powerful and their social structures. Rowland passionately contends that Jesus' message was not a retreat into other-worldliness nor a renunciation of the political world. Much of the novelty of Rowland's thesis lies in his claim that apocalyptic—the framework for the message of Jesus—has been misunderstood. Apocalyptic does not issue in a quietistic view of life. In fact, properly understood, it is an "ancient Christian form of the critique of ideology."[68] Through the use of apocalyptic images and symbols the ideology of the rich and the powerful is unmasked and denounced.

It is both interesting and enlightening to compare the approach of Hollenbach, Rowland, and others to that of Ben F. Meyer,[69] who helped launch the so-called Third Quest[70] of the historical Jesus. Meyer, like Rowland, Hollenbach, and most other New Testament scholars, lives in the shadow of Schweitzer. It is accepted that eschatology is indeed the key to understanding the message of Jesus. But in spite of this common starting point, Meyer's conclusions are quite different from those of Rowland and others. How he reaches these conclusions not only sharpens the differences in his approach, but also sheds light on some of the buried issues in historical Jesus research.

Meyer recognizes, like Hollenbach, the importance of one's own presuppositions. This is why he spends about half of *The Aims of Jesus* laying bare the presuppositions of those previously involved in the quest. Meyer delineates the contours of his own approach: a historical-critical methodology influenced by the work of Collingwood, Lonergan, and others. Meyer takes intentionality and the understanding of the "inside" of an event to be crucial to fruitful historical reconstruction. When he applies his method to the Gospels he finds they focus quite clearly on Jesus as an eschatological figure who saw himself as inaugurating the Kingdom of God. The Kingdom is a supra-racial, supra-legal, supra-human reality. It is God's saving act. This saving act involves the restoration of Israel, but was not to be confined within a political agenda. Jesus, says Meyer, was "not at all absorbed by political oppression." He affirmed the "root structures of social existence and took for granted the essential goodness of the ordinary customs and daily occupations of his surrounding world."[71]

Meyer thus rejects a political interpretation of Jesus. Central to the message of Jesus was the restoration of Israel. This was God's climactic eschatological act, and participation in this act was through the *ecclesia*. Two questions inevitably arise at this point. First, was Jesus not simply mistaken in his expectation of the imminent end of the world? Second, is it not insurmountably difficult to reconcile that Jesus expected the imminent end of the world with the idea that he intended the 'Church'?

In the first place, says Meyer, it is important to realize that Jesus' view of the future was prophetic and symbolic. Thus the question, Was Jesus mistaken about the future? is too undifferentiated. Rather the question should be, Did Jesus have determinate knowledge of what God intended by the symbolic scheme of things which Jesus himself was commissioned to announce? The answer would seem to be no, but the question thus posed allows for a more nuanced understanding of this no. Jesus, as a prophet, appears to have limited knowledge, but this is not to limit the knowledge of God who speaks through the prophet. Prophetic knowledge is different from empirical knowledge, for it is only through the eye of faith that its symbolic imagery is perceived in actual events: "the actuality of events discloses to the believing community the divine intention charging the prophet's symbols."[72] Jesus had a schematic visionary view of the future—the now of the present, followed by the eschatological crisis, culminating in the resolution of this crisis with the coming of the Son of Man. How this schematic sequence translates into actual sequence, and how symbolic time is related to actual time, is thus grasped by faith in the context of history.

The problem in the second question—How could a Jesus who awaited the imminent end of the world have also intended a Church?—is set up, claims Meyer, by the false premise that 'Church' is a non-eschatological concept. But 'Church' does not belong to the present order of things, and therefore will not be swept away at the outbreak of the eschatological crisis. Jesus, in fact, did see a role for the Church prior to the resolution of this eschatological crisis. In Mt 16:13–20, for example, we have a substantial datum concerning the aims of the historical Jesus. Jesus intended the restoration of an eschatological community and Peter was the rock on which this community was to be built.[73]

Rowland and others have resolved the question of how Jesus speaks to us today by translating his message into a political critique. Meyer resolves the question by turning Jesus into an eschatological figure whose intention finds expression in the Church. These two approaches are grounded in different suppositions. One locates the message of Jesus within a culturally determined political horizon, the other within a traditionally determined religious horizon. One takes a cultural fact as its starting point: there is great injustice and oppression, and if the message of Jesus is to mean anything today it must address these issues. The other takes a religious heritage as its starting point and affirms its authenticity in spite of a massive cultural rejection of much of its horizon of meaning.

Meyer's position is grounded in the same suppositions as Turner's. Hollenbach, Rowland, and the Liberation theologians do not seem to share these assumptions. But it is evident that there is much more at issue than a dispute about how far the politicization of Christianity can be justified from the historical origins of Christianity. What we have uncovered is the essentially theological nature of the question about politics and Christianity. This is apparent in the work of scholars with such divergent approaches as Turner, Norman, Meyer, and Rowland. We need to probe deeper still to get to the root of the real issues. Nobody has done this better than Ernst Käsemann, whose views are particularly fascinating because they emerge out of an examination of the Johannine literature.

Ernst Käsemann: The Fourth Gospel
and the Nexus of History and Theology

The Gospel of John was dubbed by Clement of Alexandria as "the spiritual Gospel" and has been regarded traditionally as unworldly, and by implication, apolitical.[74] Of all of the New Testament writings the Gospel of John would seem the best one to look to in support of Norman's thesis and the least promising to appeal to in support of a political theology. Certainly many liberation theologians have in the past tended to neglect the Fourth Gospel because of its apparent lack of the same historical ground as the Synoptics. If one were to appeal to the historical Jesus one would not do so on the basis of what is said in the Fourth Gospel. And yet in recent years there has been a noticeable trend toward believing that the designation of John's as "the spiritual gospel" is essentially misleading. Many now claim that the Gospel is not spiritual and unworldly in the sense of endorsing quietism. It may well be unworldly in the sense that it proclaims a message which the world cannot accept, but this is clearly not the same as saying it endorses political inaction. This new perspective on the Gospel can be seen especially in the work of some liberation theologians.[75] To many historical critics this will come as no surprise, suspicious as they are of the political agenda of liberation theology. The surprise is, however, that a recognition of the political dimensions of John's theology is also found within the gates of traditional historical criticism. A particularly illuminating example of this may be seen in the dialogue between two fine exemplars of this tradition, Rudolf Bultmann and Ernst Käsemann.[76]

Rudolf Bultmann is regarded by many as the interpreter of the Gospel of John *par excellence*. His great commentary on the Gospel,[77] and his numerous articles on various aspects of Johannine thought, set the agenda for Johannine studies for over a quarter of a century. Ernst Käsemann is perhaps his most renowned student, a man whose iconoclastic views combined with a deep personal commitment to the Christian faith have made him one to be reckoned with in theological debate. In the course of his very distinguished career, Käsemann moved from being the most prominent disciple and supporter of Bultmann to breaking with him and becoming one of his severest critics. It is the reasons for this break which are of interest to our inquiry and which demand our attention.

Both Bultmann and Käsemann shared certain basic assumptions, especially about the nature of early Christianity. In particular, they were both influenced by Walter Bauer. Bauer, however, never considered whether the disputes in the New Testament were instances of his own thesis. As we have seen, it was Bultmann who saw the real significance of Bauer's thesis when applied to the New Testament when he said that the New Testament "reflects a multiplicity of conceptions of Christian faith or its content."[78] The origin of Christian theology is to be found in the disputes and debates reflected in the New Testament documents. It follows, of course, that once we better understand the nature of these disputes and debates we will understand more clearly the theology of individual New Testament authors. We will understand Johannine theology better by trying to grasp more precisely its relationship to early Christianity—the crucible in which it was forged. In comparing the thought of Bultmann and Käsemann it is interesting to note that it is Käsemann and not Bultmann who consistently adheres to this basic point of departure. In Bultmann's theology, Paul and John are central and normative. This is evident in the arrangement of his *Theology of the New Testament*, which is divided into four parts: (1) "Presuppositions and Motifs of New Testament Theology," (2) "The Theology of Paul," (3) "The Theology of the Gospel of John and the Johannine Epistles," (4) "The Development Toward the Ancient Church." A chiastic arrangement can be discerned: ABBA. A is primarily historical, while B is primarily theological and normative. That is to say, the two central sections on Paul and John are the normative pillars on which Bultmann builds his New Testament theology, while the beginning and concluding sections are somewhat like historical "bookends" enclosing this theology. For Bultmann, Paul and John are normative because they, more than other New Testament writers, afford the possibility of an existential interpretation of the Christian Gospel. Paul and John do not, therefore, function as normative for historical reasons, but because they approximate closely to Bultmann's anthropological presuppositions.[79]

In terms of the history of John's Gospel, Bultmann conceives of it as having been written within the first century, in an environment heavily permeated by Oriental Christianity, by a person who was influenced by Gnosticizing Judaism. Bultmann therefore considers all references to the traditional doctrines of eschatology (5:27–29; 6:39, 40, 44, 41b–58; 12:48), sacraments (3:5; 6:51b–58; 19:34b), and the atonement (6:53–56; 19:34b) to have been added by an "ecclesiastical redactor." This redactor's concern was to bring the Gospel of John into line with the broad stream of Christian tradition. The implication is that the Fourth Evangelist had produced a work which was unacceptable to the church at large.

Käsemann is logically working out his teacher's thought when in "Ketzer und Zeuge" ("Heretic and Witness"),[80] a public lecture given on the occasion of taking up Bauer's position at Göttingen, he reverses Bauer's thesis that Diotrephes was the heretic in the Johannine letters. In this article Käsemann begins by acknowledging the influence of Bauer on his own thinking. He then criticizes Bultmann's thinking on the Johannine authorship problem. Says Käsemann:

> It is no accident that the last great commentary on John, that of R. Bultmann, is highly sceptical of the view that the controversy over the authorship problem is of any value for its essential exegesis. Such an assertion seems to me to go too far. Every detail that allows us to grasp more exactly the historical placement of the work keeps us at the same time from losing ourselves in the realm of speculation. Moreover, scepticism would be justified only if all the available possibilities had been really exhausted. In my view that has not happened, for in the whole debate the third letter of John has been unduly left out of account.[81]

Accordingly, Käsemann proceeds to argue that the author of 3 John (and the Gospel) was a presbyter who had refused to accept the verdict of orthodoxy, and was thus excommunicated by a representative of monarchical episcopacy. As Käsemann puts it:

> The essential point, if my argumentation proves right, lies in this: this presbyter is excommunicated and therefore forced to be a lone wolf. Despite the verdict of orthodoxy he has held fast to his title as well as his work and organized his own Church association with its own Gentile mission alongside the orthodox community, without giving up the hope or the will to reach an agreement with the other side.[82]

Käsemann is standing the traditional understanding of the Johannine literature on its head. Traditionally the Johannine epistles had been thought to have been written by a significant and authoritative presbyter who, according to 3 John, had encountered opposition from a certain Diotrephes, thought to be some kind of troublemaker and heretic. Käsemann is suggesting that it is Diotrephes who is the person of authority, and the author of the epistles is the trouble maker and heretic. Diotrephes has had to assert his authority and throw him out of the Church. As the author of the epistles was also the author of the Gospel of John, says Käsemann, it raises intriguing questions about whether we should regard its writer as a heretic or a witness.[83]

In a later work, *The Testament of Jesus: A Study of the Gospel of John in the Light of Chapter 17*,[84] Käsemann deals specifically with the Gospel of John. He is concerned to find the historical situation in which to locate the Gospel of John. For Käsemann, "A world without shadows and historical contours cannot be investigated. He [the historian] must be able to localize an historical object in order to recognize it."[85]

Käsemann chooses to focus his attention on chapter 17 because it is a summary of the last discourses and a counterpart of the prologue. In particular, Käsemann chooses for attention certain "key words"—the glory of Christ, the community under the Word, and Christian unity.

Käsemann's basic assertion is that the beginning of chapter 17 is dominated by the key word "glorification." The category of the Galilean teacher, which we find in the Synoptics, does not apply to the Johannine presentation.[86] "The Word became flesh" (1:14a) is almost always made the central and proper theme of the Gospel. But, asks Käsemann, in what sense is he flesh who walks on water and through closed doors, cannot be captured by his enemies nor deceived by men, and permits Lazarus to remain in the grave four days so that the miracle of raising him might appear more impressive? Does the statement "The Word became flesh" mean any more than that he descended into the world of man "and there came into contact with earthly existence, so that an encounter with him might be possible?" Käsemann believes that "the Word became flesh" receives its meaning from "We beheld his glory" (1:14b). The verse is stressing, in other words, that the glory of God is shining through the Word. It does not stress the humanity of the Word.[87]

Käsemann finds in the Gospel of John evidence of traditions reflecting the "Corinthian enthusiasm" which Paul attacks in his correspondence with the Church at Corinth. For example, John 5:24 says: "Truly, truly, I say to you, he who believes my word and him who sent me, has eternal life; he does not come into judgement, but has passed from death to life" (cf. also 3:36; 6:47; 8:51; 11:25 f.). This is very much like the heresy that Paul counters in his Corinthian letters, for the Corinthian enthusiasts rejected not Christ's resurrection, but the believer's future resurrection. As shown in 2 Timothy 2:18, which warns against those who have swerved from the truth by holding that the resurrection is already past, this did become a major heresy in the Church. Käsemann says, "It is quite disturbing that the Evangelist, at the very centre of his proclamation, is dominated by a heritage of enthusiasm against which Paul had struggled violently in his day and which in the post-apostolic was branded as heretical."[88]

Käsemann does admit, however, that the Evangelist modified this "heretical" heritage. He detached it from the understanding of baptism as an initiation rite into mysteries and placed it "at the service of his Christology"; yet he still affirms what "the enthusiasts of Corinth and the heretics of 2 Timothy 2:18 had proclaimed, namely that the reality of the general resurrection of the dead is already present now."[89] Moreover, neither the incarnation nor the passion has "those emphases which were taken from the ecclesiastical tradition." The Johannine account sees a change in terms of "coming" and "going," "ascending" and "descending," and not a change in Christ according to his nature.

Contrary to most exegetes, Käsemann finds in the Gospel of John "a dogmatic controversy taking place," for only in Paul do we find the "same passionate discussion," so that for Käsemann the historical situation of the Fourth Evangelist is decisive in shaping its presentation. The Jews in the Gospel are representatives of the world "as it is comprised [sic] by its religious traditions." A struggle within the Church is "reflected and hidden in these debates with the Jews." Thus the origin of the Gospel may well be in the circle of Hellenistic enthusiasm opposed by 1 Corinthians 15 and 2 Timothy 2:18, and the controversy may well be over the slogan *solus Christus.* That the Gospel of John is anti-docetic is, says Käsemann, "completely unproven" and the danger of Docetism in the Gospel's Christology of glory is very apparent.

In the chapter "The Community under the Word," Käsemann begins by making the observation that the Gospel of John seemingly does not unfold the kind of ecclesiology we might expect from a first-century representative of the Christian Church—he has a very insignificant interest in sacraments, worship, and ministry. The Gospel does, however, presuppose an organized communal life. Yet the whole presentation is different; the community is not troubled by questions of order, neither is it viewed from "the aspect of corporateness, but rather from the aspect of its individual members."[90] This is against the trend to incorporate the individual into the community by sacramental, cultic, and organizational means.

Käsemann concludes that although the Gospel is connected with the main stream of Christianity, the historical context seems to be that of a side tributary; the Evangelist is on the periphery of the Church. Commentators perhaps attribute an "other-worldly" quality to the Gospel of John simply because it does not reflect the realm of the Church known to us through the rest of the New Testament.

In conclusion, Käsemann proclaims that the inclusion of the Gospel of John in the canon is "not without irony." He says:

> If historically the Gospel reflects the development which led from the enthusiasts of Corinth and of II Tim. 2:18 to Christian gnosticism, then its acceptance into the Church's canon took place through man's error and God's providence. Against all its own intentions, and misled by the picture of Jesus as God walking upon the face of the earth, the Church assigned to the apostles the voice of those whom it otherwise ignored and one generation later condemned as heretics.[91]

From the historical point of view the Church was in error when it declared the Gospel of John as orthodox. But, Käsemann suggests, perhaps from a theological viewpoint it was fortunate.

Käsemann's lecture "Ketzer und Zeuge" may be envisaged as a defense of Bultmann. At this time there was talk of a heresy trial for Bultmann,[92] and so Käsemann seems to be casting him in a similar role to the writer of the Gospel of John. Just as the Fourth Evangelist and his theology ran afoul of authority in the shape of Diotrephes and yet was ultimately vindicated by the inclusion of the Gospel of John in the canon, so, Käsemann is implying, will Bultmann's theology be vindicated even though now it is seen as suspect. In his book *The Testament of Jesus*, however, Käsemann seems to be deliberately correcting his former teacher. In his claim, for example, that the focal point of the Gospel is not "And the Word became flesh" but rather "And we beheld his glory," Käsemann is decisively and significantly repudiating a fundamental premise of Bultmann's theology.[93]

For Käsemann the Johannine Christ acts as the Exalted One on earth. The glory of Christ is the central theme of the Gospel, the incarnation is only the means for his revelation. Käsemann is the true heir of Bauer. Bauer attempted to show the theological diversity of early Christianity. Käsemann sees theological diversity as present in the New Testament itself.[94] Bultmann had also seen this. But by making Paul and John the two normative pillars of the New Testament and interpreting them existentially, he had sought to unite New Testament theology by tying his anthropology to a doctrine of the incarnation. Käsemann rejects this. The Gospel of John is *the example* in the New Testament which shows that one cannot unite New Testament theology under one theological rubric.

Käsemann's break with Bultmann, then, is more than simply a repudiation of a former teacher. It is a rejection of a New Testament interpretation that had been dominant for many years. It is a rejection of an interpretation that privatizes the New Testament's message and leaves it without any social content. Käsemann was not disputing Bultmann's point that human existence was rooted in history (*Geschichlichkeit*). He was saying that this concern with the historicity of existence was too narrow. For Käsemann, the meaning of Christ's universal Lordship is the key to understanding the New Testament.

The Gospel of John, then, like the rest of the New Testament, emphasizes the Lordship of Christ. This is the first major point to emerge from Käsemann's dialogue with Bultmann. The second—equally crucial—point is Käsemann's insistence that the New Testament canon reflects a multiplicity of interpretations. It is the implications of this assertion for the ecumenical movement which is of profound significance and which Käsemann seizes upon. Today's ecumenical plurality is, according to Käsemann, already prefigured in early Christianity. Thus he says, "The worldwide body of Christ, composed of members differing in time and space, is held together by its Lord alone, and manifests this reality at any given time in a specific manner in confession of faith and discipleship."[95]

Bultmann once declared that "humanity" was an abstraction. Käsemann declares that it is the word *individual* that is the abstraction. The focus of the New Testament is not the individual quest for salvation. The New Testament is about the world Lordship of Christ.[96] This is the central thrust of the Gospel of John and indeed, of the New Testament. It is the Lordship of Christ over creation that unites the New Testament. As Käsemann puts it:

> Christian mission comes to fruition in world wide service to humanity, to whom salvation shall come. This does not happen without doctrine, and it has to develop on its own in various places and times in order to be able to gain entry in general. In this case, however, pure doctrine is instruction for the practice of discipleship, and theology is a necessary function of the community, not a lord over faith.[97]

Käsemann's study of the Gospel of John, then, liberated him from a narrow confessional vision. The Gospel of John had been included in the canon despite the fact that it had stood, in Käsemann's estimation, on the periphery of the Church. By accepting the Gospel of John into the canon, Christianity had accepted the principle of theological diversity. It had accepted that there were many paths to the same goal. (Which is not to say that all paths lead to the same goal.) And it is this very richness and diversity of the Christian tradition that ensures that biblical theology has a political dimension. In Käsemann's estimation, the only unifying factor in the variety of New Testament theologies is the Lordship of Christ. And in making the statement that Christ is Lord over all creation, we are making a political statement.

We began this chapter by speaking of Edward Norman, who attacked liberation theology. He is not alone in thinking that liberation theology has interpreted Christianity by means of a fundamentally alien Marxist philosophy. But Käsemann is not a Marxist, and he has arrived at a conclusion very similar to that of the liberation theologians. The similarities between them are striking. Both emphasize that the starting point of theology is not the individual, but the community. Both focus on real life and actual history. Both, in short, emphasize history and context. Both proclaim a Christianity in which Christians have a commitment to following Jesus, identifying with the outcast and the oppressed, and which plunges deep into divergent cultures.[98] Käsemann uses the image of the Church as the wandering people of God. The liberation theologians speak of a band of pilgrims celebrating a mystery that suffuses the world.[99]

If a Lutheran pastor like Käsemann, steeped in the Germanic philosophical tradition and the historical-critical method, can essentially endorse many of the conclusions of liberation theology, it certainly means that those conclusions have to be taken seriously. And if, furthermore, these conclusions are reached through penetrating the deeper meaning of the "spiritual Gospel," then this makes the Fourth Gospel one of the more fascinating texts when discussing Christianity and politics. It is no longer sufficient to dub the Gospel of John "spiritual" and therefore apolitical. It should now be accepted that there are political dimensions to Johannine thought. The task facing Johannine interpretation is thus to seek a deeper understanding of the relationship between Johannine spirituality, politics, and modernity. In order to accomplish that task we must first try to understand the message of the Fourth Gospel. It is to that task that we now turn.

CHAPTER 2

Understanding the Fourth Gospel

1. THE STUDY OF THE NEW TESTAMENT

Historical Criticism and Biblical Studies

We now turn to our examination of the Fourth Gospel, setting our inquiry within the general context of historical criticism. The basis of historical inquiry is the asking of questions. In order to understand the questions which are pertinent to the study of the Fourth Gospel it is useful to begin with a brief overview of the discipline of New Testament studies and the major figures who have had a significant impact on its development.

It was toward the end of the seventeenth century that Biblical Studies developed as an independent discipline. Crucial to its emergence were the efforts of Richard Simon, John Mill, and others to shape a critical text of the Bible and of such pioneers as J. D. Michaelis and J. S. Semler to clarify introductory questions essential to the work of interpretation. It has subsequently progressed as a discipline through the asking of new and significant questions which have in turn led to new insights and better understanding. In particular, the quest for a better understanding of introductory questions has focused on historical issues.

H. S. Reimarus (1694–1768) was the first to formulate clear and methodical questions in this area. He raised the question: What was Jesus' intention? And he answered: Jesus intended to throw off the Roman yoke and replace it with the reign of the Messiah. After he failed, his disciples attempted to rationalize events by casting his life in a spiritual light. The Gospels, then, Reimarus argues, are intended to be read historically but their actual historical account is fraudulent. The Evangelists had put out a false historical record of Jesus' life.

The importance of this part of Reimarus's work lay in his distinction between Jesus' intention and the intention of the Evangelists. By making this differentiation he created a horizon within which historical Jesus questions could be asked which in turn led to an intense interest in source criticism. The basic idea behind source criticism was to uncover the sources which had been used by the Evangelists. This was not intended to be a destructive enterprise. In 1826, for example, Gottlieb Wilke wrote an article in which he argued that Mark was used by Matthew.[1] Scholars built on Wilke's thesis by attempting to show that not only was Mark the first Gospel to be written, but his Gospel was objective (if somewhat unsophisticated) history. Therefore when Matthew (and Luke, as it turns out) used Mark they were using a reliable historical source. By arguing in this way they hoped to show that such scholars as Reimarus were wrong in their assessment of the Gospels as fraudulent history.

This was, however, only the beginning of the questions about the New Testament. In 1835–36, in the two-volumed work *Leben Jesu,*[2] the German scholar D. F. Strauss asked a different question. Reimarus had argued that the Gospels *intended* the reader to read the Gospels as history, even though what they reported was not what happened. They wanted us to think that that was what happened. Strauss, however, asked whether the Gospels really did intend us to read them as history. He answered in the negative and asserted that they belonged to the genre of myth. "Myth," for Strauss, is the embodiment of an idea in story. In other words, the Gospels were narratives or stories that embodied important truths and ideas. Readers should look for these ideas and not get caught up in distracting questions about the historicity of the narratives themselves. To put it very simply, the Evangelists meant us to read the Gospels as stories which conveyed ideas, not as narratives which conveyed history.

Strauss's ideas were ultimately to have a major and irrevocable effect on later formulations of questions of faith and history. His influence, however, was slow to manifest itself. Scholarly study of the New Testament immediately after Strauss took place largely under the banner of liberal theology, a school of thought which all but ignored his contributions. The core of this school's ideas was an assumed timeless love ethic founded on the fatherhood of God and the brotherhood and sisterhood of humanity as expressed in the Sermon on the Mount and the parables. The center of its attention was the personality of Jesus, which "combined complete open-ness towards the world with perfect inwardness towards God so as to become the source of a new religion, in which self-surrender and liberty, humility and energy, enthusiasm and lucidity, are blended and the chasm of previous ages between God and man are filled up."[3] The Gospels, then, were essentially about love.

The liberal theologians were positive in their goal. Their aim was to reveal a Jesus who would be both acceptable to people of the modern world and at the same time challenging to their spiri-tuality. Jesus' teaching, they argued, was, at its core, ethical and timeless and therefore open to appropriation by people in any era. Its main elements were not especially difficult to understand. The concept of the Kingdom of God, for example, refers to "the moral task to be carried out by the human race . . . it is the organization of humanity through action inspired by love."[4] It is the message of the teaching, not its historical setting, which counts for the mid–nineteenth century liberals.

Near the end of the nineteenth century the emphasis changes again, this time radically, with the rise of the *Religions-geschichtliche Schule* or "History of Religions School." For mem-bers of this school it was precisely the historical context of ancient Judaism and non-Judaic Hellenism which gave early Christianity its distinctiveness. Thoroughly rejecting the liberals' efforts at mod-ernizing Jesus, they focused on the New Testament world in which he lived and taught, and they found it a strange and, at times, per-plexing milieu. The world of Jesus and his contemporaries was decidedly unmodern, a world characterized by "enthusiasm" and ecstasy and by a Kingdom of God that was outside the person, a supernatural catastrophe reserved for the end of time. The most notable proponents of this view were Johannes Weiss and Albert Schweitzer. It was mostly through their efforts that eschatology came to be viewed as an important element in the perspective of Jesus and his early followers. Moreover, the History of Religions school left its mark through its preoccupation with historical con-text. The latter gave rise to the development of form criticism.

Despite this influence, however, form criticism was not pri-marily concerned with the historical context of Jesus and the Gospel authors. Rather it was the proclamation (*kerygma*) of sal-vation through the crucified and risen Christ that most interested this school. Hence, Rudolph Bultmann, the most celebrated of the form critics, saw "kerygma theology" as the core of the New Testament and the Christ of faith rather than the Jesus of history as the key to its illumination.

Consistent with this, Bultmann and other form critics centered their interpretive questions on the horizon of meaning of the early Church community rather than on those of the individual Gospel writers. The latter they viewed as mere *Sammler* (collectors) of traditions. In commenting on Mark, for example, Bultmann states unequivocally that he was not "sufficiently master of his material to venture a systematic construction himself."[5] Instead, he was merely recording the already preformed traditions of the early Church itself.

It was in reaction to this de-emphasizing of the creative role of the Gospel authors that redaction criticism sprang up, the English translation of *Redaktionsgeschichte,* a phrase coined by the German scholar Willi Marxsen. He proposed that when examining the Synoptic tradition we keep in mind three *Sitze im Leben:* the *Sitz im Leben* of Jesus, that of the early Church, and that of the Evangelist. We should take into account not only the transmission of tradition within the community but also the editing (redacting) of the individual Gospel writer. And each evangelist of necessity wrote within his own particular theological framework.[6] The primary aim of redaction criticism is the uncovering of that theology by an examination of the structure of the Gospel and its author's handling of the early Church traditions incorporated in it; in other words, the uncovering of the individual Evangelist's redaction of the material he received.

Within redaction criticism there are two approaches. One studies a redaction by focusing on its origins, the other by examining its overall design. The difference between the two reflects different emphases. The first highlights the redactor's distinctiveness—what sets him apart from his predecessors. The second looks at the redactor's total theology, including, as well as differences, features it shares with his predecessor's position. E. Haenchen coined the phrase "composition criticism"[7] to describe this latter approach. Composition criticism is, in the words of Stephen Moore, "a holistic variation of redaction criticism in which the work itself . . . viewed rigorously and persistently in its entirety, becomes the primary context for interpreting any part of it."[8] It is, in fact, very close to literary criticism. Of course, it differs from literary criticism in that its purpose is historical: to sift out the author's intention and in the process learn more about the theological history of early Christianity. As Perrin has noted, redaction criticism helps us move from the theological position of the Evangelist to the historical situation which gave rise to that theology.[9]

Redaction criticism, then, takes the spotlight off the historical Jesus and the early Church tradition and places it on the individual Gospel author and his intention. It shifts the emphasis away from studying the Gospels to find out what Jesus actually said and did, to studying the Gospels to find out more about the historical situation that gave rise to them. This is a most important shift in methodology, and in our study of the Fourth Gospel we too will leave aside historical Jesus questions and focus rather on the historical circumstances that gave rise to the Fourth Gospel, and how these circumstances further illustrate the Gospel's meaning. Logically, this seems to be a circular method, for we look at the text to find out more about the historical circumstances that gave rise to it, and we look at the historical circumstances to find out more about the text! It is not, however, a circle in the strict sense, but more of a spiral. We go to and from the text to the historical circumstances, and each time we do so we gain more and more insight so that we "spiral into the meaning of the text." In fact, there are many such circles or spirals operative in the way we study texts and history. We will now say more about these "hermeneutical circles" or "circles of interpretation."

Hermeneutical Circles

Interpretation is not, of course, always necessary. The sense of many texts is often quite clear and no interpretation is needed. But interpretation *is* necessary where the presuppositions, conceptual and linguistic idiom, and world of thought are foreign to us. This is the case with the New Testament. Interpreting ancient texts is, moreover, a difficult and challenging task. Something of its challenge and difficulty can be seen in the following "hermeneutical circles."

The Circle of Reader and Text   In what has become a well-known comment, the German philosopher Wilhelm Dilthey observed that texts are "expressions of life." Digging out the expression of life in a given text helps us reach beyond straightforward historical criticism to a situation in which interpreter and text, as it were, communicate with each other. To discern the expression of life in a text we must uncover its view of existence. The process of doing this produces a lively interaction between interpreter and text, brought about when the interpreter's worldview challenges that of the text with questions on human existence.

This involves much more than the uncovering of past details by means of historical research. It leads as well to some insight into the past's "universe of discourse." Historians might do a very good job of describing and comparing isolated bits of past experience and action, but without some grasp of the past's paradigm(s) for explaining and interpreting human existence the research amounts to little more than an antiquarian activity devoid of relevance for the present.

This, certainly, was the view of Rudolph Bultmann, for whom the recovery of "past particulars" of New Testament history was never just an end in itself. It was rather—as reflected in his well-known demythologizing program—the pursuit of the meaning of existence embodied in the New Testament texts. According to Bultmann, we are never simply impartial "viewers" of history because history cannot be reduced to a "museum of antiquities." It must be encountered. Only those who approach history for answers to the questions that "agitate" have a chance of hearing history speak. "When we encounter the words of Jesus in history . . . they meet us with the question of how we are to interpret our own existence." "Directly or indirectly" the words of the text express an understanding of existence which engages the interpreter in a "living relationship" with the text. The interpreter interrogates the text and in turn must be open to being "interrogated by the text, [and] he must listen to its claims."[10]

Bultmann has had fundamental influence on other New Testament scholars, most of whom now recognize that historical criticism, despite its usefulness, does not cover all possibilities of textual meaning. In a new context any text can assume a new meaning. Hermeneutics, then, has to consider the dynamic interaction between text and interpreter and not restrict itself to the analysis of a text in its historical setting only.

One activity that is helpful in this regard is literary criticism. Specifically, it has pointed out the basic paradox characterizing the dynamic interaction of reader and text. A text can only be understood via what we as readers understand; such understanding sometimes involves the probing of worlds of meaning radically different from our own. Hence the paradox and challenge: how to understand texts which are not expressed in terms we understand. The challenge is especially strong as far as historical texts are concerned. As R. P. C. Hanson points out, historical investigations "depend upon estimating the motives and intentions, the thoughts and desires, of people in the past."[11] To make these estimations and to avoid abandoning history as an "indecipherable chaos," we must somehow see beyond our own horizon of meaning.

Most literary critics believe this is not possible, for we are time- and culture-bound. Hayden White, for example, argues that "there can be no such thing as a non-relativistic representation of historical reality."[12] Although he is not commenting specifically on White, Hanson does, in effect, counter his position in this sharp statement: "It must be obvious to the meanest intelligence that if we are bound by our cultural context, and we can neither make generalizations about history nor enjoy any continuity of truth in history, then we cannot make the generalization that there are no universal truths surviving through history."[13] But in spite of Hanson's criticism, there are many who see no contradiction in maintaining that there are many comprehensive views, each as legitimate as the other. And each view develops within a horizon—a horizon set for us by circumstances or fate.

Literary critics are right, therefore, to demand that historical critics give a fuller explanation of how they know the past. One scholar who takes this challenge seriously is Ben Meyer. He argues that we learn about other worlds of meaning cumulatively, starting with simple, isolated acts of understanding and gradually progress toward compound, multirelational ones. Growth in understanding is always dependent on what we already know. It proceeds, however, not just by addition but by differentiation as well. That is, not only do we come to understand more but we understand it in a more detailed and sophisticated way.[14]

Of course, our knowledge is gained largely as a result of our questions, and these vary according to the inquirer's background.

Each age asks its own questions and in getting them answered rewrites history. Ultimately, what we know about the past is shaped and limited by a "perspectivism of questions." Both the questions themselves and the habitual knowledge we bring to the interpretative activity in which they are raised are distinctly our own. Yet, this does not mean we are forever and totally ignorant of the past. We come to understand the past's other worlds of meaning in a piecemeal and continuing manner.

The Circle of Things and Words   The interaction of reader and text, Meyer maintains, is in reality a hermeneutical circle, which implies other hermeneutical circles. For example, implied in the points made so far is a circle of "things and words" (*Sache und Sprache*). We grasp the meanings of words by means of our knowledge of the things to which they refer. And vice versa: we understand things by understanding the words that refer to them. A person who has been blind from birth, for example, will likely have difficulty learning much from a lecture on color. In the words of Martin Luther: "*Qui non intelligit res non potest ex verbis sensum elicere.*" ("He who does not understand the things cannot draw sense from the words.")

It is true, of course, that when we encounter a word we do not understand, we can consult a dictionary or some other reference guide and thereby relate it to the relevant "thing." But this does not always work; for various reasons the meaning of the word may remain elusive. In the words of the philosopher Bernard Lonergan:

> There can arise the need for a long and arduous use of the self-correcting process of learning. Then a first reading yields a little understanding and a host of puzzles, and a second reading yields only slightly more understanding but far more puzzles. The problem, now, is not of understanding the object or the words, but of understanding the author himself, his nation, language, time, culture, way of life, and cast of mind.[15]

We understand the author through his/her words but these get their meaning from the world of meaning in which the author functions. Our "understanding of things," is, in effect, one interpretation of reality, reality mediated through the author's world of meaning. Our "understanding of words" comes through our encounter with whole literatures. By exploring the circle of "things and words," then, we get to the heart of what interpretation is ultimately all about: participation in a common human heritage through which, understanding others, we come to understand ourselves.

The Circle of Whole and Parts   The third, and most familiar, hermeneutical circle is the circle of "whole and parts." This principle states that we can understand the whole only in terms of its constituent parts and the parts only in terms of the whole. Although this appears to be a vicious circle, we do better to look at it as a spiral. Our vision, or expectation, of the whole helps us grasp a part of the whole; our knowledge of a particular part will be informed largely by our grasp of the whole. Alternating between the two, we "spiral into the meaning of the text."

2. INTRODUCTION TO THE FOURTH GOSPEL

Having examined some of the larger issues raised by historical inquiry and the study of texts, we turn now to our specific study of the Fourth Gospel. We have seen how every interpreter proceeds on the basis of certain assumptions about the work to be interpreted. These are often clarified and discussed in the special discipline called "Introduction" (in German, *Einleitung*). In the present instance "Introduction" defines the "Johannine Problem," a network of questions concerning the relation of the Fourth Gospel to the Synoptics, its background, unity, composition, and author. It is necessary to clarify introductory questions to indicate what presuppositions will guide this study of the Fourth Gospel and to offer a summary justification of the presuppositions adopted.

Understanding the Fourth Gospel is inextricably tied to understanding the intention of the "decisive redactor." The decisive redactor is that person who, more than any other, has given the Gospel its peculiar thrust and present form. This implies a particular position on how the Fourth Gospel was produced. Negatively, it says that the Gospel was not a free composition of a single writer at a single point in time. On the contrary, its composition had a history; and in this history there was one redactor decisively responsible for its present contours and content. Our remarks on the

Johannine problem, then, will turn mainly on the decisive redactor, distinguishing this stage in the history of the Gospel's composition from what preceded and followed it.

The question of what preceded the decisive redaction of the Fourth Gospel is currently dominated by a renewal of source-critical efforts. In his *magnum opus* on the Fourth Gospel, Rudolf Bultmann posited three principal sources: the *Semeia-Quelle* or Signs-Source; the *Offenbarungsreden* or Revelatory Discourse Source; and a source underlying the Passion and Resurrection story.[16] The Signs-Source is a written document used by the Fourth Evangelist in writing chapters 1–12. Bultmann thinks that the existence of such a source is detected in the enumeration of the signs in 2:11 and 4:54, for the Evangelist himself attributes to Jesus a much larger number of signs (2:23; 4:45). Thus the enumeration of the signs belongs to the source. Moreover, 20:30 ("Now Jesus did many other signs in the presence of the disciples"), although not a fitting ending to the whole of the Gospel, is an appropriate conclusion to the Signs-Source. The *Offenbarungsreden* are found throughout the Gospel and form the basis of the discourses of Jesus in the Gospel, but their use is particularly apparent in the prologue. The source is identified by its poetic structure and its Gnostic mythological motifs. A third written source used by the Evangelist undergirds the Passion story (18:1–19:41). Elements of the Resurrection narrative (chapter 20) are also found in this source.

Bultmann believes that these three sources were woven together by the Fourth Evangelist who reworked the sources to make them the vehicle for his own unique theological exposition. Unfortunately, the text produced by the Evangelist fell into disarray, and the order as we now have it was established by an "ecclesiastical redactor." This ecclesiastical redactor—whose own concerns were primarily ecclesial—added chapter 21 and interpolated into the text such passages as 5:27–29; 6:39, 40, 44, 51b–58; 12:48 (on eschatology); 3:5; 6:51b-58; 19:34b (on the sacraments); 6:53–56; 19:34b (on the atonement); and 4:1; 6:23; 11:2; 20:9.

Bultmann's work stimulated further research along these lines, and the question of sources continues to generate controversy. Various studies, for example, have attempted to disprove on linguistic grounds the hypothesis of sources in the Fourth Gospel. Of these, E. Schweizer's and Ruckstuhl's[17] are especially significant. Ruckstuhl sought, first of all, to determine the linguistic and stylistic peculiarities of the Gospel, and second, to show that these peculiarities traverse the whole of the Gospel. He hoped to show that inasmuch as such stylistic peculiarities are found in all of the supposed sources, it cannot be shown that sources were drawn upon in the composition of the Fourth Gospel.

Schweizer was more cautious than Ruckstuhl. He sought to show that the unity of style in the Fourth Gospel is such that the distinguishing of sources on the basis of style is impossible. But Schweizer did not go so far as to say that sources were not used in the composition of the Fourth Gospel. Indeed, in the preface to the second edition of his book, Schweizer grants that sources for the prologue and the miracle stories probably do exist.

Objections were raised to the work of Ruckstuhl by those who maintained that the linguistic characteristics which supposedly traverse the whole of the Gospel may have been inserted by the Evangelist into his sources. "Thus by means of these linguistic observations nothing decisive against this or that source hypothesis has been established."[18] But if we are to conclude that the linguistic peculiarities of the Evangelist are distributed over the whole of the Gospel then it also follows that the "identification of connected sources on the basis of linguistic and stylistic arguments is hardly possible."[19]

Stylistic studies aimed at the refutation of the hypothesis of sources in the Fourth Gospel have not impeded the continuing quest for sources. The most recent trend is to focus particularly on the Signs-Source, which the Fourth Evangelist purportedly used. The most noteworthy contribution here is that of R. T. Fortna. Fortna has argued that it is possible to isolate the Signs-Source in the Fourth Gospel by using stylistic criteria and "aporias" (breaks and inconsistencies in the narrative).[20] This effort, however, although highly ingenious, cannot be said to have been successful. As C. K. Barrett has commented:

> That John used source material is almost certainly true; that here and there we can trace his editorial activity is probable; that we can write out one of his sources *in extenso* is not yet proved—though if it could have been proved it would have been proved by Dr. Fortna . . . If the case fails in the end to convince, the fault does not lie with the advocate.[21]

All the indications are that the Evangelist radically transformed his material, so that any source he might have used is now impossible to isolate.[22] This is not to say that, for example, a Signs-Source did not exist. The question is whether the source can be isolated. The difficulties of reconstructing any source in the Fourth Gospel appear to be insurmountable. At this point it is salutary to recall the comment of B. H. Streeter: "If the sources have undergone anything like the amount of amplification, excision, rearrangement and adaptation which the theory postulates, then the critic's pretence that he can unravel the process is grotesque. As well hope to start with a string of sausages and reconstruct the pig."[23]

In any case, the question of sources has only a limited impact upon our inquiry. If it could be shown that the decisive redactor inherited the substance of his work, it would perhaps reduce our estimate of his genius. But it would not make the decisive redactor any less decisive precisely as redactor; it would mean only that when referring to "the theology of the Fourth Evangelist" (decisive redactor) we mean "the theology sponsored by the Evangelist."

In accordance with the strategy outlined at the beginning of this chapter, we have thus far summarized the efforts of source critics to determine the history of the Johannine redaction before the decisive redactor. But this aspect of Johannine research has yielded no clear consensus of opinion. We must now move on to a discussion of the extent to which the Fourth Gospel has been edited. This is a complex problem, but one with which we must now deal in order to explain the use of the term *decisive redactor*. Our task is not, however, to deal with the whole range of the authorship question.

Our attempt to indicate what we believe to have been the history of the composition of the Fourth Gospel will of necessity be conjectural. The very nature of the problem means that we cannot offer a definitive "proof" of our conclusions. It is, rather, an attempt to put forward a working hypothesis for the study of the Gospel.

There are almost as many theories on the origin and composition of the Fourth Gospel as there are commentators on the Gospel. Most agree now, however, that the Gospel was composed in stages. R. E. Brown posits five. Stage one is the existence of "a body of traditional material pertaining to the works and words of Jesus."[24]

"One principal disciple" is responsible for stages two through four. Stage two is the "development of this material into Johannine patterns." Stage three is the first edition of the Gospel. Stage four is a revised edition by the same author. Stage five is the same edition revised and put out by the final redactor, a person other than the Evangelist.[25] It should be noted that for Brown the decisive redactor[26] (stages two through four) is not John the Apostle.

Other scholars, such as F.-M. Braun, have tried to retain the Apostle John as the authority behind the Gospel, while acknowledging that he did not write it. Braun argues that a "secretary" is responsible for the actual writing. He is in fact limiting the role of the actual writer of the Gospel. But as Schnackenburg says:

> Since he makes much of the fact that he was a writer with roots in the Jewish diaspora, he is obviously inspired by the idea that the style and language have a character of their own which cannot be associated with the Apostle John. We must surely concede a far greater measure of independence to the Hellenistic disciple of the Apostle who committed the Gospel to writing, because form and content, language and thought, cannot be separated . . . Thus the evangelist would have been both the spokesman who transmitted the tradition and the preaching of the Apostle John, and a theologian in his own right and a teacher of the readers whom he addressed.[27]

C. K. Barrett is more willing than Braun to acknowledge the identity and independence of the actual writer. In fact, Barrett's theory is very similar to Brown's. He suggests that the Apostle John migrated to Ephesus, where he attracted a group of disciples. Because of such predictions as Mark 9:1, it was thought as he aged that he would survive until the Parousia. Accordingly, his eventual death engendered apocalyptic fervor. One of his disciples wrote the Apocalypse of the New Testament. Another wrote the Epistles. And another, "a bolder thinker, and one more widely read in Judaism and Hellenism, produced John 1–20,"[28] the work first used by the Gnostics. Only when the church realized how usefully one might employ the Gospel against the Gnostics was it now edited together with chapter 21:

> The evangelist, perhaps the greatest theologian in the history of the Church, was now forgotten. His name was unknown. But he

had put in his Gospel references to the beloved disciple—the highly honoured apostle who years before had died in Ephesus. These were now partly understood, and partly misunderstood. It was perceived that they belong to John the son of Zebedee, but wrongly thought that they meant that this apostle was the author of the gospel. 21.24 was now composed on the model of 19.35, and the book was sent out on its long career as the work of John, foe of heretics and beloved of his Lord.[29]

This is an attractive theory, but it has not received wide acceptance. There is no manuscript evidence at all that the Gospel was ever circulated without chapter 21. If at first it remained unpublished, it is difficult to see how the Gnostics got hold of it. If it was first published without chapter 21, it seems strange that there is no evidence of this, especially as it would have had to have been in this form (at least in Barrett's theory) for some time to allow the references to the Beloved Disciple to be misunderstood. Moreover, it is very doubtful whether the Evangelist meant to refer to the Apostle when he spoke of the Beloved Disciple, as we shall argue later.

Chapter 21 is of vital significance in discussing the authority and composition of the Fourth Gospel, for it is the key to any redaction theory. It seems clear that this addition to the Gospel was written by someone else. There are three principal reasons for this. In the first place, the Gospel seems to conclude at 20:31. Second, the presence of chapter 21 leaves an unlikely sequence. It hardly seems likely that having been commissioned by the risen Christ in Jerusalem the disciples would return to Galilee and continue fishing. Third, the Greek style of chapter 21 leads one to believe that it is by another hand, although the evidence here is ambiguous.[30]

Accordingly the question arises whether this redactor is at work elsewhere in the Gospel. Many scholars reply in the affirmative, but it is noticeable that each exegete has very different ideas on which verses are the work of the final redactor. As we have seen, Bultmann posits an "ecclesiastical redactor" who is responsible for 3:5; 4:1; 5:27–29; 6:23, 39, 40, 44, 51b–58; 11:2; 12:48; 20:9; and chapter 21. The subjectivity of such conclusions is rather disconcerting. We have already stated that isolation of additions by a redactor on the basis of style is highly problematic. Therefore, out of necessity the interpreter has to supplement linguistic criteria with content (*sachlich*) criteria. But this only makes the subjectivity of the exegete more apparent. The inescapable conclusion seems to be that Bultmann begins with the supposition that the Gospel was unsacramental and then isolates all sacramental references and attributes them to an ecclesiastical redactor. Wilkens, on the other hand, locates sacramental allusions and futuristic eschatology in the first stages of the Gospel.[31]

It is one thing to attribute chapter 21 to a final redactor; it is quite another to see him responsible for insertions into the Gospel. The arguments for attributing chapter 21 to a final redactor turn upon placement, content, purpose, and style; taken together they make a reasonable case. But the very way chapter 21 is added suggests, contrary to most exegetes' conclusions, that the redactor did not tamper with the rest of the Gospel.[32] If he had regarded his task as editing the Gospel in the fullest sense of the word he would presumably have removed 20:30f. and the "aporias" noted by many scholars. Moreover, the person who added chapter 21 is no mere inept collator of traditions; he is a skillful writer. It is difficult to see how this same writer could have altered the main body of the text to create the "aporias." It seems more likely that the final redactor left the "aporias" in the text than that he was responsible for them.[33]

Although the alleged "aporias" in the text may be overemphasized, it cannot be denied that the Gospel does have rough edges, and we have insisted that these go back to the final redactor. What, then, is the explanation for this?

The problem of chapter 21 presents us with one of three alternatives. First, chapter 21 was always part of the Gospel and was written by the same person who wrote chapters 1–20. This seems, on the basis of what has already been said, to be unlikely. Second, the Gospel was without chapter 21 for some time and then it was added before the Gospel was circulated. Again, we have maintained that this is unlikely. Third, chapter 21 was added almost immediately to the Gospel by a different hand. This we regard as most probable. The question then arises: Why, almost as soon as the Gospel was completed in rough draft form, was 21 added by a different hand? Why did the Evangelist (i.e., the decisive redactor) himself not add it if there were a need?

There is one very simple answer. The Evangelist had died. Many critics agree with this, but seem to think that this implies that he left behind an incomplete work that required much editing. But this need not necessarily have been the case. There is nothing at all improbable about the suggestion that he had completed his work in draft form before he died. A fellow disciple undertook the task of circulating the Gospel and, having read it, decided to add a postscript emphasizing 19:35 and commenting upon the position and fate of the Beloved Disciple; but he did not tamper with the rest of the text.

The scenario just sketched envisages a situation in which the Beloved Disciple had gathered around him a number of disciples (later reasons will be given for believing that it is he who is behind the Johannine circle). Some of his disciples wrote: one wrote the Apocalypse, one (or possibly two) wrote the Johannine epistles, and another wrote the Gospel. The latter, however, died soon after the completion of a draft of his work, and another of the group undertook the task of circulating it. It was this person who added chapter 21, possibly using Johannine material with which he himself was familiar. Thus, the Beloved Disciple is the authority behind the work, but one of his disciples is the decisive redactor responsible for chapters 1–20 and another of his disciples is responsible for chapter 21. It was the former of these disciples—whom we call "the Evangelist"—who used and shaped the Johannine tradition, stamping upon the work his own unique theological insight.

So, then, chapters 1–20 were written by a single hand, and another added chapter 21. We have called the former the decisive redactor, or the Evangelist, and the latter the final redactor. It is now time to give a brief account of the redaction of the decisive redactor—its thematic concerns, structure, and so forth—and then clearly set out the method by which we intend to proceed.

3. THE JOHANNINE REDACTION

As a preliminary to our proposed sketch of the structure of the redaction of the Fourth Gospel, we shall deal briefly with Johannine themes. This attempt at a short explication of the Fourth Gospel's thematic concerns is a necessary preliminary inasmuch as it is helpful to have some notion of Johannine thematic complexes before we can discern how their organizational disposition gives us clearer insight into the author's exact intentions and meaning.

All the themes of the Gospel center on Jesus as the incarnate Word. He is God's only Son, the true life, the light that enlightens every man. His "signs" ("Christophanies") reveal him: in witnessing them, the disciples have seen his "glory" and testify to him. His mission is not condemnatory, but inasmuch as he is the light that shines in the darkness he shows up evil for what it is, and this is the judgement (e.g., 3:19). As he is one with the Father and abides in him, so his disciples must be one and abide in him through love. Begotten of the Father from above (e.g., 8:23), he is the Way, Truth, and Life; whatever is opposed to him is from below, especially darkness, lies, and death, the progeny of sin and the devil (cf. 8:44). He is sent into the world because the Father loves the world and wills its salvation (3:16 f.). The heart of his mission is his hour: the supreme moment of his glory and of the judgment of the world. He is the true shepherd, and his own recognize his voice; he is the true vine and his disciples abide in him like branches. He is the new Paschal lamb and the new Temple. He sends the Paraclete as a "guide into the whole range of truth." He empowers his own to forgive sins.

The transcendent nature of the Johannine Christ is asserted at the very beginning of the Gospel in the Prologue—he is the pre-existent λόγος, the agent of creation. What is remarkable about the section following the Prologue (1:19–51) is the thematization of "testimony" and the number of appellations applied to Jesus. Testimony to Jesus is given by John the Baptist, Andrew, Philip and Nathanael. In this section Jesus is given the titles Lamb of God, Son of God, Rabbi, Messiah, King of Israel, Son of Man—all of which are Jewish titles. In other words, from the very beginning the Evangelist is asserting that Jesus is the fulfilment of Jewish religious hopes. He goes further when, in the incident of Jesus and the Jewish Samaritans (4:1–42), he presents the Samaritans as professing Jesus to be the "Saviour of the World." At the end of the Gospel, Thomas confesses Jesus as his Lord and his God. But although the Johannine Christ is thus presented as transcending the boundaries of exclusively Jewish hopes, there can be no mistake that the Fourth Evangelist begins with the assertion that Jesus fulfills those hopes.

That Jesus is the fulfilment of Jewish messianic hopes is also thematized throughout the Gospel by repeated references to him as fulfillment of the Scriptures. This is done both allusively and directly. There are many allusive references to the Old Testament in the Fourth Gospel, for it is one woof woven into the Gospel's fabric.[34] Besides 1:1–19 this is especially evident in 2:1–11 (Jesus as the agent of the new dispensation), ch. 6 (Jesus is the Bread of Life), 10:1–27 (Jesus the Good Shepherd), and 15:1–17 (Jesus the True Vine). The redactor specifically refers to the fulfilment of Scriptures in 12:37–41, 18:9, 18:32, 19:24, 19:28, and 19:36.

Thus by using testimonies to Jesus, Old Testament allusions, and specific Scriptural citations, the Fourth Evangelist presents Jesus as the climactic revelation of God's plan. In this sense the Johannine Christ is at one with the Christ of the Synoptics. But the Fourth Evangelist's presentation of Christ goes further. Throughout the Fourth Gospel runs the theme of the Son's relationship to the Father. This relationship is explicated in such a way as to leave no doubt that it is this very relationship which causes the Jewish authorities to reject Jesus (cf. chapters 7 and 8). Jesus is presented unambiguously as the revealer of the Father (cf. 1:18; 6:37–40; 8:28f.; 10:30; 14:9–11; 14:31; 15:15).[35] Bultmann finds the depiction of Jesus as a man who has descended and ascended to be a puzzle in the Fourth Gospel, inasmuch as Jesus never divulges what he has "seen and heard," but only discloses that he is the revealer.[36] But the Johannine Christ is the revelation itself (John 14:9). He reveals the Father; thus he is the way, for he is truth and life (14:6). As he alone is "truth" (and, therefore, "life"), he is the only way. This concern for truth belongs to the substance of Johannine soteriology.

Now, our intent is to understand the redaction of the Fourth Gospel in its own terms, to enter its world of meaning. We have focused briefly on the Gospel's presentation of Jesus as unique revealer. Discerning the organizational disposition of these thematic concerns in the redaction, however, also gives us clearer insight into the author's exact intentions and meaning. For the organization of the whole further indicates the principle of intelligibility operative in the redactor's writing. This is why we will now examine the structure of the whole and seek to isolate its parts. This strategy of inquiry is undertaken not only with a view to understanding the whole in terms of the parts and the parts in terms of the whole (the hermeneutical circle of "whole and parts"), but also in an attempt to grasp the peculiarity and particularity of the whole by discerning the function of the meaning of the parts. In other words, our effort is to enter the Johannine world of meaning by an examination of the Johannine constellation of themes, and to relate them to the thrust of the whole. Moreover, "the whole" in writing and music is sequential; it is not grasped all at once as in such art forms as sculpture and painting. It follows that the strategy of understanding the whole in terms of the parts and the parts in terms of the whole calls for the understanding of the author's strategy of sequence. Our effort, then, of drawing up a plan of the redaction will be followed by a few remarks on the strategy of sequence in the work.

Among those scholars who have not concerned themselves with displacement theories, most have tended to agree that the structure of the Fourth Gospel is "simple in outline, complicated in detail."[37] The Gospel can easily be divided along the following lines: the Prologue (1:1–18); Narratives, Conversations, and Discourses (1:19–12:50); the Discourse of Jesus to "his own" (13:1–17:26); the Passion and Resurrection (18:1–20:31); and the Postscript (21:1–25). We seek to determine the function of the meaning of each of these parts in the redaction.

Our search begins with the Prologue. In its present form, the Prologue is indissolubly linked to the rest of the Gospel. J. A. T. Robinson has maintained that the Prologue (minus verses 6–8, which originally began the Gospel) has been tacked on to the completed Gospel.[38] His thesis falls on stylistic grounds.[39] Schnackenburg correctly maintains that "we are, therefore, dealing with a deliberate piece of redaction which, as is also suggested by the presence of criteria of Johannine style, can be attributed only to the Evangelist himself."[40]

What, then, is the meaning of the Prologue in relation to the rest of the Gospel? It has been variously described as an overture, a dramatic introduction, and a summary. How are we to see it?

There are four units within the Prologue: verses 1–5, 6–8, 9–13, 14–18. The first describes the preexistent status of the Logos; the second the testimony of John the Baptist; the third returns to the role of the Logos as creator and as existing in creation as the Light and Life of men—he enters the world and is rejected; the fourth deals with the economy of salvation—grace was manifested to those who believed.

The Prologue is evidently an announcement of theological themes. To this extent Bultmann is correct when he says that the Prologue leads the reader "out of the commonplace into a new and strange world of sounds and figures, and singling out particular motifs from the action that is now to be unfolded."[41] The Prologue thus functions as a hermeneutical key to the sense of the narratives, conversations, and discourses to follow.[42]

The section 1:19 through 12:50 contains a great deal of apparently disparate material, but its function is quite clear. As we have noted briefly, 1:19–50 is remarkable for the number of appellations applied to Jesus. It leaves the reader in no doubt that Jesus is the fulfilment of Jewish salvific hopes. 2:1–4:54 then elaborates on this theme. Jesus is not only the fulfilment of Jewish salvific hopes, his work has a universal significance (4:42). The meaning of the cleansing of the Temple (2:13–22) for the Evangelist is clear from the redactional comment in 2:21–22: the crucified and risen Christ would take the place of the Temple. This same theme had been anticipated in the incident at Cana (2:1–11). The dialogue with Nicodemus (3:1–15) stresses that only by rebirth can one enter eternal life and not simply by virtue of one's Jewish heritage. Chapter 4 then makes the universal significance of Jesus' work clear: he is "Saviour of the World" (4:42).

The healing story beginning in chapter 5 provides the introduction for the important and recurrent explication of the relation of Jesus to the Father. As this healing takes place on the Sabbath (to the chagrin of Jewish authorities), the ensuing dispute provides the occasion for a discourse by Jesus explaining his unity with the Father. This is the real stumbling block to Jewish authorities, who fail to realize that their own religious heritage points to Jesus (5:45 f.).

Chapter 6 (an obvious midrash on the Exodus theme) further elaborates on the true nature of Jesus the Christ, the Bread of Life. Chapters 7 and 8—masterfully interpreted by Dodd[43]—present a series of discourses on the dispute between Jesus and the Jewish authorities. These chapters continue analyzing Jesus' relationship to the Father, and the opposition that these claims evoke from the

Jewish authorities. Chapter 9 delineates the conflict by using dramatic irony: the Jews are blind to the Light within their midst.

In 10:1–18 (to be set against the background of Jewish salvific hopes) Jesus refers to himself as the Good Shepherd. A discourse follows, once again explaining the relationship of Jesus to the Father. In 11:1–53 the first half of the Gospel reaches its climax. In raising Lazarus from the dead, Jesus is clearly presented as the way to triumph over death.

Although 1:19–12:50 does contain much seemingly disparate material, it all coheres in its explanation of the true nature of the Johannine Christ. In particular, Jesus' relationship to the Father is examined repeatedly. It is, moreover, evident that the Evangelist does not conceive of the Jewish scriptures as the norm against which Jesus must be measured; rather, the Evangelist presents the scriptures as being incomplete without the climactic revelation of Jesus the Christ. In other words, the thrust of the first part of the redaction is not to present Jesus as *part* of God's plan—he *is* God's plan: human salvific hopes are consummated in him.

The next part of the Gospel—the discourse of Jesus to "his own" (13:1–17:26)—opens with the symbolic action of Jesus washing the disciples' feet, after which Jesus gives an almost uninterrupted discourse to the disciples. As Bultmann says:

> The subject-matter of the new section of the Gospel becomes clear from its opening scene: it deals with the relation of Jesus to his disciples, with his ἀγάπη to his ἴδιοι. His mission, seen as a whole, is itself the divine ἀγάπη (3:16) as it becomes operative in the world. The first part (chs. 3–12) has shown this ἀγάπη in its struggle to win over the world to itself; it had shown how ἀγάπη necessarily implies σκάνδαλον for the κοσμος, and how the latter allows the σκάνδαλον to become its own condemnation. The second part shows the ἀγάπη revealing itself to the community of "his own," firstly by direct means, in the farewell scenes of the night before the passion, and then indirectly in the passion itself, and in the Easter event.[44]

Chapters 13–17 are a hermeneutical key to the following narratives of Jesus' suffering, death, and resurrection appearances. These chapters do not solely focus on "the Twelve," and the disciples present at the Last Supper represent "his own" in a general sense. The whole of the Last Discourse embraces the life of the community and its relation to Jesus and the Paraclete. The guiding principle of the community is Jesus; the community is united to him in its knowledge, faith, and love.

The Passion narrative in the Fourth Gospel is highly charged with theological significance. Furthermore, the sparse comments of the redactor inescapably etch the meaning of Jesus' crucifixion: this is "the hour" of Jesus (13:1), the consummation of his salvific action as foretold by the scriptures (19:24; 19:28; 19:36–37).

The meaning of the resurrection appearances is specified in 20:17, where the Evangelist is making the theological assertion that "the elevation of Jesus which affected man's salvation involves the chain of crucifixion, resurrection and ascension."[45] Moreover, the meaning of Christ's first appearance to the disciples (20:19–23) forms the crux of verses 21–23, when they are divinely commissioned and receive the Holy Spirit to accomplish their mission. They are the chosen agents of the messianic economy of forgiveness. The central intent of the second appearance at which Thomas is present is given in 20:27–29. The climactic response of Thomas, "My Lord and my God," is followed by a blessing of Jesus on those who believe and yet have not seen. The Gospel concludes with 20:30 f. (As we have seen, ch. 21 is a postscript.)

From this brief analysis it is evident that there is indeed a strategy of sequence in the redaction of the Gospel. Moreover, the meaning of each part is grounded in the transcendent nature of the Johannine Christ. The unfolding of the meaning of the Gospel is governed by the author's prime concern: to present Jesus as the revealer of the Father. In this respect, at least two "hermeneutical keys" are prominent in the sequential strategy of the writing: the Prologue and the Last Discourse. As we observed, the Prologue singles out the motifs of the Gospel. The second part of the Gospel features the revelation of Jesus to "his own." In the first part of the Gospel Jesus is presented as the revealer to the world. He is "Saviour of the world"; the judge of the world. In this sense, he is the norm of all religion. The second part of the Gospel embraces the life of the specifically Christian community and its relation to Jesus and the Paraclete. That is, here the concern is with the revelation of Jesus as the norm for Christians.

4. STUDYING THE FOURTH GOSPEL

The following study of the Fourth Gospel is predicated on two basic methodological points. First, that the study of the Fourth Gospel tells us not only about the life and ministry of Jesus, but also about the circumstances of the Evangelist and his community.[46] Second, that redaction criticism is a most fruitful way of studying the Fourth Gospel. A brief discussion of these points follows.

The Johannine Transposition

The Fourth Evangelist, when he was writing, was giving expression to his own theology. This theology is expressed in a narrative about the past (concretely, about the life and ministry of Jesus). To put it another way, the Fourth Evangelist, writing many years after Jesus had been crucified, retrojected his own (contemporary) theology into a story of the past. He thus transposes his present theology into the past story of Jesus. This signifies a transposition with two facets: theology is transposed into story, and present into past. Now it is true that this kind of transposition is also found in the Synoptics, for all the Gospels are narrated in a confessional witness form, with the narrative itself reflecting a communication that transcends the historical. But in the Johannine redaction this transposition and retrojection is bolder, more central to the redactor's intention and more thoroughgoing than in the Synoptics. The distinctiveness of the Johannine transposition lies in the Evangelist's depiction of Jesus. The Christ of the Fourth Gospel is transposed from the realm of historicity (in the sense of "the literal actuality of the past" as well as in the sense of "the reality of ordinary human existence") to metahistoricity. The Fourth Gospel is not concerned with history in the sense of the recovery of "past particulars," and in this sense it is the furthest removed of all the Gospels from the actualities of history. Yet the Evangelist's own Christian experience penetrates the record of the events that brought it into being, and reveals their deepest significance. In the performance of this transposition, the Fourth Evangelist reveals his deepest concern. He wishes to present Jesus as the way, to show that Jesus is truth and life, Jesus alone is truth (14:6). This concern is the key to the Johannine transposition.

Redaction Criticism and the Fourth Gospel

Redaction criticism, by focusing upon the Gospel framework and the articulation of traditions, attempts to uncover the theological position of the Evangelist. Most redaction critics do this by examining how the Evangelist has changed his sources—what he has added, omitted and modified. It is by looking at these changes that one hopes to gain insight into the Evangelist's own theology. There are, however, difficulties in doing a redaction-critical study of the Fourth Gospel, for it presents special problems in distinguishing the superimposed redaction from traditional elements; for we have seen that chapters 1–20 are a unity, written by an author who, if he did use sources, used them so freely that they are impossible to isolate. However, this does not preclude redaction-critical inquiry into the Fourth Gospel. First of all, we acknowledge that in places it is possible to see certain verses as comments of the decisive redactor. Second, we must not forget that the author sponsors the whole of his work including the traditional elements he employs. Indeed, there is a danger in overemphasizing the tradition history approach. James Robinson says, for example:

> New Testament theology cannot be carried on apart from a reconstruction of the history of the transmission of traditions, since apart from such a reconstruction the hermeneutical activity carried on within the Gospel itself cannot be identified. This in turn means that progress in understanding Johannine theology depends on progress in defining Johannine sources, such as the resolution of the problem of the miracle source.[47]

The danger of such an over-statement is that the study of the Gospel sources—and it is doubtful whether this can successfully be done in the Fourth Gospel in any case—inevitably creates a tendency to make the distinctive central, irrespective of the status of the common material in the total design of what the writer finally produces.

In the final analysis the study of the history of forms and tradition in the Fourth Gospel has yielded highly unsatisfactory and debatable results. As we have seen, many studies of the Fourth Gospel have concluded that one cannot isolate various independent literary strata, and certainly cannot write out *in extenso* whatever written sources he might have used. Such conclusions are, however, very valuable if, as Schnackenburg puts it, "they serve to underline the evangelist's predominant role in the making and shaping of the Fourth Gospel, and as the distinctive theologian who gave its doctrine its unified character."[48]

The approach taken in this text can perhaps be silhouetted more sharply by pointing out that there are two distinct tendencies within redaction criticism. One is to study the redaction primarily by reference to its sources. The other is to study the redaction primarily by reference to its total design. These approaches are motivated by different aims. The former tends to focus on the redactor's uniqueness vis-à-vis his predecessors; the latter tends to focus on the redactor's whole theology, underscoring not only what sets him apart from others but what unites him to them. As we have already noted, this latter approach has been called "composition criticism."[49] As Fowler says:

> As a piece of literature, the Gospel has an integrity, a certain wholeness to it which should be acknowledged by those who interpret it. It is a fatal error to move from the standard axiom that the Gospel tradition originally circulated as individual sayings and stories to the conclusion that the gospels are simply collected pieces with no great coherence. The whole is more than the sum of its parts. The gospels do in fact display unity and coherence, but that can only be seen if one entertains the possibility of a holistic approach to them and avoids an overly fragmented, pericope-by-pericope reading of the texts. Only by approaching the gospels as literary works, i.e., as integral wholes, can we see how all the individual pieces fit together to make a whole.[50]

Thus, although major contemporary works on the Fourth Gospel have often undertaken the task of consistently distinguishing between materials inherited by the redactor and, on the other hand, the redactor's own additions, alterations, and omissions, our study of the Gospel is not so methodically ambitious. Our inquiry will be conducted within the limits of the redaction as such, focusing upon the hermeneutical circle of whole and parts. We will make no attempt to figure out what the decisive redactor might have added to an original text. We will focus on the text as it now stands.

5. JOHANNINE MOTIFS

We must now focus more specifically on our task of recovering the message of the Fourth Gospel. One aspect of this message is very clear: Jesus is the one and only way to salvation. Jesus—to the complete exclusion of all others—is the way to salvation. He alone has seen the Father, so he alone can reveal him. It follows that he alone can give eternal life. It is clear that the Fourth Gospel prominently features themes of revelation and response, the unique saving revelation brought to the world by Jesus Christ and the call for unreserved adherence not simply to it but to him, for he is not simply the revealer but the revelation itself. Jesus is indeed the very norm of religion; normative religion can be nothing other than the response to Jesus.

There is, however, a further development of this theme of normative religion. The Fourth Evangelist also presents us with a theology of normative Christianity. Here the Johannine concern is not thematic but pragmatic. The Evangelist has not presented normative Christianity as a theme; rather he has orchestrated such themes as "truth" and "witness" to secure it as a fact. In chapter 17, for example, we are told that the Johannine community taught what Jesus taught, and that this comes from the Father himself (17:6c, 14a, 17; cf. 7:16b).

There is obviously a legitimizing interest here. In 17:8 the Johannine community is presented as having accepted the Christological doctrine that the Father sent the Son, and that the Son has communicated to them the λόγος which they have in turn communicated to the second generation (17:20). Other major themes such as the sending of the Paraclete and the witness of the Beloved Disciple have also been pressed into the service of the Evangelist's concern for legitimacy, and this concern is equally the key to what we have called the Johannine transposition.

The theology of the Fourth Gospel is preeminently a theology of revelation. This note is struck in the Prologue and continues throughout the Gospel. The Word is the light that shines in the darkness. John the Baptist is "sent by God" but he is not the revealer. He is a witness to the revealer; his sole role is to testify to the light.

The dramatic element of the Fourth Gospel is epitomized in "divine initiative" versus "human response": the initiative of revelation Ἦν τὸ φῶς τὸ ἀληθινόν . . . ἐρχόμενον εἰς τὸν κόσμον ("The true light was . . . coming into the world" [1:9]) and the response of unbelief ὁ κόσμος αὐτὸν οὐκ ἔγνω ("the world knew him not" [1:10]). Yet the divine initiative did win a positive response. There were those who welcomed the light, who not only "saw his glory" but who "knew" him, "accepted" him, "believed in his name" and thereby became "children of God." The Prologue concludes with a charged epitome of the Gospel's theology of revelation (1:14e–18). We will return to this passage of the Prologue, but first we must say more about the sense of "truth" (ἡ ἀλήθεια) in the Johannine redaction.

The theme "truth" is so interwoven with the theme "word" (ὁ λόγος) in Jn. 8:31–55 that the two appear to be reciprocally defining. The relationship between them finds a first expression in vss. 31f.: Ἐὰν ὑμεῖς μείνητε ἐν τῷ λόγῳ τῷ ἐμῷ . . . γνώσεσθε τὴν ἀλήθειαν, καὶ ἡ ἀλήθεια ἐλευθερώσει ὑμᾶς ("If you continue in my word . . . you will know the truth, and the truth will make you free"). Those who seek to kill Jesus do so because his word finds no place in them (v. 37). Says Jesus: νῦν δὲ ζητεῖτέ με ἀποκτεῖναι, ἄνθρωπον ὃς τὴν ἀλήθειαν ὑμῖν λελάληκα ἣν ἤκουσα παρὰ τοῦ θεοῦ· τοῦτο Ἀβραὰμ οὐκ ἐποίησεν ("but now you are trying to kill me, a man who has told you the truth that I heard from God. This is not what Abraham did" [v. 40]). The accusers of Jesus are not truly Abraham's descendants; if they were they would love Jesus. The Son claims no independent rights; he has been sent from God (v. 42). They do not understand Jesus' word because their father is the devil, and the devil is the father of lies: ὑμεῖς ἐκ τοῦ πατρὸς τοῦ διαβόλου ἐστὲ καὶ τὰς ἐπιθυμίας τοῦ πατρὸς ὑμῶν θέλετε ποιεῖν. ἐκεῖνος ἀνθρωποκτόνος ἦν ἀπ᾽ ἀρχῆς, καὶ ἐν τῇ ἀληθείᾳ οὐκ ἔστηκεν, ὅτι οὐκ ἔστιν ἀλήθεια ἐν αὐτῷ. ὅταν λαλῇ τὸ ψεῦδος, ἐκ τῶν ἰδίων λαλεῖ, ὅτι ψεύστης ἐστὶν καὶ ὁ πατὴρ αὐτοῦ. ("You are from your father the devil and you choose to do your father's desires. He was a murderer from the beginning and does not stand in the truth, because there is no truth in him. When he lies he speaks according to his own nature, for he is a liar and the father of lies" [v. 44]). Therefore they cannot comprehend the truth: ἐγὼ δὲ ὅτι τὴν ἀλήθειαν λέγω, οὐ πιστεύετέ μοι ("but because I tell you the truth, you do not believe me" [v. 45]). They would believe Jesus if they were of God (v. 47). The word of Jesus, which is truth (v.

45), is also eternal life (v. 51). The texts of John 8:31 ff., in which the theme "truth" is interwoven with the theme "word," therefore justify the general agreement among scholars that the theology of the Fourth Gospel is a theology of revelation.

There is, however, some disagreement over the background against which ἡ ἀλήθεια is to be understood. Does the Johannine usage of ἡ ἀλήθεια reflect a Hellenistic rather than a Hebraic background? The background reflected by the Johannine usage of ἡ ἀλήθεια must be determined to facilitate our understanding of its intended sense in the redaction. The etymology of the word ἡ ἀλήθεια suggests the root meaning of "non-concealment"; that is, "the full or real state of affairs." Thus for historians ἡ ἀλήθεια would be real events as opposed to myths, while for philosophers it would indicate real being in the absolute sense. The two adjectives derived from ἡ ἀλήθεια are ἡ ἀληθίνος and ἡ ἀλήθης. Ἡ ἀλήθης means "corresponding to facts," "true" or "veridical," i.e., a thing really is as seen or represented. Ἡ ἀληθίνος, when applied to objects of experience means "real" as opposed to "pictured" objects. As the adjectives indicate, ἡ ἀλήθεια is susceptible to two nuanced interpretations. When the truth of a statement means "that which corresponds to the real facts," ἡ ἀλήθεια can refer to the abstract quality of truthfulness or the content of a statement. Ἡ ἀλήθεια can also mean "reality" as opposed to "appearance."

In Hellenism ἡ ἀλήθεια thus comes to refer to eternal or divine realities. As Rudolf Bultmann says, "It still retains its sense of genuineness, since the divine being is that in which man comes to share in order to be saved . . . and thus attain to his own genuine or proper being."[51] But the presupposition that ἡ ἀλήθεια is accessible to thought has been abandoned; it is accessible only when human limitations are transcended (as in ecstasy or revelation). In this sense ἡ ἀλήθεια has become an eschatological concept.[52]

The LXX translates the Hebrew word אמת as ἡ ἀλήθεια. But the two words are not equivalent. אמת primarily has the connotation of "trustworthiness" or "steadfastness" and is used as an attribute of God in this sense. The Hebrew concept of truth is different from that of the Greek; for the Hebrew truth is moral rather than intellectual.[53]

Dodd and Bultmann contend that the background against which the Johannine concept of ἡ ἀλήθεια is to be understood is

Greek rather than Hebraic. Dodd, in his *Johannine Epistles* defines ἡ ἀλήθεια as "the ultimate reality as revealed in Christ."[54] In *The Interpretation of the Fourth Gospel* he describes ἡ ἀλήθεια as "the eternal reality as revealed to men—either the reality itself or the revelation of it."[55] Dodd admits to only one passage in the Fourth Gospel where a reader would see ἡ ἀλήθεια used in a way strange to the natural idiom of the Greek language, namely Jn 3:21. He also admits that in 16:13 the Hebrew expression may "find an echo" but argues that the context rules out the Hebrew connotation: "This is clearly not the sense of ἡ ἀλήθεια in John xvi.13. The context speaks of things to be spoken, announced and heard. The Paraclete hears the words of Christ, receives them, and announces them to the disciples. The content of these words is precisely summed up in the word ἡ ἀλήθεια, which is therefore not אֱמֶת, 'faithfulness,' but 'truth.'"[56] And in 1:14 the phrase "full of grace and truth" derives from a Hebrew source, but again, argues Dodd, "while the mould of the expression is determined by Hebrew usage, the actual sense of the words must be determined by Greek usage."[57]

There are some scholars who take a mediating position on ἡ ἀλήθεια by maintaining that the Johannine concept combines biblical and Greek philosophical ideas. De la Potterie argues, however, that the choice should not be restricted to Greek or biblical background, nor does he believe that those form the background. In the apocalyptic and sapiential literature of post-biblical Judaism one finds a new usage and sense unrestricted by specifically Greek thought-forms. This new sense is moral, as in the Bible, but nuanced to include more than fidelity and, in fact, to signify "uprightness." Moreover, ἡ ἀλήθεια in these writings often intends revealed truth (as in the doctrine of Wisdom), and so is synonymous with the Greek word μυστήριον: the divine plan revealed to men. For example, in the "book of truth" (Dn 10:21) is written the plan of God for the time of salvation (cf. Wis 3:9; IQH 7, 26 f.; IQH 6,6).[58]

De la Potterie notes that the following expressions are missing from Greek and Hellenistic literature, but are paralleled in the Bible, *The Testament of the Twelve Patriarchs*, the writings of Qumran: "doing the truth" (Jn 3:21); "in spirit and truth" (Jn 4:23 f.); "in truth" (Jn 17:19). Still more probative of de la Potterie's hypothesis on the background of ἡ ἀλήθεια is the close tie with word, which we have already discussed. In fact in Johannine usage "to speak" signifies revelation (e.g., Jn 17:17: "thy word is truth"; Jn 8:40: "I told you the truth which is from God"). In Hellenistic and Gnostic dualism, ἡ ἀλήθεια is not a word which is heard, but the divine essence seen or contemplated on arrival at the spiritual goal (CH 8, 3). In apocalyptic literature, however the explanation of enigmas is heard, and in Daniel this explanation is אמת.[59]

The ultimate test of this hypothesis is, however, exegetical. We shall examine those texts concerning the "Spirit of Truth" later. This point in our inquiry will focus on two texts: John 1:17b–18 and 14:6. Our purpose in focusing on these texts is not only to test de la Potterie's hypothesis, but also to understand the Johannine concept of ἡ ἀλήθεια.

The text of John 1:17b–18 reads:

ἡ χάρις καὶ ἡ ἀλήθεια διὰ Ἰησοῦ Χριστοῦ ἐγένετο
θεὸν οὐδεὶς ἑώρακεν πώποτε ·
μονογενὴς θεὸς ὁ ὢν εἰς τὸν κόλπον τοῦ πατρὸς
ἐκεῖνος ἐξηγήσατο.

(Grace and truth came through Jesus Christ.
No one has ever seen God;
the only son, who is in the bosom of the Father,
he has made him known.)

Here, "grace" and "truth" are probably reciprocally defining, thus giving the sense: "The gracious gift of revealed truth (came through Jesus Christ)."[60] God is not directly accessible to humans ("no one has ever seen the Father"); he is accessible only through Christ. (There may be a polemic here against the desire to see the "glory of the Lord" [cf. Ex 33:18] and mystical visions of the divine.) Christ reveals God because he has a special relationship with God—he is in τὸν κόλπον τοῦ πατρὸς. In fact the Greek literally means "*into* the bosom of the Father," which is probably meant to indicate a dynamic relationship with God. It is because of this relationship that Christ is able to "make [God] known."

A text which similarly deals with the idea that God is revealed through Christ is found in John 14:6. The text reads:

λέγει αὐτῷ ὁ Ἰησοῦς, Ἐγώ εἰμι ἡ ὁδὸς καὶ ἡ ἀλήθεια καὶ
ἡ ζωή · οὐδεὶς ἔρχεται πρὸς τὸν πατέρα εἰ μὴ δι᾿ ἐμοῦ.

(Jesus said to him, 'I am the way, and the truth, and the life;
no one comes to the Father, but by me.)

The real problem posed for exegetes is the precise relationship
between the concepts of "way," "truth," and "life." Bultmann
finds here the dualist and Gnostic theme of the ascent to light and
truth, and he interprets this verse as meaning that Jesus is simulta-
neously the way *and* the goal.[61] De la Potterie argues that this is
mistaken, and points out that the view of ancient writers was that
Jesus was the way *to* the goal.[62]

De la Potterie substantiates his own interpretation of the verse
("C'est moi, le chemin") by a literary analysis and an examina-
tion of the milieu out of which 14:6 springs. In the first place,
John 13:33–14:6 is dominated by the theme of the departure of
Jesus (a theme introduced by the departure of Judas in 13:30). The
motifs of "going" and "following" are dominant.

In 14:1–4 Jesus seeks to console the disciples: all will be
reunited in the Father's house, for he goes to prepare a place for
them. The topic of the next few verses is specified in 14:4: "you
know the way"; that is, the issue is "the way." In 14:6 a chiastic
structure is displayed:

6a *I* am . . .
6b . . . through *me*

Moreover, of the two questions of 14:5:

(a) We do not know where you are going
(b) How can we know the way?

14:6 emphasizes the answer to (b):

(b) I am *the way*
(a) no one comes to the Father
(b) except through me

The significance of this literary analysis lies in the fact that in it
"truth" and "life" play no significant role; they are no more than
explanatory comments on "the way." The sense is this: Jesus is
the way to the Father precisely inasmuch as he is truth and life: "I
am the way (for I am) truth and (therefore) life."

This conclusion of de la Potterie is quite in accord with what we have asserted about the background of the Johannine concept of truth. Certainly, its sense as defined above is neither Gnostic nor Greek. Neither in this text nor in any other Johannine text can it be legitimately claimed that ἡ ἀλήθεια is equivalent to God.

So then, "the way" is here metaphorical, and does not suggest anything of the Gnostic ascent to the realm of light and truth. Furthermore, truth is not "the reality of the divine," nor is it the goal. Its sense is perhaps best given by reference to the Acts of Thomas, where Christ is "the richness of truth," he who "mounts the way to truth," the "teacher of truth." This guides the exegesis of Jn 14:6—Jesus is "the truth" as "perfect revealer," as "plenitude" of revealed truth.[63]

In the Fourth Gospel, then, ἡ ἀλήθεια is not "an object of intellectual research, but the essential principle of the moral life, of sanctity; for it is the thought of God on man, perceived and heard in faith."[64] "To be of the truth" is to cultivate an interior disposition, bringing oneself into harmony with ἡ ἀλήθεια, remaining habitually under its action, acquiring a connaturality and affinity with the truth.

The truth "frees" the follower of Christ (Jn 8:32). It is the word of Jesus which frees us from sin. Η ἀλήθεια is a divine, power-charged concept. Thus 17:17 ("sanctify them in the truth") means, in effect: "Set them on a course of holiness by the [power of the] saving word of revelation." Expressions such as "doing the truth" and "walking in the truth," now take on a rich, specifically Christian connotation. Even a seemingly colorless expression such as "in truth" becomes "a magnificent compendium of [John's] whole moral teaching."[65] It is a pure semitism. To love one's brother "in truth" is not to love them "really" but to love them with the power of the ἡ ἀλήθεια that abides in us.

In conclusion, the Johannine concept of truth is to be differentiated from the intellectualist concept of the Greeks and the cosmic dualism of theosophy. For the Fourth Evangelist ἡ ἀλήθεια is the word of the Father addressed to humankind, incarnated in Christ and illumined through the action of the Spirit.[66] The Johannine concept of truth shows that salvation consists in communion with "the Father"; that such communion is communicated by the gift of "eternal life," and that this "gracious gift" is nothing other than "truth." As Jesus is not simply the revealer but the revelation itself, he alone is the way to salvation.[67]

This presentation of Jesus as the unique revealer is further emphasized by the way the Evangelist presents the two images of the Shepherd (10:1–21) and the Vine (15:1–17).

In John 10:1–21, Jesus speaks figuratively about how the person who does not enter the sheepfold by the door, but by another way, is a "thief and a robber": Ἀμὴν ἀμὴν λέγω ὑμῖν, ὁ μὴ εἰσερχόμενος διὰ τῆς θύρας εἰς τὴν αὐλὴν τῶν προβάτων ἀλλὰ ἀναβαίνων ἀλλαχόθεν ἐκεῖνος κλέπτης ἐστὶν καὶ λῃστής ("Truly, truly, I say to you, he who does not enter the sheepfold by the door but climbs in by another way, that man is a thief and a robber" [10:1]). He who enters by the door is the shepherd of the sheep (ὁ δὲ εἰσερχόμενος διὰ τῆς θύρας ποιμήν ἐστιν τῶν προβάτων [10:2]). The Greek ἀναβαίνων, which the RSV translates as "to climb," more accurately means "to go up" or "ascend." It is possible therefore that the Fourth Evangelist means us to see a second or double meaning here. The word not only refers to the thief and bandit gaining access to the sheep by surreptitious means, but also to those "who would ascend to heaven by some other means than the cross."[68] It refers not to one particular figure but to "every corrupter of the faithful or of those who are called to the faith, to everyone who might be a temptation to them—always, that is, in a particular concrete situation."[69] Such pretenders will be unable to deceive Christ's elect sheep (10:5; cf. I John 4:6). But since the shepherd calls "his own" (10:4), it follows that there are sheep in the fold who are not his and who do not respond to his voice. Who are "his own"? And with what group are the sum of the sheep in the fold to be identified? Some interpreters see the fold as that of Judaism (cf. v. 16: "But I have other sheep who are not of this fold"). Others have identified the flock with the Christian community.

What is the Evangelist's intention? With which set of characters within the story line are the readers to identify, if any? The false teachers and heterodox belief that were problems in I John (especially I John 2:19), can illuminate our understanding of this text. For the shepherd is to be identified with Jesus (v. 11), and the bandits and robbers with false teachers. The flock is the Christian community, the church. But if this is the case, how are we to understand the sense of "his own"? Who are the other sheep in the fold who do not recognize the shepherd's voice? Evidently they do not know the voice of the shepherd and are thus all the more susceptible to the bandit and thief; they are those in the community who are susceptible to false teachers. But what of v. 16? In v. 3 there is a distinction between sheep within the same fold; in v. 16 sheep of other folds are mentioned. If the fold of v. 3 is the Christian community, it follows that the other folds of v. 16 refer to non-Christian communities.

Many commentators have found considerable difficulty with "For all who came before me are thieves and robbers" (10:1). Does the verse refer to Old Testament prophets? Or the Pharisees and priests of Jesus' time? This seems most unlikely. On the basis of the interpretation above, it refers to all pretended revealers and saviours.[70] The verse is in fact a condemnation of the religions of the age, inasmuch as they appeal to supposed revealers of earlier ages.[71]

In 10:17 there is a shift from the shepherd of the previous pericope to the "door." There is also an ambiguity: 10:7 seems to mean "I am the door of the sheep," that is, the shepherd approaches the sheep through Jesus; 10:9 seems to mean "I am the door through which the sheep enter the fold," that is, Jesus is the door not for the shepherd but for the sheep. But this ambiguity should not be given too much emphasis. It seems unnecessary to seek an explanation by resorting to composite source theories. Barrett has observed, "The only unity in the discourse is Christological, Jesus draws to himself every epithet which the picture of sheep and shepherd suggests."[72] This is precisely the point: the only protection the sheep have from pretenders breaking into the fold is to know the shepherd and his function. Jesus is the only means of entry into the salvific community. All pretenders or unauthorized persons can only bring death (v. 10).

Jesus, then, is the good shepherd who is willing even to die to protect his sheep (10:11). The "hirelings" betray the flock (10:12). They are those entrusted with the care of the flock who, when danger threatens, flee—the leaders of the Christian community who allow the sheep to be scattered. This kind of imagery of the flock being scattered is used elsewhere in the New Testament (cf. Acts 20:29–30); there is every reason to think that John was reflecting a situation familiar to him. Jesus is the good shepherd because he knows his sheep (10:14), a mutual knowledge analogous to that of the Father and the Son (10:15). The unity of the flock is possible only through Jesus.[73]

This image of unity only being possible through Jesus is taken up again in John 15:1–17, where Jesus is the "true vine" (ἡ ἄμπελος ἡ ἀληθινή). There has been much discussion of the background to this image of the vine.[74] Is it Jewish, or is it gnostic? If the background is Jewish and the Old Testament, John radically transforms the sense in that the vine no longer refers to Israel: it is a Christological definition applied to Jesus. Moreover, a comparison with similar sayings in the synoptics (Mk 12:1–9; Mt 21:33–44; 20:1–16, 21:28–32; Lk 20:9–16) reveals that in the Johannine redaction it no longer refers to the eschatological crisis of the ministry of Jesus but to the continuous life of the Christian community.

One of the other major points lies in determining whether the passage has a (secondary) eucharistic significance. Such commentators as Bultmann totally reject such a suggestion.[75] But although the eucharistic institution is lacking in John, it was probably familiar to the readership, for it is part of an early faith formula (I Cor 11:23–26). Moreover, the cup designated as "the fruit of the vine" was also probably familiar to them (Mk 14:25; Mt 26:29; cf. also Didache 9:2). The theology of the eucharist in the early church (I Cor 10:16–17) and that of the vine in John both stress intimate union with Christ. It is therefore not unreasonable to think that this passage in John would evoke eucharistic thoughts from the readership.

This possibility is given more weight by the remarkable parallels between John 15:1–17 and its eucharistic section, 6:51–58. (Cf. 15:5b with 6:56; 15:5c with 6:57; 15:13 with 6:51c; 15:1 with 6:51a.) These parallels have led R. E. Brown to comment: "Perhaps, when it was brought into the context of the Last Supper, the *mashal* of the vine served in Johannine circles the paraenetic purpose of insisting that eucharistic union must last and bear fruit and must deepen the union between Jesus and his disciples already existing through love."[76]

The emphasis in 15:1 falls on Jesus as the "true" vine; only through him is life to be found. It has been suggested that here the author intends a polemic against Judaism, but this seems unlikely. As Barrett says: "There is abundant evidence that John was well aware of the historical fact of the rejection of Jesus by Judaism (see especially 12:36b–50). But this rejection he has already set forth, and here, as regularly in the last discourses, his major interest is in the life of the Church, in the question of who are and who are not disciples of Jesus."[77]

In 15:2 we are told that every branch that bears no fruit is taken away. This leads us to question who the branches are that do not bear fruit. Brown suggests that the author may have been thinking of the "anti-Christs" of I John 2:18–19. Certainly Christian apostates are intended, as shown by "in me." Furthermore, the theme of the unity of Christ with the faithful is accented in verses 4–5. If the followers of Jesus remain in him through faith he will remain in them through love and fruitfulness.

In 15:6 we come upon the most crucial part of this image of the vine. For here we are told that anyone who does not abide in Jesus is "cast forth as a branch and withers." What is the force of "cast forth" (ἐκβάλλω)? Often it is taken as referring to eschatological punishment, but this does not cohere well with Johannine thought. The Greek ἐκβάλλω often carries the connotation of "banishment from a family or society." In John 9:34f, it seems to have the double sense of "to expel from the synagogue and to expel from the audience room"; cf. also I John 2:19.[78] Therefore it is very possible that here it refers to expulsion from the Christian community. The meaning then would be that the unfaithful or apostate Christian suffers the fate of the unfruitful branch in that he or she is cut off from that which gives life (the Christian community).

The two images of the shepherd and the vine again emphasize the theme of Jesus as the unique revealer. There is only one shepherd (10:16) and that is Jesus. Jesus is the true vine (15:1), and apart from him the Christian can do nothing (15:5). But these passages also stress that the response to the revelation of Jesus must be "in truth." There is a recognition that within the Christian community itself there are those who betray the flock. Moreover, in the passage on the vine, the Fourth Evangelist is stating that errant believers must be put out of the Christian community, a fate which, as the denial of eternal life, is death (15:6).

The Fourth Evangelist's concern, then, is not only to present Jesus as the unique revelation of the Father, but also to characterize the response that the revelation calls for. The very nature of the revelation of Jesus calls forth a response "in truth." This requires the cultivation of a certain inner disposition that has an affinity and connaturality with the revelation itself.

The first phase in the development of the Evangelist's theology is the presentation of Jesus as the unique revealer. In the second phase this presentation is inextricably bound with the Evangelist's concern to legitimize his own theology. This becomes especially apparent when we examine the motif of the Paraclete.[79] Much has been written on the Paraclete. We will not review all the literature here, but rather will focus on two particular questions: What is the function of the Paraclete in the Johannine redaction? And what are we able to discern from a study of the Paraclete passages of the contemporary historical horizon of the Evangelist?

In 14:15–17 Jesus promises his disciples that he will send them "another Paraclete":

> Ἐὰν ἀγαπᾶτέ με, τὰς ἐντολὰς τὰς ἐμὰς τηρήσετε κἀγὼ ἐρωτήσω τὸν πατέρα καὶ ἄλλον παράκλητον δώσει ὑμῖν ἵνα μεθ᾽ ὑμῶν εἰς τὸν αἰῶνα, τὸ πνεῦμα τῆς ἀληθείας, ὃ ὁ κόσμος οὐ δύναται λαβεῖν, ὅτι οὐ θεωρεῖ αὐτὸ οὐδὲ γινώσκει· ὑμεῖς γινώσκετε αὐτό, ὅτι παρ᾽ ὑμῖν μένει καὶ ἐν ὑμῖν ἐστιν.

> (If you love me, you will keep my commandments. And I will pray the Father, and he will give you another Paraclete, to be with you for ever, even the Spirit of truth, whom the world cannot receive, because it neither sees him nor knows him; you know him, for he dwells with you, and is in you.)

The sense of these verses is not that when Jesus is present in the disciples, they will keep his commandments; rather the verses attempt to define the nature of love. This section addresses itself to a question that is most easily understood in the context of the Last Discourse: Can the disciples continue to love Jesus, even after he is gone? The disciples who love Jesus must continue to keep his commandments and it is promised that they will receive the Paraclete. Thus the disciples will not be without that which they had in Jesus. This Paraclete is defined as the "Spirit of Truth," a title used three times in the Fourth Gospel. By this phrase the Fourth Evangelist means "the Spirit who communicates truth."[80]

The second text that features the Paraclete is 14:26, which reads:

ὁ δὲ παράκλητος, τὸ πνεῦμα τὸ ἅγιον ὃ πέμψει ὁ πατὴρ ἐν τῷ ὀνό-
ματί μου, ἐκεῖνος ὑμᾶς διδάξει πάντα καὶ ὑπομνήσει ὑμᾶς πάντα
ἃ εἶπον ὑμῖν [ἐγώ].

(But the Paraclete, the Holy Spirit, whom the Father will send in
my name, he will teach you [the disciples] all things, and bring to
your remembrance all that I [Jesus] have said to you.)

Teaching and bringing to remembrance (or reminding) are not
here to be taken in different senses; the same function is being
described. Thus there is no independent revelation through the
Paraclete, but by carrying on Christ's work the Paraclete ensures
that the revelation does not die out with his departure.[81]

The third text (15:26–27) which features the Paraclete reads:

Ὅταν ἔλθῃ ὁ παράκλητος ὃν ἐγὼ πέμψω ὑμῖν παρὰ τοῦ πατρός,
τὸ πνεῦμα τῆς ἀληθείας ὃ παρὰ τοῦ πατρός ἐκπορεύεται, ἐκεῖνος
μαρτυρήσει περὶ ἐμοῦ· καὶ ὑμεῖς δὲ μαρτυρήεῖτε, ὅτι ἀπ᾽ ἀρχῆς
μετ᾽ ἐμοῦ ἐστε.

(But when the Paraclete comes, whom I shall send to you from
the Father, even the Spirit of truth, who proceeds from the
Father, he will bear witness to me; and you also are witnesses,
because you have been with me from the beginning.)

This passage again expresses the idea that Christ's mission parallels that of the Paraclete (cf. 8:42; 13:3; 16:27;17:8). It prepares
the reader very well for the next section on the Paraclete (16:7–11),
where we have a forensic description of his work. The gap is thus
bridged between what has been said about the Paraclete and what
will be said in the next reference to him. The Paraclete represents
Jesus among the disciples, and this explains why the world will
treat them in the same way it treated Jesus.

The final reference (16:7–11) reads:

ἀλλ᾽ ἐγὼ τὴν ἀλήθειαν λέγω ὑμῖν, συμφέρει ὑμῖν ἵνα ἐγὼ ἀπέλθω.
ἐὰν γὰρ μὴ ἀπέλθω, ὁ παράκλητος οὐκ ἐλεύσεται πρὸς ὑμᾶς· ἐὰν δὲ
πορευθῶ, πέμψω αὐτὸν πρὸς ὑμᾶς. καὶ ἐλθὼν ἐκεῖνος ἐλέγξει τὸν
κόσμον περὶ ἁμαρτίας καὶ περὶ δικαιοσύνης καὶ περὶ κρίσεως·
περὶ ἁμαρτίας μέν, ὅτι οὐ πιστεύουσιν εἰς ἐμέ· περὶ δικαιοσύνης
δέ, ὅτι πρὸς τὸν πατέρα ὑπάγω καὶ οὐκέτι θεωρεῖτέ με· περὶ
δὲ κρίσεως, ὅτι ὁ ἄρχων τοῦ κόσμον τούτου κέκριται.

(Nevertheless I tell you the truth: it is to your advantage that I go
away, for if I do not go away, the Paraclete will not come to

you; but if I go, I will send him to you. And when he comes, he will convince the world of sin and of righteousness and of judgment: of sin, because they do not believe in me; of righteousness, because I go to the Father, and you will see me no more; of judgment, because the ruler of this world is judged.)

The sense of this passage is indeed difficult. It is possible that behind the imagery there is the notion of a trial of cosmic dimensions, in which the world is proved guilty before God. But, as Bultmann himself observes, even if that were originally the case, in the text before us the "mythical side of the picture has faded away." Brown says:

> Moreover, the trial is only indirectly a trial of the world. It is properly a rerun of the trial of Jesus in which the Paraclete makes the truth emerge for the disciples to see. Its effect on the world stems from the fact that, having been assured by the Paraclete of the victory of Jesus in that trial, the disciples go forth to bear witness (xv 27) and thus challenge the world and its interpretation of the trial. In being the moving force behind this the Paraclete is simply continuing the work of Jesus, who himself bore evidence against the world that what it does is evil (vii 7).[82]

The three nouns "sin," "righteousness," and "judgement" are used without the article in Greek and therefore are to be understood in a general and not in a particular sense. These verses thus indicate that first, the world is guilty of sin by refusing to believe in Jesus. Second, the Paraclete shows the irony of the world's judging Jesus to be guilty, for in fact he was just and innocent. Jesus' death was really his glorification (cf. Jn 17:5; Rom 3:21–31). Third, in condemning Jesus, the world itself is judged. The paradox is that, through the Paraclete, Christ is still present after his death. Thus the world—which thought that its crucifixion of Jesus was a victory—is, in fact, defeated.

On the basis of all of this we can draw the following conclusions about the function of the Paraclete in the Johannine redaction. First, that he functions as a guarantor of continuity between Jesus and the disciples; that is, he guarantees the continuity of the Christian tradition (cf. 14:16). We saw how 14:15–17 specifically focuses on the question of how the disciples can continue to love Jesus after he is gone. This is done through the Paraclete, who is the

"Spirit of truth," i.e., "the Spirit who communicates truth." The divine truth is that which works in revelation. The function of the "Spirit who communicates truth" is to continue the work of revelation in the community. Related to the Paraclete's revelatory activity is the forensic aspect of his work, for he glorifies Jesus by continuing the work of revelation (16:14) which continually calls for a response from the world (16:8–11). Interpretations which focus solely on the charismatic function of the Paraclete are essentially defective, for the primary emphasis falls on the Paraclete's function as the communicator of truth; he is the nourisher and sustainer of that interior disposition which in faith grasps and responds to the revelation of the Father.

Brown is probably right in observing that the Evangelist had in mind the problem caused by "the death of apostolic eyewitnesses who were the living chain between the church and Jesus of Nazareth."[83] But can this observation be nuanced? Can we give a more concrete historical dimension to the concern of the Evangelist to show that his own community stands in direct continuity with Jesus of Nazareth? A more concrete historical dimension is, in fact, provided through the motif of the disciple whom Jesus loved (the "Beloved Disciple"). A study of this motif gives us direct access to this concrete aspect of the Evangelist's concern to legitimate his own theology.

6. THE BELOVED DISCIPLE IN THE FOURTH GOSPEL

The study of the Beloved Disciple helps us to determine the kinds of responses the Fourth Evangelist wished to inculcate in and elicit from his readership, and to relate these aims to contemporary concerns.[84] Although this aspect of the critical task must be distinguished from examining the relationships within the story line, we should be aware that the two sets of relations are themselves related, for there is the question of how the author wishes the readers to identify with the groups and characters within the story line. That is, the redactional story line is functional to religious purposes.

Our strategy of inquiry will continue to take account of "the hermeneutical circle" of the whole and the parts; the whole is intelligible in terms of the parts and the parts in terms of the whole. As we have already noted, although this is logically a circular method, the circle is in fact broken open by acts of insight.

The organizational disposition of the Johannine redaction has already been discussed. In that discussion, chapters 13–17 (the Last Discourse) were described as a "hermeneutical key" to the subsequent narratives of suffering, death, and resurrection appearances. We need now to look more closely at this.

The composite nature of the Last Discourse has often been remarked upon. Brown makes the following observations, which seem to militate against the unity of the section:

(a) The words of 14:30–31 seem to mark the end of the Discourse.

(b) There are duplications and repetitions, e.g., 13:31–14:31 and 16:4b–33.

(c) Some material in the Last Discourse is placed in the public ministry in the Synoptics, suggesting that some of the Johannine material was not always associated with the Last Supper.

(d) Some of the material, for example the allegory of the vine (15:1–6), does not seem to be connected with the characteristic theme of the Last Supper (Jesus' departure).

(e) There seem to be differing theological outlooks present in the Last Discourse, which suggests to some scholars that not all the sayings were delivered at the same time.[85]

These considerations militating against the unity of the Last Discourse have been met in various ways. Bultmann rearranges the Last Discourse along the following lines: 13:1, 17, 13:31–35, 15, 16, 13:36–38, 14.[86] Bernard has a different arrangement: 15, 16, 13: 31–38, 14, 17.[87] These two examples serve to illustrate the problem of rearrangement theories: often, either consciously or unconsciously, they reflect the interests and ingenuity of the commentator rather than strictly exegetical considerations. We shall attempt no rearrangements of the text.

Verses 1–30 in chapter 13 fall into two parts, each closely connected. The first part (13:1–20) has further subdivisions: 13:1 introduces the narrative; the footwashing scene (vss. 2–11) is followed by an interpretative discourse (vss. 12–20). The second part (13:21–30) concerns the prophecy of the betrayal.

What is the meaning of this complex of material in 13:1–30? The footwashing scene focuses on the self-abasement and humility of Jesus. There may also be a secondary sacramental motif.[88] As for the betrayal scene, Bultmann remarks:

There can be no talk of the community, without reckoning with the possibility that one of its number is unworthy. But in the circle of those who have received Jesus' service, unworthiness is synonymous with betrayal. The consciousness of belonging to the body of disciples must not seduce any of them into the illusion of security. The Evangelist has emphasized this immediately after the emergence of the body of disciples as a limited circle (6.66–71), and has twice drawn attention to the fact in the previous scene which dealt with the founding of the community (vv. 11, 18). He now uses a special scene, that of the prophecy of the betrayal (13.21–30), in order to express the idea in tangible form.[89]

At the end of the section Judas leaves into the night. The Discourse proper now commences to the faithful.

Chapter 13, verses 31–38 are an introduction to the unit 13:31–14:31, and they announce its theme—Jesus' departure and new commandment. Chapter 14 subdivides into two parts: 14:1–14 focuses on the way to the Father for the community, and 14:15–31 on the promise of the Paraclete and his work.

The next unit is easily discernible. It begins at 15:1 and ends at 16:33. There are four subunits: (a) 15:1–17; (b) 15:18–16:4a; (c) 16:4b–15; (d) 16:16–33. The first three of these units have been cleverly woven together: "The theme of choosing the disciples in (a) overlaps into (b); cf. 15:16 and 19. The theme of love in (a) is matched by the theme of hatred in (b). The theme of the world's opposition in (b) prepares the way for the description of the Paraclete as the prosecutor of the world in (c)."[90]

The unit stresses the community in the world. Undoubtedly there are parallels between 13:31–14:31 and 16:4b–33, but these should not be overstressed. There is a progression in the two units we have isolated (13:31–14:31 and 15:1–16:33) from the departure of Jesus to the community he leaves behind (and the work of the Paraclete within the community) to that community's work in the world. Moreover, these two units introduce the final unit in the section, the prayer of Jesus for the community (17:1–26). The point to notice at this juncture is how important the life of the community is for the Fourth Evangelist. The guiding principle of the community is Jesus, and this community is united with him by its knowledge, faith, and love.[91]

The whole of the Last Discourse embraces the life of the community and its relation to Jesus and the Paraclete. This emphasis on the community life of the Christian, expressed so clearly in this part of the Gospel, may give us valuable insight into the meaning of the Gospel as a whole. To this we shall return later.

The Passion of Jesus (18:1–19:42) divides into the following sections:

Prologue	18:1–12
Act One	18:13–27
Act Two	18:28–19:16
Act Three	19:17–37
Epilogue	19:38–42

The "Prologue" (the capture of Jesus) and the "Epilogue" (the burial) are linked in that both are garden scenes. Act one is the interrogation of Jesus by Annas with all the historical problems that raises. This anecdotal narrative is framed by the denials of Peter.

Act two is set at Pilate's praetorium. Here there are seven scenes:[92]

Scene 1	18:28–32	(outside the praetorium)
Scene 2	18:33–38a	(inside)
Scene 3	18:38b–40	(outside)
Scene 4	19:1–3	(inside)
Scene 5	19:4–8	(outside)
Scene 6	19:9–11	(inside)
Scene 7	19:12–16	(outside)

Why do the scenes alternate between outside and inside the praetorium? The answer is presented in an ironic way in scene 1: Jewish officialdom's fear of defilement. Act two is, in fact, charged throughout with dramatic irony gravitating around the kingship of Jesus theme and his rejection by the Jews, as evidenced by the central scene 19:1–3. Act three similarly continues this theme.

In act three we are presented with five tableaux:

Scene 1	19:17–22
Scene 2	19:23–24

Scene 3	19:25–27
Scene 4	19:28–30
Scene 5	19:31–37

The first scene has the ironic witness of the pagan to the king-ship of Jesus. Jesus is "guilty" of being the messiah, King of Israel. Scene 2 demonstrates the fulfillment of the Book of Psalms. Fur-thermore, the reference to the seamless robe (exclusively Johannine) is probably intended to present Jesus as both king and priest. Scene 3—the central one—features the Beloved Disciple, and we shall examine this in more detail shortly. In scene 4 the work of Jesus is depicted as now finished. He dies having fulfilled another scripture. Moreover, the mention of the hyssop branch recalls a detail of the Passover liturgy. The intention of scene five is quite clearly con-veyed in the comment of the redactor in verses 36–37.

The Fourth Evangelist's presentation of the Passion of Jesus gives us valuable insight into his intentions. In particular, we should note that scene 4 is the centerpiece of act two and scene 3 is the centerpiece of act three. Especially important for our inquiry is that the latter scene features the appearance of the Beloved Disci-ple.

The Resurrection appearances in the Fourth Gospel divide clearly into two scenes, each comprising two episodes. In each of the scenes the first episode is concerned with disciples and the sec-ond with specific individuals (Mary and Thomas respectively). In the latter case, however, the faith of the individual is related to a wider audience.

Even though our comments on the structure of the latter half of the Gospel have been brief, one fact emerges very clearly: the Evan-gelist has constructed his work carefully. Our task now is to dis-cover the author's intentions in so constructing his work. In accor-dance with the strategy of examining the whole and the parts, we shall now focus our attention on those specific parts of the redac-tion which feature the Beloved Disciple. Our examination so far indicates that although this disciple appears only three times (excluding the postscript), the placement of the incidents which feature him give him central significance. That is, he appears at the beginning of the Discourse of Jesus to "his own" (13:23), in the Passion narrative (19:26), and in the Resurrection narrative (20:2).

He thus appears at crucial points in all three sections.

There have been various attempts to identify the Beloved Disciple with a particular historical figure.[93] These attempts cannot be regarded as having been successful.[94] The attempts to interpret the Beloved Disciple as a purely symbolic figure[95] are also open to serious objections.[96] He is rather a historical figure with paradigmatic significance.[97] But the historical question of who the Beloved Disciple might have been is to be distinguished from the question of how he functions in the Johannine redaction. To pursue this question we must first delimit and examine the texts which refer to him.

If, for the moment, we exclude the postscript, the Beloved Disciple is explicitly mentioned in three places: 13:23, 19:26, and 20:2. It seems no accident that he appears for the first time in 13:23–26. In our examination of the outline of the whole Gospel, we noted that chapters 13–17 are the Discourse of Jesus to "his own." It is evident that the Christian readers of the Gospel are meant to identify with the group at the Last Supper, which is representative of the Christian community. The scene itself can hardly be maintained to be historical—rather it is an "ideal" scene[98] freely created by the Evangelist.

The text of 13:23 reads:

ἦν ἀνακείμενος εἷς ἐκ τῶν μαθητῶν αὐτοῦ ἐν τῷ κόλπῳ τοῦ ᾽Ιησοῦ, ὅν ἠγάπα ὁ ᾽Ιησοῦς·

(One of his disciples, whom Jesus loved, was lying close to the breast of Jesus.)

Now it is certainly no accident that the first reference to the Beloved Disciple refers to him as "lying close to the breast of Jesus." Many commentators have gone to great lengths to discover who was sitting where and how it was possible for the Beloved Disciple to be "lying close to the breast of Jesus." But the primary purpose of the phrase is surely to evoke a comparison with 1:18 where Jesus is said to be in the breast (or bosom) of the Father. That is, just as Jesus has a special relationship with the Father, so the Beloved Disciple has a special relationship with Jesus.[99]

This special relationship is illustrated by means of the story of the betrayer (13:24–30). After Jesus says that one of his disciples will betray him, Simon Peter "beckons"[100] to the Beloved Disciple to ask Jesus who the betrayer is. The identity of the traitor is then revealed to the Beloved Disciple.

This incident has several strange features. Besides the difficulty of why Peter himself did not ask Jesus who the betrayer was, there is the problem that once the identity of the traitor is revealed to the Beloved Disciple it is not conveyed to Peter. Indeed, verse 28 says that "no one" at the table knew why Jesus told Judas to do what he had to do immediately, when in verse 26 Jesus does reveal to the Beloved Disciple that Judas is the betrayer.[101]

It can hardly be cogently maintained that the purpose of the pericope is to represent the Beloved Disciple as the "mediator" between Jesus and Peter and the disciples.[102] This is simply not true to the text. Nothing is mediated to Peter! Peter is mentioned only once in the pericope in verse 24. Certainly in this pericope nothing of significance is said about the relation of Peter to the Beloved Disciple.[103]

What, then, is the point of the pericope? In Matthew, Jesus tells Judas himself that he is the betrayer; in the Fourth Gospel the secret is imparted to the Beloved Disciple. It is here that the point of the pericope is located. The whole scene specially introduces the "disciple whom Jesus loved," by which designation we are to understand him as having a special knowledge of, and relationship to, Jesus. This point is then illustrated in a simple story: the Beloved Disciple alone at the Last Supper knew of the identity of the betrayer. He was the special confidant of Jesus.

The next pericope in which the Beloved Disciple is explicitly mentioned is 19:25–27. The text of 19:26–27 reads:

Ἰησοῦς οὖν ἰδὼν τὴν μητέρα καὶ τὸν μαθητὴν παρεστῶτα ὃν ἠγάπα, λέγει τῇ μητρί, Γύναι, ἴδε ὁ υἱός σου. εἶτα λέγει τῷ μαθητῇ, Ἴδε ἡ μήτηρ σου. καὶ ἀπ᾿ ἐκείνης τῆς ὥρας ἔλαβεν αὐτὴν ὁ μαθητὴς εἰς τὰ ἴδια.

(When Jesus saw his mother, and the disciple whom he loved standing near, he said to his mother, "Woman, behold, your son!" Then he said to the disciple, "Behold, your mother!" And from that hour the disciple took her to his own home.)

Two preliminary points are worth making. First, Mary, mother of Jesus, rather than Peter, figures in this incident. Secondly, the passage hardly squares with the Synoptic tradition that Jesus' disciples deserted him after his arrest, a tradition the Fourth Gospel does preserve: "The hour is coming, indeed it has come, when you will be scattered, every man to his home, and will leave me alone . . ." (16:32). The Evangelist records the presence of the Beloved Disciple at the Last Supper, and so this desertion should apply to him as well. However, one has to be wary of concluding that this, too, is an "ideal scene," especially in view of 19:35, which can hardly refer to anyone but the Beloved Disciple under the cross, and the wording of which strongly suggests that he was there as an eyewitness.

The questions to be considered are: First, how are we to understand the figures of Mary and the Beloved Disciple here? Second, what is the essential thrust of the whole pericope?

Bultmann interprets Mary as symbolic of Jewish Christianity and the Beloved Disciple as representative of Gentile Christianity.[104] Others see the Beloved Disciple as replacing the unbelieving brothers of Jesus (7:3) and Jewish Christianity as being replaced by Gentile Christianity.[105] But these suggestions are hardly true to the text. A. Dauer does not think that the emphasis in this pericope falls on Mary but on the Beloved Disciple. Moreover, he sees the presence of the women as evoking one of the Evangelist's main themes—the revealer is presented as the crisis of the world, calling forth unbelief and belief (represented by the soldiers [vss. 23–24] and the women [v. 25] respectively).[106]

We must look elsewhere for a plausible explanation of Mary's presence in the pericope. We begin with the text itself. In our examination of "the whole" we saw how scene 4 (19:1–3) was the centerpiece of act two (18:28–19:16). Similarly here, this scene is the centerpiece of act three (19:17–37). Its theological significance lies in its thematic conjunction with the Cana scene (2:1–11) through the term γυνή derived from Genesis 3:15, where the serpent is crushed by the seed of the woman.[107] Mary is representative of the woman, the woman who is mother of the faithful, and the Beloved Disciple represents the faithful.

Dauer has pointed out the similarity of "Woman! Behold your son!" and "Behold your mother!" to an adoption formula, and sees an emphasis on the disciple taking over the obligation of Mary as a *grown-up* son.[108] There is much in this insight. In the light of it, what response did the Evangelist wish to evoke from the readership in this pericope? The Evangelist is inviting his readership to identify with the Beloved Disciple, the disciple who was commissioned by the dying Jesus to be a witness and propagator of the new salvific dispensation, born under the shadow of the cross. The death of Jesus gives life to the Christian community.

The last pericope (apart from the postscript) in which the Beloved Disciple is explicitly named is 20:2–10. Chapter 20, verses 1 and 2 speak of Mary Magdalene coming to the tomb, finding the stone rolled away, and then rushing to Peter and the Beloved Disciple with the story. The two disciples then run to the tomb. The Beloved Disciple arrives first, but does not enter. Peter arrives and enters. The Beloved Disciple enters, and he "saw and believed" (καὶ εἶδεν καὶ ἐπίστευσεν). The second episode with Mary standing at the tomb is taken up in 20:11.

For the purposes of our inquiry we must pose two questions: First, in what sense did the Evangelist wish us to see the juxtaposition of Peter and the Beloved Disciple? Second, what is the significance of the whole pericope?

Here, as in 13:21–30, it must be noted that Peter and the Beloved Disciple are not placed in opposition.[109] It is stated that the Beloved Disciple "saw and believed"; this is not stated explicitly of Peter. But as Bultmann has observed that: "Clearly, it is presupposed that Peter before him was likewise brought to faith through the sight of the empty grave; for if the writer had meant otherwise, and if the two disciples were set over against each other with respect to their πιστευσαι, it would have had to be expressly stated that Peter did not believe."[110]

Bultmann sees the relation of the two disciples as the key to the interpretation of the scene. The race to the grave illustrates how each achieves precedence over the other. Thus, "The meaning manifestly then is this: the first community of believers arises out of Jewish Christianity, and the Gentile Christians attain to faith only after them. But this does not signify any precedence of the former over the latter."[111]

The relation of the Beloved Disciple to Peter is certainly the key to interpretation here.[112] Clearly, their relationship is not one of rivalry; in this Bultmann is also correct. The narrative is constructed in such a way that each can claim precedence over the other. But Bultmann is wrong to identify the Beloved Disciple with

Gentile Christianity and Peter with Jewish Christianity. It is evident that the Johannine community is meant to identify with the Beloved Disciple. The key to the problem of interpretation is to determine in what sense the Johannine readership would understand the representation of Peter.

Certainly, Peter was a figure of great importance in early Christianity. There is a very strong tradition that he is a witness to the Resurrection (Lk 24:34; I Cor 15:5; cf. Mk 16:7). He is known as an apostle (Acts 1:13) and is recognized as the leader and spokesman of the disciples (Mt 16:16–19; Mk 8:27–29; cf.: Mk 3:16, 9:2; Lk 5:3–11, 22:31). The first chapters of Acts record him as being leader of the Jerusalem church in the early days,[113] and he is an authority in Corinth (I Cor. 1:12, 22) and Galatia (where his apostleship seems to have been contrasted favorably with Paul's). Moreover, there is the strongest evidence that he was an important authority in Syria, Antioch, and Rome. (The Apocryphal *Gospel of Peter*, the *Kerygmata Petrou* and the Gospel of Matthew probably originated in Syria,[114] and there is a tradition that he was bishop of Antioch[115] and Rome.)[116]

The Fourth Gospel itself retains the tradition of the prominence of Peter in early Christianity (cf. 1:42; 6:68; and, of course, he is the first witness to the Resurrection—20:6–7). In the light of these observations, how is the figure of Peter to be understood in the Fourth Gospel? It seems justified to see him not as a representative of Jewish Christianity, but in a wider context: he is representative of the *Gesamtkirche* (the whole church or church at large). That is, Peter represents the whole church, while the Beloved Disciple is representative of the Johannine *Einzelkirche* (the individual or local church).

What, then, of significance is being said in this pericope? Simply this: the Johannine *Einzelkirche* (the Beloved Disciple) has an equal claim to that of the *Gesamtkirche* (Peter). Its faith and belief are just as authentic, indeed go hand in hand with that of the *Gesamtkirche*. The two disciples run to the grave together; one reaches the tomb first, but the other enters first. There is no attempt to denigrate Peter; rather the emphasis falls on the fact that the Beloved Disciple believed. It is not so much that the importance of Peter is played down; rather the attempt is to elevate the importance of the Beloved Disciple. The whole thrust of the pericope seems to be to show that just as Peter and the Beloved Disciple share the same faith experience, so the faith of the Johannine local church can be correlated with that of the church at large.[117]

The Beloved Disciple is also explicitly mentioned in the postscript (21:7 and 21:20). Although added by an editor, the references are instructive in confirming our conclusions. It seems unlikely that this editor misunderstood or intentionally falsified the Evangelist's picture of the Beloved Disciple.

This observation is borne out by the text. Chapter 21, verse 7f. shows the same bias as 20:2–10. The Beloved Disciple recognizes Jesus first, but Peter reacts quickly and jumps into the sea in his desire to reach Jesus. Moreover, and this is of vital significance, 21:15–17 confers upon Peter a great honor. In response to Jesus' question "Do you love me more than these?" (i.e., the disciples, including the Beloved Disciple, who are present), Peter does not reply specifically to the question. He only asserts that he loves Jesus. This is important. The Johannine church, identifying with the Beloved Disciple, would probably see this in a positive manner. The sense is this: the authenticity of the faith of the Johannine community is acknowledged, inasmuch as Peter does not claim to love Jesus more; moreover, in the Fourth Gospel the theme of love is closely bound with the concept of unity. Christians are one in love. Jesus then proclaims Peter as leader of the community.

In 21:20 the Beloved Disciple is represented as following Jesus, something that Peter has already been doing. Again, it is difficult to see how this verse implies the Beloved Disciple's superiority to Peter; they share the same faith.

In 21:21 Peter questions Jesus about the Beloved Disciple: "Lord, what about this man?" To which Jesus replies, "If it is my will that he remain until I come, what is that to you? Follow me!" "What is that to you?" can hardly be construed as a denigration of Peter, who after all had died a martyr's death (vss. 18–19). Verse 23 then corrects an apparent misunderstanding: Jesus did not predict that the Beloved Disciple would live until the Parousia. Presumably this was now a problem because he had died.[118] One cannot use this verse as evidence that he is thus John the son of Zebedee, around whom legends had grown to this effect because of his immense age; for the earliest Christian belief was that the Parousia would take place before the first generation of Christians disappeared (I Thess 4:15 and I Cor 15:51). In other words, it was a general belief not attached to specific persons. Thus the Beloved Disciple could be anyone of the first generation of Christians.

Chapter 21, verse 24 reads: Οὗτός ἐστιν ὁ μαθητὴς ὁ μαρτυρῶν περὶ τούτων καὶ γράψας ταῦτα, καὶ οἴδαμεν ὅτι ἀληθὴς αὐτοῦ ἡ μαρτυρία ἐστίν. (This is the disciple who is bearing witness to these things, and who has written these things; and we know that his testimony is true.) This verse thus appears specifically to identify the Beloved Disciple with the author of the Gospel. If we accept the general verdict of scholarship that this is not the case, we are left with three alternatives. First, that the identification was a "tactical ploy" by the author to bolster the importance of the work. The work would thus be pseudepigraphical. Second, that the identification was a misunderstanding of the editor. This seems unlikely. Or, third, that the Greek word γράψας is to be taken in its causative sense. That is, "This is the disciple who *caused* these things to be written."[119]

In favor of this latter view is the fact that the causative is used elsewhere, for example 19:1. Moreover, in 21:24b the emphasis falls on the witness of the disciple. Bultmann is surely wrong in thinking that a definite circle is not meant by "we know."[120] He says, "For either the readers know the circle which is editing the Gospel, and then the appeal is superfluous; or they do not know it, and then it is meaningless." But the appeal is not superfluous if the attempt is to authenticate this community's standing in the church at large.

This verse is important, for it shows the singular significance of the Beloved Disciple in the Johannine community as a witness of tradition. The truth of the Johannine Gospel depended on it. Such an affirmation is also found in the Gospel proper in 19:35. The person who saw the blood and water gushing from Jesus' side is quite evidently the disciple who stood under the cross, that is, the Beloved Disciple. This is the most explicit reference within the Gospel to the Beloved Disciple as Christ-witness.

We are leaving out of our discussion the possibility that the Beloved Disciple is referred to in either 1:35 or 18:15 ff.[121] There is thus one other question left to consider before we proceed to a conclusion about the significance of the Beloved Disciple in the Fourth Gospel. That is the question of the anonymity of the figure.

We have maintained that he is an historical figure with paradigmatic significance. But if he is historical, why is he not named? There have been various proposed resolutions to this problem. For example, the British scholar W. Sanday argued:

> The Beloved Disciple had a special reason for not wishing to protrude his personality. He was conscious of a great privilege that would single him out for all time among the children of men. He could not resist the temptation to speak of this privilege. The impulse of affection responding to affection prompted him to claim it. But the consciousness that he was doing so, and the reaction of modesty led him at the same time to suppress, what a vulgar egotism might have accentuated, the lower plane of his own individuality. The son of Zebedee (if it was he) desired to be merged and lost in the "disciple whom Jesus loved."[122]

Such tortuous psychologizing explanations are neither appealing nor convincing. Much more convincing is the explanation given by J. Roloff.[123] He compares the Beloved Disciple to the Teacher of Righteousness who also is not named, yet who was of great significance in the community. Lorenzen has appropriated this insight:

> The parallels [of the Teacher of Righteousness] to the Beloved Disciple are obvious. Whereas the Teacher understands himself to have an intimate relationship to God, the Beloved Disciple stands in an intimate relationship to the revealer of God. As a result of this intimate relationship both are exegetes and interpreters of God and Jesus respectively. Where the Teacher grounds his authority in the words of the prophets, the Beloved Disciple depends on the way of Jesus; both distinguish themselves in that they are both initiated into the divine secret which they then communicate to the community. Both are crucial personalities in their communities and thus so well known that they need not even be mentioned by name.[124]

Our conclusion is that we do not know who the disciple is, and that the Evangelist makes no attempt to tell us. What we can say is that the Evangelist regarded him as an eyewitness to Jesus' earthly existence and that he was one of the disciples, though not necessarily one of the Twelve. It is quite possible that he was a Jerusalem disciple, but beyond that we cannot go.

In conclusion, what is the significance of the Beloved Disciple for our particular question? How does he function in the redaction? There is no doubt that he is an important authenticator of and witness to the tradition. He witnesses those things most important in the Christian faith—the death and resurrection of Jesus (this is evidenced by his strategic placement in the redaction). His association with Peter is not to be seen as rivalry. The readership identifies with the Beloved Disciple but not against Peter. Rather the association is a further effort on the part of the Evangelist to legitimate the theology of the Johannine community.

Such a conclusion, if generally correct, has far-reaching implications for any discussion of the place of the Fourth Gospel in the early church. The author of the Gospel is claiming through the figure of the Beloved Disciple to stand both theologically and historically within the Christian fellowship. The Beloved Disciple was the confidant of Jesus, and the Lord recognized this disciple as one who understood him. The theology of the Johannine community is dependent upon this same person; it is through him that the Evangelist can claim that his work coheres with the truth of divine revelation. And around the central affirmation that Jesus is the way to communion with the Father, the Fourth Evangelist has orchestrated "truth," "Paraclete," and "witness" to thematize communion with Jesus.

In the Fourth Gospel we have a two-tiered argument. At the primary level the central affirmation is that Jesus is the one and only way to salvation. He alone has seen the Father; so he alone can reveal him. It follows that he alone can give eternal life. It is clear that the Fourth Gospel prominently features themes of revelation and response, the unique saving revelation brought to the world by Jesus Christ and the call for unreserved adherence not simply to it but to him, for he is not simply the revealer but the revelation itself. On a secondary level the concern of the Evangelist is not thematic but performative. That is, the decisive redactor has employed such themes and motifs as truth and witness, shepherd and vine, Paraclete and Beloved Disciple, to secure the legitimacy of his own theology.

7. BEYOND THE FOURTH GOSPEL

How successful was the Fourth Evangelist in his attempt to legitimize his own theology? The Fourth Gospel did, of course, become part of the Christian canon and in this respect the Fourth Evangelist was successful in gaining acceptance for his work in the church at large. But his Gospel was certainly open to misunderstanding. We have seen how Käsemann regards the Fourth Gospel as "naively docetic." A look at the Johannine Epistles shows us that in its own historical context the Johannine tradition was subject to a similar misunderstanding. As R. E. Brown comments:

> E. Käsemann has described the christology of the Fourth Gospel as a naïve, unreflected docetism which has not yet been recognized as such by the evangelist and his community. I think that Käsemann has mistakenly gone beyond the evidence in judging this to be the christology of the Gospel itself, and he is anachronistic in applying the term docetism to the Gospel. Yet he shows how the Gospel *can* be read, and he may well have approximated in the twentieth century the way in which the opponents of I John interpreted the Johannine tradition in the first century, namely, in terms of an earthly career that did not really involve an appropriation by Jesus of the limitations of the human condition.[125]

It behooves us therefore to look beyond the Fourth Gospel to the Epistles to see what light they shed on our inquiry into the theology of the Fourth Gospel.

The first, second, and third epistles of John have been traditionally attributed to John the "presbyter" and linked with the author of the Fourth Gospel. In our hypothesis concerning the authorship question, we suggested that the Epistles and the Gospel came out of the same community, and were probably written by different hands. C. H. Dodd, among others, agrees that the author(s) of the Epistles is different from the one of the Gospel. He differs from many, however, in how he conceives of the relationship between the two. Focusing especially upon 1 John he argues that this Epistle differs from the Gospel in important respects. He claims, for example, that the Epistle is more naively open to gnosticism in that its terminology is less guarded. (This is therefore different from Käsemann's position.) The Epistle makes statements such as "God is Light" and "God is love," speaks of "the divine seed," and echoes a gnostic sentiment when it says, "We know that if he is manifested we shall be like him, because we shall see him as he is." But most scholars do not accept Dodd's arguments and affirm that the Epistle is more *anti*-Gnostic than the Gospel. The Epistle carefully clarifies things that the Gospel leaves open. Whereas the Evangelist emphasizes the divinity of Christ (as opposed to the Jewish account, which never denied Jesus' manhood), the Epistle emphasizes the humanity of Jesus (over the gnosticizing tendencies that denied it). There is a growing consensus among scholars that the Epistles were written after the Gospel, by a different author, but someone who was from the same community—the "Johannine community." They reflect an internal situation sometime after the Gospel and focus in particular on a situation in which there is dissension in the community and significant differences of interpretation over christology and ethics.[126]

The Epistle is addressed to a congregation which is threatened by schismatics (Bauer would say "heretics") who, according to the writer of the Epistle, have cut themselves off from the authority of apostolic witness to Jesus (2:19, 4:6). Their beliefs were incompatible with Christian faith and had eventually caused a schism in the community (2:19). They had then left the community, but there was still much turmoil among those who were left.

What was it that these schismatics said that caused this turmoil? They denied that Jesus was the Christ (2:22f.). This was not, however, the simple denial that it seemed. When the schismatics used the term "Christ" they did not use it in its traditional Jewish sense. Rather they meant by it a higher power, which they believed had descended on Jesus before his baptism and left him before his passion. Therefore it could not be identified with the earthly Jesus. This was the typical Gnostic position in the second century. The writer of 1 John answers that Jesus is the Christ (5:1), the Son of God (4:15; 5:5ff.), who came in the flesh (4:2). To reject this was to reject the Father who sent Jesus (4:5; 5:1).

The first epistle of John is structured as a response to the claims and behavior of these schismatics and their gnosticizing tendencies. The schismatics seemed to have made seven basic affirmations. These can be reconstructed from the Epistle where the writer uses an introductory formula that attributes affirmations to the schismatics:

a threefold use of "If we say . . ." (1:6, 8, 10)

a threefold use of "He who says . . ." (2:4, 6, 9)

a single use of "If anyone says . . ." (4:20).

The writer of the Epistle sees the schismatics as raising two crucial issues: (1) Is it essential to confess that Jesus Christ came in the flesh? and (2) Is it necessary to pursue a life of love for one's fellow human being? The author of the Epistle answers a resounding "Yes!" to both of these questions. The seven affirmations of the schismatics to which the author of the Epistle alludes are:

1. "If we say we have fellowship with him while we walk in darkness, we lie and do not live according to the truth; but if we walk in the light, as he is in the light, we have fellowship with one another, and the blood of Jesus his Son cleanses us from all sin" (1:6f).

2. "If we say we have no sin we deceive ourselves, and the truth is not in us. If we confess our sins he is faithful and just, and will forgive our sins and cleanse us from all unrighteousness" (1:8f).

3. "If we say we have not [ever] sinned, we make him a liar and his word is not in us" (1:10).

4. "He who says 'I know him' but disobeys his commandments is a liar and the truth is not in him; but whoever keeps his word, in him truly love for God is perfected" (2:4f).

5. "He who says he abides in him ought to walk in the same way in which he walked" (2:6).

6. "He who says he is in the light and hates his brother still is in the darkness still" (2:9).

7. "If anyone says, 'I love God', and hates his brother, he is a liar." (4:20).

From these statements it is possible to reconstruct the beliefs of the schismatic community. It appears that they thought that it was possible to have fellowship with God without the mediation of Christ. When they claimed to "walk in the light" they meant mystical enlightenment, which was not predicated on a historical revelation and did not imply ethical conduct. The schismatics also appear to have believed (as the Gnostics did later) that mystical fellowship with Christ meant sinlessness; therefore there was no need for redemptive activity (i.e., a redemptive death). Moreover, when the schismatics spoke of "knowing" him, they meant they knew the power which was Christ, not the historical or earthly Jesus. There-fore the commandments of the earthly Jesus were of no salvific importance either. They were illuminated by a supernatural knowl-edge that was independent of the earthly Jesus and which had no ethical implications such as "loving" one's brother.

The writer of the Epistle finds all this unacceptable. He affirms that the historical revelation of Christ was efficacious in salvation; that this implies "fellowship"; that one must confess one's sins; that loving God means keeping his commandments, which means believing in Jesus and loving one another as he commanded. He believed the schismatics' love for God to be a self-centered love.

The writer of the Epistle thus works out his own view in dia-logue with the positions of the schismatics. All Christians have been anointed in baptism (2:20) and therefore have knowledge. This anointing involves faith in the apostolic testimony to Jesus. "Knowing" is tested by keeping the commandments (2:3), thus exposing false claims (2:4). The commandments affirm one's belief in Jesus and in loving one another (3:23). What emerges from the author's dialogue with the schismatics are two criteria that must be applied to their claims. The claim to know God is found wanting because it does not conform to the standard of apostolic testimony to Jesus (4:1; 3:6). Apostolic testimony says that Jesus came in the flesh and that his commandments are to be obeyed. The second cri-terion follows from this: right belief issues in right conduct. The author of the Epistle sums up his position thus: "Believe in the name of his Son Jesus Christ and love one another as he (Jesus) gave you commandment" (3:23; cf. John 13:34).

Reconstructing what was happening in the Johannine commu-nity provides a historical perspective for understanding the Fourth Gospel. By far the most interesting reconstruction of what the Johan-nine community was like, what it believed, and what happened to it, is given by R. E. Brown in *The Community of the Beloved Disciple*. Brown paints a picture of a community originating in or near Pales-tine, with Jews of "relatively standard expectations," including fol-lowers of John the Baptist, who accepted Jesus as the Davidic mes-siah. This originating group was joined by Jews of an anti-Temple bias who understood Jesus against a Mosaic rather than a Davidic background. Jesus had been "with God, seen him, and brought down his words to people" (p. 166). This led to the development of a high preexistent Christology in this group. This high Christology alienated them from the Jews who remained more traditional and could not transpose their beliefs to this higher plane. The Beloved Disciple, however, was able to do this and became the leader of the group. It was out of these circumstances that the Gospel arose.

Brown believes that after the Gospel there was a split in the community, and this is the situation reflected in the Epistles. Some of the Johannine group believed that the One from Above was not fully human. They left the community and continued along a road that eventually led to gnosticism. The adherents of the author of the first Epistle maintained that Jesus Christ had come in the flesh. They were gradually assimilated into the Great Church despite the distinctive nature of their Johannine faith.[127]

What is interesting about Brown's reconstruction is that he sees that the dispute within the Johannine community arises over the interpretation of the tradition handed down from the Beloved Disciple (and which is embodied in the Gospel). The trouble reflected in the epistles was not caused by a group which came from outside of the community, but rather from a group within the community which interpreted this Johannine Gospel differently. The author of the first epistle does not deny the affirmations of the secessionists, but qualifies them. He also appeals to "what was from the beginning" (1:4; 2:7). This clearly indicates that this argument was over a common tradition.

Brown's view of what was going on in the Johannine community is particularly interesting in the light of the debate between Turner and Bauer over Christian origins. What Brown is saying is quite in accord with Turner's understanding of early Christianity. It was not immediately obvious where some beliefs would lead. Only concentrated theological reflection, arising out of situations of intense discussion and debate, led to the clarification of many issues of faith. This is clearly what happens in the Johannine community. A closer look at Brown's reconstruction supports this view.

Whereas both proclaim Jesus to be the Son of God, the Gospel stresses the *Son of God*, says Brown, and the first Epistle stresses *Jesus*. Does this mean that the secessionists were thorough-going docetists, that is, they denied completely the humanity of Jesus? We know something about the Docetists of the second century. As Brown tells us:

We now have much more evidence of such Christian docetism in the gnostic works discovered in Egypt in the mid-1940s. The *Timorphic Protenoia* (XIII 50:12–15), written *ca.* 200, shows a heavenly Word saying aloud: "I put on Jesus, I bore him from the cursed wood and established him in the dwelling places of his Father. And those who watch over their dwelling places did not recognize me." In the third century *Apocalypse of Peter* (VII 81:15–25) a living Jesus laughs at persecutors who torment the external Jesus. The *Tripartite Tractate* (I 113:37), which has affinities with Valentinian gnosticism, speaks of an "unbegotten, *impassible* Word [*Logos*] who came into being in the flesh." In particular, scholars have thought of the adoptionistic docetic theory attributed to Cerinthus by Irenaeus: "After Jesus' baptism the Christ, coming down from that Power which is above all, descended upon him in the form of a dove . . . In the end, however, the Christ withdrew again from Jesus . . . the Christ, being spiritual, remained unable to suffer."[128]

Brown does not think, however, that the secessionists were thorough-going Docetists of this type. He argues that they thought that the human existence of Jesus, while real, was not salvifically significant and claims that such an interpretation could easily have been based on Johannine theology as we know it from the Fourth Gospel. "First, the Gospel gives a portrait of Jesus which somewhat relativizes his humanity"—the stress is on the glory of God which shines through him. (Here we should recall that Käsemann interprets the Fourth Gospel in precisely this way.) "Second, there are elements in John which lessen the salvific import of the public ministry of Jesus." Such statements as John 17:3 and 17:8 "centre salvation in the sending by God rather than in the actions of the Son on earth."[129]

In trying to refute the position of the secessionists the author of I John obviously could not deny the preexistence of Christ, as this was clearly given in the Johannine tradition. He rather stresses the earthly career of the Word made flesh, a strategy that is apparent from the very beginning. If we compare the Prologue of the Gospel with the opening of the Epistle we notice common terms—*beginning*, *word*, and *life*—but the stress is significantly different. "Beginning" is used in the Gospel in the sense of before creation, but in the Epistle "what was from the beginning" is paralleled with "What we have seen . . . heard . . . looked at . . . felt"—that is, the beginning is located in the earthly ministry of Jesus. "Word" and "life" in the Gospel echo the Genesis story, but in the Epistle the author speaks of eternal life "as it has been revealed to us," and the "word of life" was manifested in the earthly career of Jesus. The Epistle opens by announcing that what "we have heard, and seen with our own eyes . . . we looked at, and felt with our own hands." The Prologue of the Gospel ends on a different note: "We have seen his glory." For the author of the Epistle, the earthly career of Jesus and his death are central.

The author of the first Epistle also ties an ethical life to belief in an earthly Jesus: Christians must keep the commandments given through Jesus. It is interesting that although he attacks the ethics of the secessionists (cf. 2:4) he does not catalogue their particular failings. He appears rather to be taking issue with the theoretical base of their beliefs: they did not think that the earthly life of Jesus was important, and (logically!) they attached no salvific importance to ethical behavior. If Jesus' earthly life was not important for salvation, then neither is ours and therefore it does not matter what we do. It is particularly interesting that the Johannine Gospel does not, in fact, stress the ethical life. What is stressed is adherence to Jesus' word (John 8:31; 15:3; 8:24; 9:41), not obedience to particular ethical commandments. The writer of the Epistle on the other hand comes back several times to the earthly life of Jesus as an ethical model (2:6; 3:3; 3:7).

8. THE FOURTH GOSPEL IN THE MODERN CONTEXT

What are some of the implications for us today of what we have said about Johannine theology? How does our reconstruction of the beliefs of the Johannine community square with trends in recent Johannine scholarship?

Much of recent Johannine scholarship has emphasized the sectarian nature of the Johannine community[130] and how its theology differs and is distinctive. The works of Meeks and Neyrey are particularly important here. Meeks's magisterial essay, "The Man From Heaven in Johannine Sectarianism"[131] argued that the Johannine portrayal of Jesus as a man who had descended from heaven implied that he was a stranger and an alien to this world and that this Christological perspective reflected the experience of the Johannine community itself, which was alienated from the world. The significance of Meeks's approach is that he sees the enigma of the Gospel of John not as a literary or theological problem, but primarily as a social one. That is to say, for Meeks the Christology of the Fourth Gospel is occasioned by a particular social situation.

> The christological claims of the Johannine Christians resulted in their becoming alienated, and finally expelled, from the synagogue; that alienation in turn is "explained" by a further development of the christological motifs (i.e., the fate of the community projected onto the story of Jesus); these developed christological motifs in turn drive the group into further isolation.[132]

In *An Ideology of Revolt: John's Christology in Social Science Perspective*,[133] Jerome H. Neyrey takes a similar tack to that of Meeks. He argues that the Christological confession that Jesus is equal to God also emphasizes that he is not of this world. His approach is, moreover, more sophisticated than that of Meeks in that he uses an explicit social science methodology based upon the work of anthropologist Mary Douglas. He concludes:

> Despite the great marriage of heaven and earth supposedly heralded in 1:14, the Fourth Gospel ultimately put value only in spirit, not flesh, only in being from above, not from below, and only in being not of this world, not in being of this world. Ultimately the gospel argued that the flesh is of no avail. In support of this, texts such as 1 John 4:3 and 2 John 7 appear as summaries of a christology in which Jesus is exclusively perceived as a divine heavenly figure, a perception that vigorously denies any value to flesh, matter, or earth, and even to Jesus' former involvement in things material. Finally, further investigation of the social perceptions of spirit as a code for the relative degree of systematization and control in a social group led us to see more clearly that the high christology that valued the heavenly, spiritual Jesus as superior to anything earthly and material, functioned as an ideology of revolt against the past and all previous controls, structures, and classifications. Thus the figure who is equal to God is also not of this world.[134]

Our approach is certainly at odds with that of Meeks, Neyrey, and others.[135] We have argued that while the self-understanding of the Johannine community was distinctive, it was not sectarian and *the community did not see itself as alienated*. Through the use of such motifs as that of the Beloved Disciple, Johannine theology claims to have a legitimate place in the church at large. Johannine theology may well reject the values of this world—to this we will return in our final conclusion—but it does not follow from this that Johannine theology is sectarian. Neyrey suggests that the Johannine community consciously defined itself in opposition not only to this world but to the "past and all previous controls, structures, and classifications."[136] Our study suggests that such a far-reaching conclusion is entirely unwarranted, for the Evangelist sought only to legitimize his theology and have it accepted by the church at large.

What we can say, however, is that it is now clear that there exists a specifically Johannine theology. It has been recognized for some time that Pauline theology is distinctive; this recognition has now been extended to the Fourth Gospel. It has been realized that although the Fourth Gospel shares with the synoptics the *genre* "gospel," it is significantly different from them. Moreover, little attention had been given to the Johannine Epistles until recently. They have now been seen as throwing a great deal of light upon the Johannine community and its theology. We now understand that it was the distinctive nature of the Johannine community, with its special problems and interests, which gave rise to its unique theology. Knowing more about the Johannine community has helped us to see more clearly the specifically Johannine contours of belief. Before the "discovery" of the Johannine community it was difficult to gauge the significance of Johannine theology because the Gospel remained unanchored in historical circumstances.

Second, focusing upon the distinctive nature of Johannine theology has helped us to realize that there is no one New Testament theology; there are instead New Testament theologies. As E. F. Scott correctly notes: "The New Testament is not a uniform book, composed by men who were all of one mind and who were closely collaborating with one another. It presents Christianity under a great variety of forms, and for this reason presents it truly."[137]

This last point is what is at the heart of the discussion, initiated by Käsemann, which relates the Fourth Gospel to the orthodoxy/heresy debate. Käsemann emphasizes the diversity within the

New Testament itself, and the Fourth Gospel furnishes him with his best example. But if there is no uniformity of belief in early Christianity, this does not mean that there is no unity. The theology of the Fourth Gospel may be distinctive, but it is not entirely set apart from the rest of early Christianity—there are some important points of contact. The notion of Christ's preexistence, for example, is not unique to the Fourth Gospel. It is found also in Philippians 2:6–11 and Colossians 1:15–20. And when the author of the Fourth Gospel speaks in antitheses—light/darkness, truth/falsehood, slavery/freedom—he is using a dualistic manner of speaking which is also found in Paul. What is true, however, is that he has recast the Christian message in a novel and original way. Once again we should recall what Turner said about fixed and flexible elements. In the Fourth Gospel the basic elements of Christian belief are still there, but they have been reformulated by a highly original mind. The Fourth Gospel is, in other words, a good example of what Turner is talking about.

What significance does any of this have for Christian belief today? Our study of early Christianity suggests that although there was considerable diversity of belief in earliest Christianity, there was also some sense of a "center," a sense of common ground, an appeal to a common tradition. This is especially apparent in 1 John, where the author takes issue with positions that he thinks do not cohere with the basic Christian tradition. The New Testament itself, by virtue of the fact that it contains such documents as 1 John, reflects this concern. But this concern for unity is not turned into an insistence on uniformity, as the inclusion of the Fourth Gospel indicates. Käsemann may be overstating the case when he says that the Fourth Gospel was included in the canon through "man's error and God's providence," but he has done a great service by making us think about the real significance of its inclusion.

Simply stated, a Christianity based in the New Testament must recognize that the New Testament itself implies a unity in diversity. In the New Testament there are several individual emphases. Pauline Christianity, Matthean Christianity, Lukan Christianity, and Johannine Christianity are all different from each other in significant respects, and it would be improper and dishonest to gloss over these differences. But they have more in common with each other than they do with, for example, a Gnostic Christianity of the type found in the apocryphal *Gospel of Thomas*. The acceptance of the New Testament canon implies a considerable breadth in Christian belief; it endorses many different expressions, but some (e.g., gnosticism) it does not tolerate. At least, this is the conclusion if we accept that the Fourth Gospel is not Gnostic. It is here that perhaps we see clearly one of the major issues at stake in the discussion initiated by Käsemann. If he were right, and the Fourth Gospel were "naively docetic," its inclusion in the New Testament canon would imply a diversity of belief so broad that Christianity could at best be described as a syncretism—an ongoing multiplicity of interpretations with only family resemblances. There would be no intrinsic substantial identity to it. But our study of the Gospel has suggested that Käsemann is not correct, and that Turner's idea that Christianity is an interaction between fixed and flexible elements best describes what is going on as early Christianity develops. This would imply that there was room in Christianity for diversity, but that nevertheless there were proscribed limits. Exactly what those limits are is the continuing challenge presented to Christian theology.

CHAPTER 3

Understanding the Modern Context

To understand what implications the message of the Gospel of John has for us today it is necessary to understand our modern "reading site."[1] That is to say, we must understand how the socio-cultural assumptions of the society in which we live influence the way we read texts. No one comes to a text without presuppositions—with what Lonergan calls "an empty head." As we have seen in our discussion of hermeneutical circles in the previous chapter, we have all inherited intellectual baggage. Understanding the world in which we live is the first step in uncovering our deepest assumptions and, thus, toward understanding ourselves. This is necessary if we are to allow texts—especially ancient texts—to challenge us in a meaningful way. What, then, can we say about the modern world in which we live?

In 1927 Martin Heidegger published his majestic work *Sein und Zeit* in which he maintained that the definitive characteristic of the modern world is technology. Today it is almost universally acknowledged that Heidegger was correct and that any discussion of modern society must begin with technology. If the fact that we live in a technological society is easily acknowledged, however, the nature and characteristics of it are very elusive. "Technology" is derived from the Greek τεχνολογία, "the systematic treatment of an art." In English it came to be used in the nineteenth century for the study of practical or industrial arts, but in contemporary usage it can encompass techniques, tools and machines, and practical knowledge. Moreover, "technology," "technics," and "technique" are often used interchangeably. In present use, "technology" has thus come to mean much more than machines or tools ("hardware")—it also signifies the techniques used for controlling the environment and society.

Some writers, however, do still use the word *technology* in a more limited sense. There are those who stress the idea of technology as being a peculiarly human way of expressing activity. Others do not stress the making activity itself, but the *knowledge* which issues in practical activity. Others see it as a sociological phenomenon and stress that it is the defining characteristic of the modern world. It is not surprising that it has sometimes been said that people who think and write about technology do so because they think it is important, but this undertaking always carries with it a certain sense of apprehension. At the very beginning of thinking about technology one is faced with the problem of defining a term that seems to have almost an indefinite number of meanings. Technology is generally understood, however, as knowledge that issues in the techniques and hardware that humans use to shape their environment and control their destinies. Technology is thus, as George Grant has argued,[2] a *unique copenetration of knowing and doing*. It is incumbent upon us to now explain this understanding of technology.

1. THE PHENOMENON OF MODERN TECHNOLOGY

There are two very popular misconceptions about modern technology. One is that it is simply an applied science, and the other is that it is ethically neutral and may be used in any way we deem fit. These two misconceptions are at the heart of much confused discussion of technology. We will deal with each of them in turn.

During the Second Industrial Revolution there arose endeavors (in such as the chemical and electrical industries) in which the theoretical "desire to know" seemed dominant. Yet such industries as these had practical applications, which came to be labelled "technology," and so technology came to be thought of as applied science. Yet when examined closely, the idea that technology is applied science turns out to be quite problematic. There are many examples of modern inventions (such as the transistor) that cannot be explained simply as the application of previous scientific knowledge.[3] A more accurate way to see the relationship of science and technology is to see them as twin foci of the same endeavor. That is, technology is not so much a derivative of science as it is a phenomenon that is inextricably intertwined with it. The conventional separation between technology and science is based upon the idea that there is a difference between knowing and doing. In the modern paradigm of knowledge, however, there is a copenetration of knowing and doing. Science and technology are part of the same human project that manifests itself in the will to change the world.

The other misconception that we have mentioned—that technology is ethically neutral—is very much a derivative of the idea that it is applied science. The popular view is that science is somehow pure and abstract and that scientists are seekers after truth and their findings are true explanations of the world. This view is, however, quite wrong. J. Salomon has convincingly argued that the scientific endeavor is not pure and disinterested,[4] with the conclusion, as J. R. Ravetz says, that "Science, for so long the destroyer of ideologies, was itself revealed as a variety of false consciousness."[5] Thus there is every reason to question the work of scientists who are, after all, human beings who have emotions, prejudices, values, and conflicts. They live in a society and are influenced by it. They do not, in other words, live in a social or cultural vacuum. Moreover, their work reflects and is reinforced by the values of the society in which they live. This "externalist" approach to understanding scientific activity has received a great deal of attention in recent years.[6] It has become especially prominent, for example, in the discussions of the ethics of the nuclear bomb. How far can Oppenheimer and his colleagues be held responsible for the destruction wrought on Hiroshima and Nagasaki? It soon becomes apparent when the question is posed in this fashion that science is not merely some "pure desire to know," but is instead a social and political phenomenon that dramatically affects all of our lives. As we have argued that science and technology are inseparable in the modern world, it follows that technology too is no neutral phenomenon.

A further development of these arguments is the claim that technology is itself autonomous. As Reinhard Ruerup says:

> Theoretical discussion about the relationship between technology and society has in the last few years ceased to revolve around questions about the meaning, nature, and "cultural value" of technology. . . . Today's discussion is concerned, instead, with the decisive question of whether and to what extent one can speak of the "autonomy" of technology, and, resulting from this, whether

and to what extent, all other spheres of life are necessarily dependent on technology; furthermore, whether technology has developed from a means to an end in itself.[7]

The question of whether technology is autonomous is quite
crucial to understanding its relationship with society today. Accordingly, we will now focus our discussion on this issue.

2. THE AUTONOMY OF TECHNOLOGY

The idea that technology is autonomous centers around two major
arguments. The first is that, in the modern context, technology is
guided solely by a concern for efficiency.[8] There are no other
restraints placed on technology, and thus the technological society
becomes analogous to the machine, functioning efficiently and
rationally without regard to human emotions and aspirations (such
as love, spontaneity, and creativity). The second argument follows
from the first. It is claimed that modern technology has become an
artificial whole whose parts are so interrelated that they must all be
constantly sustained. Technology has replaced nature as the environment in which humans live and upon which they are dependent
for survival. Unlike nature, however, technology is artificial, and its
nonorganic nature means that it requires constant repair and mod-
ification to keep it going. It is, moreover, imperative to keep it
going because humans can now no longer manage without it.
Thus, paradoxically and ironically, the ends of technology become
primary over human ends. The best exponent of the idea that technology has become autonomous is Jacques Ellul, whose book *The
Technological Society*[9] is widely considered the best and most
provocative on the subject.

Ellul argues that it is first necessary to understand the nature
and role of technique.[10] By technique (*la technique*) Ellul means the
efficient method found in *"la société technicienne"*—a society that
uses technique in every task and enterprise. Thus the technological
society is not merely industrial but a society committed to increased
efficiency and self-management. It has as its primary objective control over non-human nature, but it does not stop there: the control
of human nature also comes under its purview. Technique is an
all-pervasive social fact: "The term *technique*, as I use it, does not

mean machines, technology, or this or that procedure for obtaining an end. In our technological society, *technique is the totality of methods rationally arrived at and having absolute efficiency* (for a given stage of development) in every field of human activity."[11]

Thus the technological society becomes analogous to the machine, which operates efficiently and rationally without regard for human emotions and aspirations. Modern technology is an artificial whole whose parts are so intertwined that they must all be constantly sustained if it is to continue to function. Humanity becomes subject to this working order because the machine embodies the ideals of rationality and efficiency, for it is created to function efficiently and rationally without human error.

In light of this, Ellul sees a dimension to technique that goes beyond the machine stage in that technique governs all of human activity. Not only do efficiency and rationality pervade modern society but they are effectively integrated into all spheres of human life. The principles of the machine govern everything:

> But let the machine have its head, and it topples everything that cannot support its enormous weight. Thus everything had to be reconsidered in terms of the machine. And that is precisely the role technique plays . . . Technique integrates the machine into society. It constructs the kind of world the machine needs. . . . All-embracing technique is in fact the consciousness of the mechanized world. . . . Technique thus provides a model; it specifies attitudes that are valid once and for all. The anxiety aroused in man by the turbulence of the machine is soothed by the controlling hum of a unified society . . . But when technique enters into every area of life, including the human, it ceases to be external to man and becomes his very substance. It is no longer face to face with man, but is integrated with him, and it progressively absorbs him. In this respect, technique is radically different from the machine. . . . The mechanization which results from technique is the application of this higher form to all domains hitherto foreign to the machine; we can even say that technique is characteristic of precisely that realm in which the machine itself can play no role. It is a radical error to think of technique and machine as interchangeable; from the very beginning we must be on guard against this misconception.[12]

The distinction Ellul makes between machine and technique is an important one. He maintains that technique functions in our society as the source and standard governing all relationships. Modern society is, in fact, a vast monolith governed by technique.[13] That modern technology was developed to serve humankind is indisputable; but we have gone beyond that and technique has engulfed human nature in order to serve itself.[14] Ellul's contention seems to be borne out by a mere casual glance at the world in which we live. How often is it said that the crises of the modern world—be they ecological or energy-related—are merely symptomatic of an incomplete stage in technology and that further development of the technology will provide the solution? The nature of technology demands more and more "fixes" in its drive toward totality.

Inherently, technique demands from us undivided allegiance to its power. This we have so far given willingly in exchange for the security of rationality and ultimate efficiency. The products of technology have become necessities for humanity, and we thus become unwilling, and perhaps unable, to change the course of technique: "We are faced with a choice of 'all or nothing.' If we make use of technique, we must accept the specificity and autonomy of its ends, and the totality of its rules. Our desires and aspirations can change nothing."[15]

Ellul's argument is that although mastery over nature through technique was originally attempted for "the relief of man's estate" (to use Francis Bacon's phrase), technique has now become an end in and of itself.[16] Those who criticize Ellul do not seem to see this, and continue to claim that the efficient and rational society in which humans reside still serves human ends, such as happiness and the alleviation of hardship. Technique is seen as devised by humans to solve problems and further modern knowledge. By comparison Ellul's conclusion is a sombre one: because technique is the sole end of the technological society, it will not be able to sustain itself and will eventually collapse.[17]

Ellul does not, however, see technique as evil as many have claimed,[18] for he says:

> I am not saying that technique is one of the fruits of sin. I am not saying that technique is contrary to the will of God. I am not saying that technique is evil in itself.[19]

> I have never attacked technology. On the one hand, I have attempted to describe the whole sociological problem of tech-

nology, with emphasis on my conviction that the benefits accruing from technology are well worthwhile. On the other hand, I have attacked the ideology of technology and idolatrous beliefs about technology.[20]

It is important to realize that Ellul is criticizing something deeper even than technique itself. He is concerned with the human motives behind the development, use, and abuse of technique, namely the human "will-to-power." From a biblical perspective, this "will-to-power" is viewed as an unquenchable thirst for power and security, which has been with us since the beginning of recorded time. Technique is the contemporary manifestation of the principalities and powers, to which modern humans give their allegiance in the blind quest to power.

It is this discussion of the essence of the human spirit which provides us with Ellul's understanding of technique. Technique can be seen as an extension of a sinful consciousness which stems from the human desire to act independently of God, to become stronger and more able to manipulate the world. "As far as power is concerned, exactly nothing has happened since Genesis," says Ellul.[21] Since the Fall humans have continued to act independently of God and thus continue to see themselves, rather than God, as the guiding principle of the world. The world is a hostile and chaotic place in which humans attempt to create order and stability. The results include "Babylon, Venice, Paris, New York—they are all the same city, only one Babylon always reappearing."[22]

In this sense, then, humanity today is doing nothing new: our use of techniques to guarantee survival has been characteristic of our existence since the expulsion from the Garden. Today, technique fulfills the requirements of what Ellul calls "the order of necessity." The order of necessity is what succeeded the spontaneous and immediate relationships of God's creation before the Fall.

> The nature which had produced everything in abundance for Adam's sustenance and joy becomes an ungrateful and rebellious nature which resists man. . . . As a result, Adam must coerce nature, must conquer this nature which gives him thorns and thistles—Adam will have to give up his wheat, his fruits etc. . . . Thus, Adam finds himself in a relationship of conflict; he gets the upper hand through the means at his disposal; that is to say, through technique—which cannot be an instrument of love but only of domination.[23]

The connection is now clear: the reliance on our own power, our own ability to control nature and act independently of God, can paradoxically lead only to our enslavement; herein lies the truly deep significance of the Fall. Our pursuit of freedom is unattainable through the use of technique. In the attempt to *use* technique we have trapped ourselves in a controlled environment which disallows creativity and freedom.

> Technique is the present source of man's enslavement. It is not simply that, of course. Hypothetically, technique could be wholly a cause of man's liberation, just as, hypothetically, the state could be the source of security and justice, and the capitalist economy could be the source of happiness and of the satisfaction of needs. But all that is hypothetical. In reality, the state, the economic structure, and technique have been sources of alienation.[24]

Ellul believes that "the qualitative change in the proliferation of techniques went hand-in-hand with a qualitative change in relationships in terms of technique. The new relationships have no historical precedent."[25]

Ellul writes as a Christian. He does not, however, seek to offer the Christian specific guidelines of response. "But I refuse . . . to offer up some Christian or prefabricated socio-political solutions. I want only to provide Christians with the means of thinking out for themselves the meaning of their involvement in the modern world."[26]

In other words, Ellul is questioning fundamental modern assumptions about freedom, power, and order. In the pursuit of freedom and independence humans alienate not only one another, through the use of technique, but also God. Like Augustine before him, Ellul claims that freedom is not rooted in the self but is only possible in the context of obedience. By obeying God we are truly free; all other quests for freedom can lead only to enslavement. "This non-obedience expresses itself, then, in a closure, a closing! In its estrangement from God, the world withdraws within itself and recognizes only its own imperatives: it is closed to all outside influences. . . . It entraps man in situations without exit, all the while promoting itself as an all-fulfilling, all-encompassing system."[27] Modern society has gone beyond the use of technology as a tool and even beyond seeing technique as a structure of society; it now sees rationality as the only definition of reality and seeks to transform everything else into its image. Modern society has ceded its total allegiance to the demands of technique. "Humanity today, in seeing the domination of nature as the guarantee of freedom, is in grave error."[28]

It is the devastating paradoxical nature of technique which Ellul seeks to illuminate. He sees a world increasingly dominated by technique, a world in which real choices and options are constantly being diminished. His sombre description of the technological society is an effort to force us to see what humanity has become. We live in a world where we have become enslaved by a phenomenon of our own devising.

3. TECHNOLOGY AND MODERN SOCIETY

Ellul's basic argument, that the essential characteristic of technology is technique and that this pervades every area of life, is very convincing. All one has to do is look at the society in which we live. Cars, for example, are an omnipresent fact of modern life. But as Jerry Mander argues, if you accept the existence of cars:

> You also accept the existence of roads laid upon the landscape, oil to run the cars, and huge institutions to find the oil, pump it and distribute it. In addition you accept a sped-up style of life and the movement of humans through the terrain at speeds that make it impossible to pay attention to what is growing there. Humans who use cars sit in fixed positions for long hours following a narrow strip of gray pavement, with eyes fixed forward, engaged in the task of driving. As long as they are driving, they are living within what we might call "roadform." Slowly they evolve into car-people. McLuhan told us that cars "extended" the human feet, but he put it the wrong way. Cars *replaced* human feet.[29]

It is in fact difficult to overemphasize the changes that have been brought about by the all-pervasive influence of technique. This is partly because we have become so inbred with technique that we fail to be surprised by its ideological power. The art of politics has degenerated into manipulation, propaganda, and social engineering. Dialogue has been reduced to the exchange of information predicated on information systems. The erotic has been reduced to technique learned from sex manuals. There is even a book that purports to help people with their married lives by providing them with "an owner's guide that tells you how to keep your marriage running smoothly with the same practical, problem-solving approach of an automobile or appliance manual."[30] When a uniquely personal relationship such as marriage is treated in such a way, it is evident that technique dominates our understanding of ourselves and the world in which we live. Moreover, when we examine the ways in which technological objects are integrated within our environment, we see that technology cannot possibly be regarded as neutral.[31]

Perhaps the best example of a technology which would appear to be quite neutral is the computer. But as George Grant points out:

> Abstracting facts so that they may be stored as "information" is achieved by classification, and it is the very nature of any classifying to homogenize what may be heterogeneous. Where classification rules, identities and differences can only appear in its terms. . . . The "ways" that computers can be used for storing "information" can only be ways that increase the tempo of the homogenizing process in society . . . [the] very capabilities [of computers] entail that the ways that they can be used are never neutral. They can only be used in homogenizing ways.[32]

That the technological enterprise, which is the hallmark of Western society today, is driven by certain assumptions about the world and human beings is nowhere seen more clearly than in our view of education. In its classical sense education involved thinking about the purpose of life and why we are what we are. We shy away from such questions in our technological society. Education is now concerned with "facts," not "values." Such questions as, What is the good life? What is a good person? are considered subjective questions, that is, they have no "right" answers. To inculcate a vision of the good is simply not a pragmatic educational goal. Thus it is that in modern educational institutions there are sexology courses in which no judgement is made on the difference between pornography and love, and humanities courses in which Mozart, Nietzsche, and Hitler receive undifferentiated treatment.

Arthur Koestler in *The Heel of Achilles*[33] claims that much of educational thinking today no longer centers around the three traditional *R*s but rather around the three *R*s of reductionism, ratomorphism, and randomness. These three "pillars of unwisdom" are in fact concrete illustrations of the technological mentality of which we have been speaking. Let us expand on Koestler's arguments by using further examples.

Reductionism is the method used by those who think that reality can be described only in scientific terms. Hence the human is described by J. B. Watson, the father of behaviorism, as "an assembled organic machine ready to run," and zoologist Desmond Morris describes the human as a "naked ape." For the reductionist, all ultimate questions—questions relating to purpose and to God—either cannot or should not be asked because they cannot be reduced to rational or mechanistic paradigms. One cannot operate rationally and efficiently with paradigms or models that resist simplification. There is no place in a rational and efficient system for mystery or spontaneity. Yet are not these qualities the very essence of being human?

Ratomorphism uses the study of the behavior of such animals as rats, geese, or pigeons as a suitable model from which to study human behavior. This view is immensely popular today due to the tremendous influence of psychology on our educational institutions, especially at higher levels. The influence of B. F. Skinner is all-pervasive here, of course, but others have exercised influence, for example Konrad Lorenz and Desmond Morris, both of whom have described as "arrogant" the refusal of humans to believe that their knowledge is not of the same kind as that of the animal kingdom.[34]

When one observes the work of some members of the modern schools of art, one can see concretely what is meant by randomness. Those who throw fistfuls of paint at canvases, or who beat material into undetermined shapes, claim that their art mirrors reality. Human beings are seen as nothing more than random mutations preserved by natural selection; civilization and culture as mere incidental products of the evolutionary process. Hence, it is implied, there is no end for humanity, because there is no ultimate purpose, except that which we create for ourselves.

These three *R*s are the unconscious presuppositions of many who are associated with education. They are concomitants of the technological world-view. The emphasis on efficiency reduces everything to technique, whilst rationality has become a way of understanding the world by simplifying and reducing it to mechanistic models. Such thinking extends to the control of both human and nonhuman nature. The modern university cultivates those very disciplines that issue in mastery of human and nonhuman nature.[35] The quantifying or behavioral sciences dominate the university curriculum. They do so because it has been generally accepted that there is a distinction between facts and values. Those who maintain this distinction asseverate that accounts of reality must not confuse the normative and the factual. Normative statements about reality are subjective; factual statements are objective. The quantifying or behavioral sciences give an objective account of reality because they deal with "facts." Thus the scientific world is separated from the world of values, which are created by humans and are subjective. In this view of things "good" and "bad" are subjective preferences and are not to intrude into the reality of the "factual" world. In this way one possible brake is removed, to use Grant's image, from the "triumphal chariot of technology."[36] Grant continues:

> "Value-free" social sciences not only provide the means of control, but also provide a large percentage of the preachers who proclaim the dogmas which legitimize modern liberalism within the university. At first sight, it might be thought that practitioners of "value-free" science would not make good preachers. In looking more closely, however, it will be seen that the fact/value distinction is not self-evident, as is often claimed. It assumes a particular account of moral judgement, and a particular account of objectivity. To use the language of value about moral judgement is to assume that what man is doing when he is moral is choosing in his freedom to make the world according to his own values which are not derived from knowledge of the cosmos. To confine the language of objectivity to what is open to quantifiable experiment is to limit purpose to our own subjectivity. As these metaphysical roots of the fact/value distinction are often not evident to those who affirm the method, they are generally inculcated in what can best be described as a religious way; that is, as a doctrine beyond question.[37]

The fact/value distinction lies at the heart of the notion that technology is neutral. It also gives credence to the idea that problems created by the technological society can, and should, be solved only by technical means.

4. THE "TECHNOLOGICAL FIX" SYNDROME AND THE LIBERAL IDEAL

Those who believe that there are technical solutions to all problems are those who would advocate for more technological intervention as the solution to, for example, ecological or medical problems. Thus we spray forests with chemicals to rid them of such infestations as the spruce bud worm. In the field of medicine, we combat heart disease by inventing artificial hearts. The truth of the matter is, of course, that it is humankind's rapacious exploitation of nature which has upset the ecological balance, and it is the modern lifestyle that has increased heart disease. Moreover, technical solutions may solve some problems, but they always create others.[38] But the technological march will not be impeded; there is no thought of turning back or even turning aside to examine the root causes of many of our problems. The only way forward is the technological 'fix,' the use of a more efficient and sophisticated technology. The crises of the modern world, whether related to ecology or energy, are seen as symptomatic of an incomplete stage in technology; the correction of the problem thereby requires a more complete technology. These examples illustrate that technology itself has a kind of inner drive to expansion and totality. To analyze the technological enterprise in this way illustrates that technology is not merely an end—it is not machines, computers, instruments, or electronic devices. In the technological process we seek to rationalize all human endeavor; that is, we direct all our efforts toward simplification, systematization, and efficiency. In short, we see the world as a thing to be manipulated, subdued, rationalized, and utilized. In ceding to technology our allegiance, we accept the autonomy of its mode of operation.

At the heart of the "technological fix" mentality that drives the technological enterprise lies a certain view of human freedom. The view of human autonomy that prevails in the technological society is "liberalism," that is, the idea that the essence of human beings is the freedom to make the world as they wish.[39] Liberalism implies open-ended progress. It offers no specific idea of a human nature that ought to be realized. Mastery of human and nonhuman nature is the end; this end is not grounded in any notion of good. If the end is defined at all it is usually in terms of "happiness," a notion which is in fact so vague it is quite incapable of checking technological progress. The conquest of chance is seen as the chief means of improving humanity, and yet there is no sense of the direction this "improvement" should take. It is one of the ironies of history that liberalism has its roots in the Christian tradition. Moreover, an examination of these roots will not only throw into sharper relief the contours of freedom in a liberal society, but also help us determine whether liberalism can possibly be reconciled with the Christian faith.

Christianity began, of course, as a sect within Judaism and therefore at its inception functioned with the basic presuppositions of Judaism concerning God, humanity, and the world. Christianity was actually an apocalyptic sect within Judaism—the earliest Christians were Jews who believed that the present world would be brought to an end by the Second Coming of Christ (cf. I Thes 4:13–8). Very quickly, however, Christianity became transplanted onto Hellenistic soil and was imbued with the Greek spirit. Greek philosophy became married to the Hebrew faith.

This liaison was not without its tensions. For the Greek view of human autonomy was different from the Hebrew one. In classical Greek thought the goal of humanity was to live according to natural law. There was an order in the world (the world was a κόσμος and not a κάος) and reason enabled us to discern that order and to live by it. In Judaism, however, what one was to do with one's life was revealed in the Torah. Thus in Greek thought our distinctive humanity lay in the rational apprehension of the cosmic order and our place in it, whereas in Judaism our distinctive humanity lay in the fact that we can choose: we can either obey or disobey the Torah. For the Greek the emphasis was on "know thyself," but for the Jew it was "choose ye this day" (Joshua 24:15; cf. 1 Kings 18:21). Moreover, choosing to obey the Torah issued in an active life on behalf of others. The early Greek fathers were aware of this tension and chose to elevate the contemplative life over the active one. Origen, Augustine, Gregory the Great, Cassian, and others all give scriptural arguments to show that although pursuing an active life on behalf of others was in accord with Christian charity, the contemplative life of beholding the Lord was better.[40] Francis Bacon, however, reversed this emphasis and in so doing paved the way for modern liberalism. Bacon equated knowledge with power. He averred that the power given to humankind by scientific knowledge should be used in a spirit of Christian charity.[41] Hence his famous call to conquer nature "for the relief of man's estate."[42] Scientific knowledge was based on action (e.g., experiments) and useful for action (e.g., control of nature). The contemplative life, claimed Bacon, was really selfish and therefore quite inferior to the life of action. It is not without significance that the biblical text quoted most often by Bacon is Genesis 1:28.

Bacon's discrediting of the contemplative life was followed by an attack upon belief in transcendental norms. The greatest and most profound expression of the view that there is no transcendental ground of permanence is found in Nietzsche. It is in Nietzsche's writings that we see most clearly the implications of emphasizing the historicity of human existence. If it is accepted that the natural sciences have demonstrated how unnecessary it is to assume purpose in unravelling the mysteries of nonhuman nature, how much more should it apply to human nature! Humans do not have purpose—the historic sense tells us so. Nietzsche was a great admirer of the Greek tragedies because he saw in them humans inspired by nobility—they understood life had no purpose but were resolutely defiant in the face of it. Socrates destroyed Greek tragedy by maintaining that life did have purpose and that this could be revealed through rationality. Nietzsche attacks Socrates. The historic sense destroys belief in any transcendent ground of purpose. We live within horizons that are our own creations, there is no transcendental sanction for them. The horizon of the transcendent has been wiped away.[43]

Bacon had attacked the contemplative life as selfish and Nietzsche had attacked its very *raison d'être*. In driving a wedge between charity and contemplation Bacon made the active life of charity intrinsically worthwhile for its own sake.[44] Thus Bacon's view of Christian autonomy was able to survive the attack of Nietzsche and others upon the rational, contemplative life. Furthermore, the active life of charity espoused by Bacon was easily accommodated to a technological society which retained the goal of the relief of man's estate. Thus liberalism, with its view of unrestrained human autonomy, has its roots in Bacon's divorce of Christian action from Christian spirituality. What implications does this have for us when thinking about the question of technology?

5. THE QUESTION OF TECHNOLOGY

There is a naive willingness in the modern era to accept arguments put forward in the name of technology. To address such arguments requires, however, a questioning of the very presuppositions of the technological society itself. People are easier to control when they cannot understand what they have become—when they do not know themselves. But to plea for questioning in the face of overwhelming ecological and economic problems will appear quite impractical to most people. How can anyone who desires to act, to make decisions, be satisfied with such a recommendation? Does not questioning simply break down and destroy? This was the very charge that was brought against Socrates by his fellow Athenians who believed his questioning destroyed the hope of the youth. Socrates' antagonists wanted only questions they could answer. They did not want questioning which shattered their world-view and left them with only ambiguity and perplexity. Ambiguity and perplexity are not something, however, that humans may shy away from, for questioning is an integral part of the human condition. As Gertrude Stein once said, it is more important to ask questions than to give answers, even good answers.

Most of the technocrats who hold sway in our society are not conscious adherents of some debased authoritarian ideology. They are people who seek to use technological power to improve the lot of humanity. But in so doing they display a blighted vision of what they consider humanity to be. The hero, Frazier, in B. F. Skinner's novel *Walden Two*, speaks for many when he claims that humans can only live in peace and freedom if they build a social structure that satisfies the needs of everyone and that everyone will want to support. New technological techniques make this possible. It is now possible to control and modify behavior so that, says Frazier, "We can achieve a sort of control under which the controlled, even though they are following a code more scrupulously than ever was the case before, nevertheless feel free. . . . By careful cultural design we control not the behaviour, but the inclination to behave—the motives, the desires, the wishes [of humans]."[45] Frazier (the typical technocrat) believes that he knows what is best for humans, and technology gives him the power to impose his vision on others. In Skinner's novel technology has become the power through which humans can be modified and transformed in accordance with the technocrat's dream. This dream is now the nightmare that is upon us. If we choose to cede our allegiance to technology we must not only be prepared to pay the price, we must know what the price is. But to put technology to the question we must have firm ground on which to stand, some norm by which to judge. Christians have such a norm—the revelation of God through Christ. In our final chapter we return to the Fourth Evangelist's portrayal of that revelation to see how it has relevance to the modern predicament which has been created by technology.

CHAPTER 4

The Politics of Eternity: Johannine Theology Today

We have seen how for Käsemann the Gospel of John is an excellent example of the New Testament's "plurality of confessions." It is representative of a very distinctive type of Christianity, one that is not in keeping with the rest of the New Testament. In Käsemann's theology the only unifying factor in Christianity is the lordship of Christ. Christ means freedom because Christians are not shackled by dogma and institutions.[1]

It is, of course, quite true that the New Testament is not uniform in its presentation of Christian belief. But uniformity is not the same as unity. This was one of the major points made by H. E. W. Turner in his argument that Christianity was marked by a dynamic unity which did not exclude differences but which, at the same time, did have a substantial identity. Christianity was, for Turner, the product of an interaction between fixed and flexible elements.

We can use Turner's general insight when speaking in particular of the New Testament. It is true that Mark's understanding of Christ—his theology—differs from, say, John's. Redaction criticism has shown us that each one of the Gospel writers has a distinctive theology. Similarly, there are significant differences between Paul and James, between Hebrews and the Apocalypse. In this Käsemann is right. What it means is that in using the New Testament as a guide, Christians do not have to conform to a uniform belief. To put it figuratively, within the Christian tradition there is room for Marcan Christians, Lukan Christians, Johannine Christians, Pauline Christians, and so on. *But*—and this is the crucial point—the New Testament does circumscribe certain limits. One cannot be, for example, a Gnostic Christian. There is nothing in the New Testament remotely like the Gospel of Thomas. Käsemann

119

himself, when speaking of the Fourth Gospel's naive docetism, was careful not to go as far as someone like Louise Schotroff, who declares that the Fourth Gospel is in fact Gnostic.[2] The books of the New Testament emerge as canonical after Athanasius's famous letter because taken as a whole they captured the spirit of the *Gesamtkirche*. Books which went too far in the direction of heresies such as gnosticism were not included. But the books which were included were sufficiently diverse to reflect the dynamic nature of early Christian development.

What this implies is not an unbounded pluralism of belief. It implies, as we noted at the end of chapter 2, that the ongoing quest of Christian theology is to find a balance between the fixed and the flexible elements. Turner labelled the fixed elements in Christian tradition "the religious facts themselves" and went on to argue that the Church's grasp on these religious facts comes through the devotional and spiritual life of the Christian—the *lex orandi*. Turner's flexible elements allow the "facts" of Christianity to be communicated through a variety of theological expressions, such as eschatology or ontology.

What Turner is saying has direct relevance for a discussion of unity and diversity, uniformity and pluralism, dogma and tolerance. Turner's religious facts cannot be reduced merely to human conceptions and descriptions. Thus they may appear in one age in the mode of eschatology, in another in the mode of metaphysics, and in another in the mode of existentialism. But they are never fully grasped—much less exhausted—by any or all of these modes. The "inexhaustible riches" (Eph 3:8) which are found in the New Testament are the riches of Christ: these riches have an *extra nos* reality. This is what it means to speak of the revelation of God in Christ.

Human reason can never plumb the depths of this revelation, because revelation is not Christology, it is Christ.[3] Each age's partial grasp of this revelation will be formulated within the philosophical and cultural parameters of that age. It follows that certain New Testament books will speak more directly to some ages than to others. This is perhaps the most significant implication of the line of argument we have been pursuing. The diversity of the New Testament is its greatest strength. It does not imply that the New Testament embraces any and every belief, but rather it implies that its very diversity allows it to speak anew to each new age. In the Middle Ages, for example, when humans were stalked by the Black Death, the Book of Revelation spoke to them in a way no other book did. In our modern age it is the Gospel of John that addresses us in a most challenging way. Through a reading of recovery we can now place it firmly in the center of the debate about human destiny in the age of modernity. Dorothy Lee puts it this way:

> John's incarnational psychology has immediate implications for the modern Western context, where a false materialistic alternative is linked to the realities of a secularised culture. In the first place, the spirituality of the Gospel challenges modern, consumerist attitudes which regard the world as dispensable. Because the world is God's creation and because, more importantly, it has the symbolic potential to reveal God, it cannot be exploited or used in a destructive way. To do so is to nullify not only its created origins but also its eschatological identity bestowed in the incarnation. Creation in John's theology can be neither abused nor manipulated, any more than human beings can. The world belongs to God, is the sphere of God's loving and saving activity, and is also the bearer of God's presence. It is sacred to God both in its origins and destiny . . . the value of the world lies precisely in its capacity to disclose, through Jesus, the life-giving presence of God.[4]

To clarify this point further we must recollect what we have said about modernity. The defining characteristic of the modern world is technology, and technology is driven by the ideology of liberalism. The beliefs of liberalism are predicated on the idea that the essence of human beings is freedom, and that this freedom expresses itself in the will to shape and control the world.[5] In the nineteenth century liberalism manifested itself in the doctrine of laissez-faire capitalism. Humans were freed to exploit each other without government restraint.[6] In our own age, however, liberalism expresses itself through the innovative power of technology. Mastery of human and nonhuman nature is the goal: technology is the agent of mastery and change. Central to liberalism is the idea of open-ended progress; the belief that the future is for humans to shape as they will; the world is theirs to manipulate and control. The conquest of chance—through technology—is seen as the chief means of improving the human lot. Unfortunately, liberalism itself does not provide us with the direction this improvement should take—the emphasis is on the journey, not the destination.[7] Moreover, in the world of technology human relationships are governed by efficiency, utility, and pragmatism.

The voice that speaks through the pages of the Fourth Gospel speaks of a different world. It is a world in which humans are seen as slaves to sin (cf. 8:31ff.) and where suffering, solitude, and death are recognized as intrinsic to the human condition. Yet it is a world permeated by the gratuitous love of God (cf. 10:18): a world for which Christ died (3:16). The voice of the Gospel of John—so long muted by quietistic interpretations—now cries out to us to look again at the world we have created. In modern parlance, the Fourth Gospel is a *critique of ideology*, a call for what Jacques Ellul has called the "desacralization of contemporary values" or—to change the image—a call for what Langdon Winner has called an "epistemological luddism."

The Fourth Gospel achieves this through its sustained emphasis upon a theology of revelation. Revelation is, as we saw in chapter 2, the central theme of the Fourth Gospel, commencing with the Prologue and continuing throughout the Gospel. The claim that Jesus is the one and only way to salvation lies at the very heart of the Johannine theology of revelation. This is evident not only in the Gospel's presentation of the motif of truth, but also in Christological affirmations such as that which sees Jesus as the Son of Man.[8] The Son of Man has ascended and descended (3:13; cf. 6:62). He alone is of heavenly origin. No one has ascended and seen the Father but the Son of Man alone who, being in the bosom of the Father, has descended to reveal him—"not the cross, nor the kerygma, nor any event, but the Lord himself is salvation."[9]

In the Fourth Gospel the revelation of God through Christ is, however, paradoxical. God gives his Son for the salvation of the world (3:16) and the world is created through him (1:3). God cares for the world, which he seeks to transform through his love (cf. 1:29). Yet the Son not only saves the world, he also condemns it (9:39; 12:31; 16:31). He is the agent through whom the world was created, yet he is also a stranger to it (17:14, 16; 18:36). The world is, in fact, controlled by the ruler of darkness (12:31, 14:30), and humans are in bondage to sin (8:31ff.). Johannine discourse recognizes that the world is in some way intractable[10]—that it is, to use later Christian terms, in a fallen state. The world resists the love of God. Thus Jesus prays for "his own" but not for the world (17:9), and promises that the Paraclete will continue the work of judging the world (14:7; 16:6ff.). It is this emphasis on the fallen state of the world that gives the Fourth Gospel its Gnostic flavor. Yet this aspect of Johannine discourse is no different from that of Paul (Rom 5:12–14; cf. 1 Cor 15:21–23). The contours of Paul's argument are clearer and less open to misunderstanding because he is writing a letter which allows him the privilege of systematic argument. The Fourth Evangelist is writing a story, and the dictates of a story line do not allow for such carefully differentiated argument. But the Fourth Evangelist is obviously in the same universe of discourse as Paul: God's love is revealed to a fallen world and is entirely gratuitous. Christian faith is rooted in the response to God's love. The love that is central to Christian faith is God's love, not human love. The revealer in the Fourth Gospel is God become man, not man become God. We are not saved by our own efforts and God's love is not called forth by qualities in those to whom he gives his love. Moreover, God's love for humans did not lead to happiness or enjoyment, but to crucifixion. His love points us beyond the horizon of this world to a mystery beyond our comprehension.

Johannine discourse thus evokes a universe of discourse which is foreign to that of the liberalism that undergirds modernity. For in liberalism human freedom is central and it issues in the will to master the world. Moreover, as an ideology liberalism is rooted in the belief that ideas are social products. Such an ideology must perforce be intolerant of mysteries. Mysteries speak of realities which are beyond the complete grasp of humans and known only through revelation. The Johannine theology of revelation points us beyond the finite to the eternal, to God himself. As Glen Tinder says:

> Because ideologies see ideas as social products, they are intolerant of mysteries, of realities that surpass every human faculty, are known only by revelation, and never under human control. The belief that the world is all and the belief that beyond the world there is God are not on the same footing; they are not reducible to mere contradictory assertions. Rather, they express dramatically different ways of approaching reality. One expresses an

attitude of mastery, the other of openness; one is unapologetically proud, the other aspires to humility; an ideological commitment represents a venture in historical sovereignty, whereas Christian faith is fundamentally responsive. The crux of the matter is that whereas worldly realities can be known and mastered by human beings, God cannot.[11]

Johannine theology calls upon us to cultivate an interior disposition and affinity with truth, which is the wellspring for Christian living. In this sense the Fourth Gospel is indeed the "spiritual Gospel," for it evokes the world of *lex orandi*. This is not to render Christianity "utterly apolitical" in order to keep it from a "vulgarized politization." To say that Christianity is not primarily concerned with correcting the rationalized imperfections of society is not the same as saying it has nothing political to say, for the *lex orandi* is a powerful source of the critique of all ideologies.

The diversification of Christianity, then, especially as embodied in the New Testament, has significant implications for Christian theology today. The very diversity of voices within its pages empowers the New Testament to speak to a great variety of times, places, and circumstances. The Fourth Gospel, which in traditional exegesis was domesticated as spiritual and unwordly and which in much of more recent exegesis has been marginalized as sectarian, in fact has a profoundly relevant (and disturbing) message for our age. This message does not negate the socioeconomic critique of liberation theology but rather goes beyond it. It challenges Christians to examine the very assumptions of modernity in which human fulfillment comes through mastery of human and non-human nature and in which efficiency, pragmatism, and utility are extolled as primary virtues. The Fourth Gospel's sustained theology of revelation and its emphasis on eternal life, spiritual renewal, and the gratuitous love of God, brings the Light into a darkened world. *Lex orandi, lex vivendi.*

NOTES

CHAPTER 1. UNDERSTANDING THE CONTEXT
OF THE JOHANNINE ENIGMA

1. W. Bauer, *Rechtgläubigkeit und Ketzerei im ältesten Christentum* (Tübingen: Mohr/Siebeck, 1936). ET: *Orthodoxy and Heresy in Earliest Christianity* (Philadelphia: Fortress Press, 1971).

2. E. Käsemann, "The Canon of the New Testament and the Unity of the Church" in *Essays on New Testament Themes* (London: SCM, 1965), pp. 95–107. H. Koester, "GNOMAI DIAPHORAI: The Origin and Nature of Diversification in Early Christianity," *HTR* 58 (1965), p. 281, in acclaiming the work of Bauer, describes Christianity as "a religious movement which is syncretistic in appearance and conspicuously marked by diversification from the very beginning."

3. Bauer, *Orthodoxy and Heresy*, p. xxi.

4. *Ibid.*, p. xxiii.

5. *Ibid.*

6. *Ibid.*

7. *Ibid.*, p. 59.

8. *Ibid.*, p. 77.

9. *Ibid.*, p. 85.

10. *Ibid.*, pp. 122f.

11. *Ibid.*, p. 114.

12. *Ibid.*, p. 231.

13. *Ibid.*, pp. 231f.

14. One can dispute Bauer's claim that the Fourth Gospel was originally a heretical Gospel. It is, however, indisputable that the Fourth Gospel was first used by the Gnostics and had difficulty gaining acceptance by the church at large. J. N. Sanders, *The Fourth Gospel in the Early Church* (Cambridge: CUP, 1943), considers whether the early Christian theologians considered it their "bounden duty" to transmit the faith without addition or diminution of content (granting that its form may change). His inquiry endorses the view that the Fourth Gospel was first used by the Gnostics and is non-apostolic. It gained acceptance by the orthodox only with Irenaeus (c. 130–200 A.D.). Sanders thinks that the

Fourth Gospel originated in Alexandria and agrees with Bauer that the early church there was not, by later standards, orthodox. Sanders himself, however, rejects both the *schema* that views the history of Christian doctrine as a degeneration and that which views it as an accumulation. He takes a third view that "allows both for the fact of revelation—of a faith once delivered to the saints—and the reality of development." This, in Sanders's opinion, is the view held by early orthodox Christian writers. He says:

> That a church should at least in an early period be what would later have to be regarded as "heretical" is by no means *a priori* impossible . . . This is not to deny that there is such a thing as heresy, but only to suggest that the question whether a doctrine is heretical depends not merely on its wording (as for instance was assumed by those who condemned Origen), but also its relationship to other doctrines along with it and to the prevailing tendencies in which it was propounded" (p. 41).

With regard to the Fourth Gospel, Sanders is in no doubt that it cannot be regarded as "heretical," because it is true to the early Christian *kerygma*:

> The Fourth Gospel itself presents the *kerygma* in the language of current religious speculation, and does it so well that, though it ultimately could be used to demolish Gnosticism because it itself was true to the *kerygma*, yet it nevertheless attracted the Gnostics, who were anxious to appropriate its teaching, and who attempted to build up a religious philosophy (if their system can be so called) on the basis of an exegesis of the Prologue which adapted it to earlier dualistic and Docetic-Gnostic ideas (p. 41).

Irenaeus is the interpreter of the Fourth Gospel *par excellence*, for it was he who put his finger on the reason why the heretics produced distorted interpretations: they sought to interpret Scripture by "means of a fundamentally alien theosophy, instead of doing it by means of the rule of truth, the Christian *regula fidei* which already, in the Apostolic *kerygma*, underlies and controls the very books of the New Testament themselves" (p. 68).

15. *Ibid.*, p. 236.
16. *Ibid.*, p. 240.
17. H. E. W. Turner, *The Pattern of Christian Truth: A Study in the Relations between Orthodoxy and Heresy in the Early Church* (London: Mowbray, 1954).
18. *Ibid.*, p. 8.
19. *Ibid.*, p. 33.
20. *Ibid.*, p. 26.

21. *Ibid.*, pp. 26f.
22. *Ibid.*, p. 27.
23. *Ibid.*, p. 28.
24. *Ibid.*, p. 30.
25. *Ibid.*, p. 31.
26. *Ibid.*, p. 80.
27. *Ibid.*, p. 79.
28. *Ibid.*, pp. 102–117.
29. *Ibid.*, pp. 117–124.
30. *Ibid.*, pp. 124–132.
31. *Ibid.*, pp. 132–148.
32. *Ibid.*, p. 498.
33. *Ibid.*, p. 488.
34. Bernard J. F. Lonergan, *Method in Theology* (London: Darton, Longman and Todd, 1972), p. 232.
35. Turner, *Pattern of Christian Truth*, p. 28.
36. N. Smart, *Philosophers and Religious Truth* (London: SCM, 1964), p. 118.
37. Turner, *Pattern of Christian Truth*, p. 498.
38. B. F. Meyer. *The Church in Three Tenses* (Garden City, New York: Doubleday & Co., 1971), p. 71.
39. E. Norman, *Christianity and the World Order* (Oxford: OUP, 1979), p. 50.
40. See, for example, John J. Shepherd, "Norman Wisdom?" *ExT* 90 (1980), pp. 262–264.
41. See C. Rowland and M. Corner, *Liberating Exegesis: The Challenge of Liberation Theology to Biblical Studies* (Louisville: John Knox Press, 1989), pp. 114–116.
42. Martin Luther, "An Open Letter on the Harsh Book against the Peasants" (1525), *Luther's Works* 6 (Philadelphia: Fortress Press, 1967), pp. 69f.
43. Leonardo and Clodovis Boff, *Introducing Liberation Theology*, trans. Paul Burns (Maryknoll: Orbis, 1988), pp. 2f.
44. *Ibid.*, p. 3.
45. *Ibid.*, p. 29.
46. *Ibid.*, p. 5.
47. *Ibid.*
48. Norman, *Christianity and the World Order*, p. 2.
49. *Ibid.*, p. 50.
50. *Ibid.*, p. 7.
51. *Ibid.*, p. 12.
52. *Ibid.*, p. 13.

128 THE JOHANNINE WORLD

53. *Ibid.*, p. 32.
54. *Ibid.*, p. 59.
55. *Ibid.*, p. 73.
56. *Ibid.*, p. 74.
57. *Ibid.*, p. 76.
58. *Ibid.*, pp. 76f.
59. *Ibid.*, p. 79.
60. *Ibid.*
61. *Ibid.*, p. 80.
62. Shepherd, "Norman Wisdom?" (See above, n. 40).
63. *Ibid.*, pp. 263f.
64. *Ibid.*, p. 263.
65. *Ibid.*
66. Albert Schweitzer, *Von Reimarus zu Wrede: eine Geschichte der Leben-Jesu-Forschung* (Tübingen: J. B. C. Mohr, 1906); ET: *The Quest of the Historical Jesus: A Critical Study of Its Progress from Reimarus to Wrede*, trans. W. Montgomery (London: A. & C. Black Ltd., 1st ed. 1910; 2nd ed. 1936).
67. Paul Hollenbach, "The Historical Jesus Question in North America Today," *Biblical Theology Bulletin* 19 (1988), p. 11.
68. Christopher Rowland, *Radical Christianity: A Reading of Recovery* (Maryknoll: Orbis, 1988), p. 75.
69. See especially B. F. Meyer, *The Aims of Jesus* (London: SCM, 1979).
70. It is N. T. Wright who has dubbed the work of Meyer and others the "Third Quest"—see N. T. Wright, "'Constraints' and the Jesus of History," *ScJTh* 39 (1986), p. 190.
71. Meyer, *Aims*, pp. 249f.
72. *Ibid.*, p. 248.
73. *Ibid.*, pp. 185–197. See also B. F. Meyer, *The Man for Others* (New York: Bruce Publishing Company, 1970), pp. 84–92.
74. See M. F. Wiles, *The Spiritual Gospel: The Interpretation of the Fourth Gospel in the Early Church* (Cambridge: CUP, 1960).
75. See, for example, José Porfirio Miranda, *Being and the Messiah: The Message of St. John* (Maryknoll: Orbis, 1977); F. Herzog, *Liberation Theology: Liberation in the Light of the Fourth Gospel* (New York: Seabury, 1972).
76. Although I have chosen to focus on Bultmann and Käsemann, the book by David Rensberger, *Johannine Faith and Liberating Community* (Philadelphia: Westminster, 1988), affords another fine example of someone who focuses upon political and social dimensions of the Gospel of John and who is also "concerned with the developments that

are more within the interests of historical-critical approaches to the New Testament than those of the various literary-critical methodologies that have come to the fore" (p. 16).

77. R. Bultmann, *Das Evangelium des Johannes* (Göttingen: Vandenhoeck and Ruprecht, 1957). ET: *The Gospel of John: A Commentary* (Oxford: Blackwell, 1971).

78. R. Bultmann, *Theology of the New Testament*, Vol. II (New York: Scribner's, 1955), p. 41.

79. Cf. the comment of James M. Robinson in his review of Bultmann's *Theology of the New Testament* (Vol II) in *Theology Today* 13 (1956–57), p. 261: "It is . . . the historian who will be concerned by the way in which normative Christianity is not explained historically, but occurs as a *creatio ex nihilo* in Paul and then independently in John. Therefore he will not rest content until he has, on a more fundamental phenomenological level, supplemented the existential norm with a description of the historical unity or continuity with the early Church."

80. E. Käsemann "Ketzer und Zeuge. Zum johanneischen Verfasserproblem," *ZTK* 48 (1951), pp. 292–311.

81. *Ibid.*, pp. 293f.

82. *Ibid.*, p. 301.

83. *Ibid.*, p. 311.

84. E. Käsemann, *Jesu Letzter Wille nach Johannes 17*, (Tübingen: Mohr/Siebeck, 1966). ET: *The Testament of Jesus. A Study of the Gospel of John in the Light of Chapter 17* (London: SCM, 1968).

85. *Ibid.*, p. 2.

86. *Ibid.*, p. 8.

87. *Ibid.*, pp. 9f. See also his "Aufbau und Anliegen des johanneischen Pologs," in *Libertas Christiana. Festschrift für F. Delekat* (München: C. Kaiser Verlag, 1957). ET: "The Structure and Purpose of the Prologue to John's Gospel," in *New Testament Questions of Today* (London: SCM, 1969), pp. 138–167.

88. *Ibid.*, p. 15.

89. *Ibid.*

90. *Ibid.*, p. 31.

91. *Ibid.*, p. 75.

92. Cf. James M. Robinson, "Basic Shifts in German Theology," *Interpretation* 16 (1962), p. 77: "This was just the time when there was talk in some Church circles in Germany of a heresy trial for Bultmann, so that Käsemann was casting the evangelist in a role not too dissimilar from what Bultmann might have become. After all, the Gospel of John is the norm of Bultmannian theology."

93. Cf. Bultmann, *Theology*, II, p. 40: "The theme of the whole

Gospel is the statement 'The Word became flesh.'" It was no surprise when G. Bornkamm chose to reply to Käsemann on behalf of the Bultmannians at a 1967 meeting of the "old Marburgers." Bornkamm criticized Käsemann on three major counts. First, Käsemann failed to see that the farewell discourses centre on Jesus' death, thus emphasizing his humanity. Second, the label "naive Docetism" may apply to the theology of the pre-Johannine tradition, but not to that of the Evangelist himself. Third, Käsemann erred in the way he applied later categories of discrimination to the New Testament. See W. Loader, *The Christology of the Fourth Gospel: Structure and Issues* (Frankfurt: Peter Lang, 1992), pp. 7ff., for a discussion of this debate. Other, non-Bultmannians, have also criticized Käsemann's position—see e.g., M. M. Thompson, *The Humanity of Jesus in the Fourth Gospel* (Philadelphia: Fortress Press, 1988). Thompson argues that the "materiality" of the signs point to the humanity of Jesus (a problematic notion which turns on what Thompson [p. 32] calls the "facticity" of the signs).

94. See especially E. Käsemann "Begründet der neutestamentliche Kanon die Einheit der Kirche?" in *Exegetische Versuche und Besinnungen*, Vol I, (Göttingen: Vandenhoeck und Ruprecht, 1960), pp. 214–225. ET: "The Canon of the New Testament and the Unity of the Church" in *Essays on New Testament Themes* (London: SCM, 1965), pp. 95–107.

95. E. Käsemann, "What I have Unlearned in 50 Years as a German Theologian," *Currents in Theology and Mission* 15 (1988), p. 332. This article is a translation of an address given by Käsemann to the Theological Faculty at Marburg on the fiftieth anniversary of obtaining his doctoral degree.

96. Cf. Käsemann, "What I have Unlearned," p. 330: "When Bultmann even pulled Ignatius of Antioch into his existential interpretation and thus, to sharpen my point polemically, transferred Kierkegaard into the beginning of the second century, I had to break with him immediately."

97. *Ibid.*, p. 333.

98. Cf. Bernard J. F. Lonergan, *Method in Theology*, p. xi: "A theology mediates between a cultural matrix and the role of religion in that matrix."

99. We can push the parallel between Käsemann and the liberation theologians even further, for the differences between Käsemann and Bultmann recall the differences between the liberation theologians and Cardinal Ratzinger's favorite theologian, von Balthazar. For von Balthazar, liberation is transcendental and individual. The Church did not arise out of Jesus' earthly life but out of subsequent events. Therefore it is mistaken to focus faith on the earthly Jesus. (For illuminating light on the rela-

tionship of von Balthazar's thought to that of the Liberation theologians see Harvey Cox, *The Silencing of Leonardo Boff: The Vatican and the Future of World Christianity* [Oak Park, Ill.: Meyer-Stone, 1988], pp. 149–157.) Bultmann too sees salvation as an individual matter. The Church began with the Easter experience. The earthly Jesus is presupposed in the kerygma, but it is the risen Christ who is the focus of faith. To focus on the earthly Jesus leads us to a kind of "Jesusology" and away from Christology. In rejecting these basic premises Käsemann and the liberation theologians stress that the Church is the development of a community created by Jesus and what Jesus said and did is important in giving content to the faith. (See E. Käsemann, "The Problem of the Historical Jesus" in *Essays on New Testament Themes* [London: SCM, 1964], pp. 15–47.)

CHAPTER 2. UNDERSTANDING THE FOURTH GOSPEL

1. Gottlieb Wilke, "Über die Parabel von den Arbeitern in Weinsberge, Matth. 20, 1–16," *ZWT* 1 (1826), pp. 73–88.
2. D. F. Strauss, *Leben Jesu*, (Stuttgart: A. Kröner, 1835–1836). ET: *The Life of Jesus Critically Examined*, trans. from the Fourth Ed. (1840) by Marion Evans (New York: Calvin and Blanchard, 1860; republished, Mich.: Scholarly Press, 1970).
3. Otto Pfleiderer, "Foreword" to D. F. Strauss, *The Life of Jesus Critically Examined*, p. xxiv.
4. Norman Perrin, *The Kingdom of God in the Teaching of Jesus* (London: SCM, 1963), p. 16.
5. R. Bultmann, *The History of the Synoptic Tradition* (Oxford: Blackwell, 1968), p. 338.
6. W. Marxsen, *Der Evangelist Markus* (Göttingen: Vandenboeck & Ruprecht, 1959).
7. E. Haenchen, *Der Weg Jesu. Eine Erklärung des Markus-Evangeliums und der Kanonischen Parallelen* (Berlin: Töpelmann, 1966), p. 24.
8. Stephen D. Moore, *Literary Criticism and the Gospels: The Theoretical Challenge* (New Haven: Yale University Press, 1989), p. 4.
9. N. Perrin, *What is Redaction Criticism?* (Philadelphia: Fortress Press, 1969).
10. R. Bultmann, *Jesus and the Word* (New York: Charles Scribner's Sons, 1934), pp. 11ff.
11. R. P. C. Hanson, *The Continuity of Christian Doctrine* (New York: Seabury, 1981), pp. 11ff.
12. Hayden White, *Tropics of Discourse* (Baltimore/London: John

Hopkins University Press, 1978), p. 117. White takes much more of a post-modernist stance in this book than in his earlier *Metahistory* (Baltimore: The John Hopkins University Press, 1973).

13. Hanson, *The Continuity of Christian Doctrine*, p. 14.

14. Ben F. Meyer, *Critical Realism and the New Testament*, (Princeton Theological Monographs Series 17, Allison Park, PA: Pickwick Publications, 1989), esp. pp. 17–55; *Aims of Jesus* (London: SCM, 1979), pp. 13–104.

15. Lonergan, *Method in Theology*, p. 160.

16. R. Bultmann, *Das Evangelium des Johannes* (Göttingen: Vandenhoeck & Ruprecht, 1964); ET: *The Gospel of John* (Oxford: Blackwell, 1971).

17. E. Ruckstuhl, *Die literarische Einheit des Johannesevangelium: Der gegenwartige Stand der einschlägigen Erforschung* (Studia Frieburgensia, n.s. 3; Freiburg in der Schweiz: Ed. E. Paul, 1951); E. Schweizer, *Ego Eime. Der Religionsgeschichtliche Herkunft und theologische Bedeutung der johanneische Bildreden, zugleich ein Beitrag zur Quellenfrage des vierten Evangeliums* (Göttingen: Vandenhoeck & Ruprecht, 1939, 2nd ed. 1965). Bultmann demonstrated he was unmoved by his critics' reproaches when he edited the posthumous work of his student H. Becker, *Die Reden des Johannesevangeliums und der Stil der gnostischen Offenbarungsrede* (FRLANT 50: Göttingen: Vandenhoeck & Ruprecht, 1956).

18. Kümmel, *Introduction*, p. 152.

19. *Ibid.*

20. R. T. Fortna, *The Gospel of Signs: A Reconstruction of the Narrative Source underlying the Fourth Gospel* (Cambridge: CUP, 1970). Also: *The Fourth Gospel and Its Predecessor: From Narrative Source to Present Gospel* (Philadelphia: Fortress, 1990).

21. C. K. Barrett, Review of *Gospel of Signs*, *JTS* 22 (1971), pp. 573–74.

22. See, for example, the article by C. Goodwin, "How Did John Treat His Sources?" *JBL* 73 (1954), pp. 61–75, who argues that the one source we know John used—the Old Testament—is utilized freely and from memory; it follows that if John did the same with his other suspected sources, they are now irretrievable. F. -M. Braun, *Jean le Theologie*, II, *Les grandes traditions d'Israel et L'accord des Ecritures selon le quatriéme evangile*, pp. 20f., has criticized Goodwin's argument by maintaining that John translated directly from the Hebrew and was not dependent upon the LXX. Fortna, *The Gospel of Signs*, pp. 10–12, is totally unimpressed by Goodwin's argument.

23. B. H. Streeter, *The Four Gospels* (London: McMillan, 1930), p. 377.

24. In his commentary Brown identifies the authority behind the Gospel as the Beloved Disciple, whom he then identifies as the Apostle John. Later on he changed his mind and came to the conclusion that the Beloved Disciple should not be identified with the Apostle John. See his *The Community of the Beloved Disciple* (New York: Paulist Press, 1979), pp. 33–34.

25. R. E. Brown, *The Gospel According to John* (Anchor Bible 29; Garden City, New York: Doubleday 1966), pp. xxxiv–xxxix.

26. *Ibid.*, p. c. Note that Fortna, *The Gospel of Signs*, p. 6, n. 5, seems to be at cross purposes with Brown when he says that Brown distinguishes between the author and the writer, whereas he prefers "to use the terms interchangeably as equivalent to evangelist." Brown makes a distinction between the authority behind the tradition (stage one) and the author who uses the material, stamping upon it his own theological outlook (stages two through four). Thus he is hardly in disagreement with Fortna over who the author is "in the true sense."

27. R. Schnackenburg, *Das Johannes Evangelium*, I (Freiburg: Herder, 1965); ET: *The Gospel According to St. John*, I (New York: Herder and Herder, 1968), p. 101. Schnackenburg has also changed his mind about the identity of the Beloved Disciple.

28. C. K. Barrett, *The Gospel According to St. John: An Introduction with Commentary and Notes on the Greek Text* (London: S.P.C.K., 1955), p. 113.

29. *Ibid.*, p. 114.

30. M.-E. Boismard, "Le chapitre xxi de saint Jean: essai de critique littéraire," *RB* 54 (1947), pp. 473–501. Whereas, for example, Barrett (*John*, pp. 479f.) thinks such evidence suggests an addition by another hand, Wilkens, *Die Entstehungsgeschichte des Vierten Evangeliums* (Zollikon-Zürich: Evang. Verlag, 1958), pp. 158f., thinks the evidence suggests the contrary.

31. Wilkens, *Die Entstehungsgeschichte des Vierten Evangeliums*.

32. It is interesting to note here that Fortna's *Gospel of Signs* marks a shift from the view that a redactor so radically tampered with the Gospel that a corrupt work confronts us, pieces of which must be excised in order to recover the true Johannine Gospel. Fortna considers that the aporias or inconsistencies are to be traced back to the decisive redactor. He even believes that chapter 21 belongs to the Evangelist (pp. 87ff.).

33. The aporias have to be attributed to either the final redactor or the decisive redactor. If we maintain that the final redactor tampered with the Gospel, we must ask why. Bultmann thinks it is because he wished to make the Gospel acceptable to the Church. But he fails to show consistently that the parts he wishes to delete as belonging to the "eccle-

siastical redactor" are in fact at odds with the rest of the Gospel. For example, he detects the work of this redactor in 6:51b–58, because of the sacramental references, but overlooks the fact that there are sacramental undertones in 6:1–50—see R. E. Brown, "The Kerygma of the Gospel According to John," *Interpretation* 21 (1967), p. 394, n. 13.

34. See C. K. Barrett, "The Old Testament in the Fourth Gospel," *JTS* 48 (1947), pp. 155–169.

35. See also E. M. Sidebottom, "The Ascent and Descent of the Son of Man in the Gospel of John," *ATR* 2 (1957), pp. 115–122.

36. R. Bultmann, "Die Bedeutung der neuerschlossenen mandäischen und manichäischen Quellen für das Verständnis des Johannesevangeliums," *ZNW* 24 (1925), p. 102.

37. C. K. Barrett, *John*, p. 11.

38. J. A. T. Robinson, "The Relation of the Prologue to the Gospel of St. John," *NTS* 9 (1962–1963), pp. 120–129.

39. Schnackenburg, *John*, p. 223: "These verses 6–8 cannot have been mechanically transplanted from, say, before 1:19 and put into the middle of the Prologue, since both the "giving testimony to the light" (v. 7b) and the second ἵνα-clause with the intransitive πιστυειν (v. 7c) presuppose the preceding verses of the Prologue."

40. *Ibid.* Schnackenburg does, however, isolate what he considers to have been the "Logos-hymn" used by the Evangelist (see his "Logos-Hymnus und johanneischer Prolog," *BZ* [1957], pp. 69–109). It consists of vss. 1, 3, 4, 9, 10, 11, and 16. There have been many other reconstructions of this supposed "Logos-hymn." But Jack T. Sanders, whose own reconstruction of the hymn omits vss. 6–8 and goes through only to v. 11, admits that "it is not entirely clear that this passage should be referred to as a hymn. There are no particles in the passage, the article is generally present, and, with the exception of v. 3, there is no *parallelismus membrorum*" (*The New Testament Christological Hymns* [Cambridge: CUP, 1971], p. 21). Barrett, *John*, pp. 125f., after dividing the Prologue into four parts, goes further: "It does not seem possible to split them up into poetic structure, either in Greek or in a conjectured original Aramaic." He maintains that the whole passage shows marked internal unity (see further his *The Prologue of St. John's Gospel* [London: University of London Athlone Press, 1971]).

41. Bultmann, *John*, p. 13.

42. Cf. A. Reinhartz, *The Word in the World. The Cosmological Tale in the Fourth Gospel* (Society of Biblical Literature Monograph Series 45; Atlanta: Scholars Press, 1992), p. 16: "The prologue not only summarizes the main divisions of the gospel and introduces some of its main themes and characters, but it also acts as the reader's guide to the

cosmological tale as it comes to expression throughout the body of the gospel narrative."

43. Dodd, *The Fourth Gospel*, pp. 345–354.

44. Bultmann, *John*, p. 457.

45. R. E. Brown, *The Gospel of John and the Johannine Epistles* (Collegeville: The Liturgical Press, 1965), p. 95.

46. The search for a discernible contemporary horizon within the redaction of John is of singular importance and touches directly upon any discussion of the Johannine enigma. For example, Barrett's discussion of the purpose of John is placed against the background of two problems: eschatology and Gnosticism. He says, however, "It may be doubted whether he was really interested in its publication. It is easy, when we read the Gospel, to believe that John, though doubtless aware of the necessity of strengthening Christians and converting the heathen, wrote primarily to satisfy himself. His gospel must be written; it was no concern of his whether it was also read . . . It seems right to emphasize a certain detachment of the gospel from its immediate surroundings; no book was ever less of a party tract than John" (*John*, p. 115). This of course contrasts quite starkly with Käsemann's "Ketzer und Zeuge" and *Testament of Jesus*. We should perhaps note that, unlike Käsemann, Barrett does not think that the author of the Johannine Epistles is the same person who wrote the Gospel. (For Käsemann's reaction to Barrett's work see his *Exegetische Versuche und Besinnungen* [Göttingen: Vandenhoeck & Ruprecht, 1970], II, pp. 141–148.) The contributors to the orthodoxy/heresy debate within the New Testament have focused attention upon the possibility that the redactional story line may be dictated by the historical circumstance of the author, so that opposition and dissent encountered by the author may well indicate how the work is to be understood and, indeed, why he wrote at all. The orthodoxy/heresy debate on Paul focuses on trying to discover who his opponents were and the exact nature of the opposition; this trend has been shifted to the Johannine writings by the work of Käsemann. Unfortunately, to pursue this tack in John is very difficult. The various studies on the opponents of Paul have produced very different results, and there are controls there which are lacking in the Johannine literature. *If* Fortna were right, and the signs-source of John could be constructed as he would have us believe, this indeed would be a great breakthrough in the interpretation of John; for then we could compare the theology of this earlier source with that of the later redaction, noting where the redactor has made additions and alterations. The developments thus apparent would give us valuable insights into the situation giving rise to the total redaction (e.g., J. Becker, "Wunder und Christologie: Zum literarkritischen und christologischen Problem

der Wunder im Johannesevangelium," *NTS* 16 [1970], pp.130–148). In the present work, however, we intend to pursue a more limited inquiry within what we consider more feasible horizons.

There have, of course, been many attempts to determine the concrete historical background of the Fourth Gospel; we do not mean to imply that such inquiry is only recent. (What is significant about Käsemann's work is that the position of the Fourth Evangelist himself is thrown into question; that is, the question is whether the Evangelist stands "on the periphery of the church.") As early as 1898, W. Baldensperger, *Der Prolog des vierten Evangeliums: sein polemisch-apologetischer Zweck* (Freiberg i. Br.), saw the purpose of the Gospel as polemic against the disciples of John the Baptist, and placed the Gospel against the background of that controversy. A polemic against the John the Baptist veneration does seem to be discernible in the Fourth Gospel, especially in 1:19–51, and it would seem as though Baptist veneration posed a problem for the readership the Evangelist had in mind. (*Clementine Recognitions*, i, 54, 60, puts on the lips of Peter the claim that "some of the disciples of John . . . have separated themselves from the people and proclaim their own master as messiah.") However the polemic is only slightly emphasized, and it cannot be correctly maintained that this is the *primary* purpose of the Gospel. (J. A. T. Robinson, "Elijah , John and Jesus," in *Twelve New Testament Studies* [London: SCM, 1962], p. 49, n. 49 doubts the existence of such a Baptist sect. See also J. H. Hughes, "The Disciples of John the Baptist," [unpublished M. A., Durham University, England, 1969]; and "John the Baptist: the Forerunner of God Himself," *NovT* 14 [1972], pp. 191–218.).

J. Louis Martyn, *History and Theology in the Fourth Gospel* (New York and Evaston: Harper & Row, 1968; 2nd, rev. ed., Nashville: Abingdon, 1979), argued eloquently that the Fourth Gospel is to be understood against the background of a church-synagogue struggle. Martyn's book is an extremely significant contribution to Johannine studies, especially in its insistence that the Gospel must be read on two levels. The first level is the story of Jesus (the "once upon a time" level), and the second level is the story of the Evangelist's community—perceived through the Evangelist's story of Jesus. It is this insight that has laid the groundwork for much of subsequent Johannine studies, and is evident in, for example, R. E. Brown's *Community of the Beloved Disciple*.

The traditional view—following Irenaeus—that the Gospel displays a polemic against docetism has received support among scholars (see especially E. C. Hoskyns, *The Fourth Gospel*, ed. F. N. Davey [London: Faber & Faber, 1947], pp. 48–57); so too has Käsemann's position that John is to be located in a gnosticizing community—see L. Schotroff, "Heil als

Innerweltliche entweltlichung," *NovT* 11 (1969), pp. 294–317; "Joh. iv 5–15 und des johanneischen Dualismus," *ZNW* 60 (1969), pp. 199–214; *Der Glaubende und die feindliche Welt. Beobachtungen zum gnostischen Dualismus und seiner Bedeutung für Paulus und das Johannesevangelium* (Neukirchener-Vluyn: Neukirchener Verlag, 1970).

47. J. M. Robinson and H. Koester, *Trajectories Through Early Christianity* (Philadelphia: Fortress Press, 1971), pp. 259f.

48. Schnackenburg, *John*, p. 73.

49. The term was coined by E. Haenchen, *Der Weg Jesu. Eine Erklärung des Markus-Evangeliums und die Kanonischen Parallelen* (Berlin: Töpelmann, 1966), p. 24. Composition criticism should be clearly differentiated from narrative criticism. Moreover, the contrasts between the two are not simply methodological—they have different agendas. See also Stephen Moore, *Literary Criticism and the Gospels* (New Haven and London: Yale University Press, 1989).

50. R. Fowler, *Loaves and Fishes: The Function of the Feeding Stories in the Gospel of Mark* (Chico, California: Scholars Press, 1981), pp. 40–41.

51. R. Bultmann, "Η ἀλήθεια" in *TWNT*, p. 240.

52. See J. Blank, "Der johanneische Wahrheits-Begriff," *BZ* 7 (1963), pp. 164–173.

53. J. Giblet, "Aspects of Truth in the New Testament," in *Truth and Certainty*, eds. E. Schillebeeckx and Bas van Iersel (New York: Herder & Herder, 1973), pp. 36f.

54. C. H. Dodd, *The Johannine Epistles* (London: Hodder & Stoughton, 1946), p. 145.

55. C. H. Dodd, *Interpretation*, p. 177.

56. *Ibid.*, p. 174.

57. *Ibid.*, p. 176.

58. I. de la Potterie, "La verità in San Giovanni," *RivBib* 11 (1963), pp. 5f. See also his "'Je suis la Voie, la Vérité et la Vie' (Jn 14,6)," *Nouvelle Révue Théologique* 88 (1966), pp. 907–942; "Οἶδα et γινώσκω les deux modes de la connaissance dans quatrième Evangile," *Bib* 40 (1959), pp. 709–725; "L'arrière-fond du thème johannique de vérité," *Studia Evangelica* I (1959), pp. 277–294.

59. I. de la Potterie, "La verità in San Giovanni," p. 8.

60. Brown, *The Gospel According to John*, p. 16.

61. Bultmann, *John*, pp. 603–612.

62. I. de la Potterie, "'Je suis la Voie, la Vérité et la Vie,'" pp. 908–910.

63. *Ibid.*, p. 925.

64. I. de la Potterie, "La verità in San Giovanni," p. 20.

65. *Ibid.*, p. 22.
66. *Ibid.*, p. 24.
67. This observation is further borne out by E. M. Sidebottom, *The Christ of the Fourth Gospel in the Light of First Century Thought* (London: S.P.C.K.,1961). The Son of Man has descended and ascended; he alone is of heavenly origin; no one has ascended and seen the Father, but the Son of Man alone, being in the bosom of the Father, has descended to reveal him. It is in love of the Son of Man and each other that men find God—"not the Cross, nor the *kerygma*, nor any event, but the Lord himself is salvation" (pp. 97f).
68. Bultmann, *John*, pp. 371f., n. 3.
69. Bultmann, *John*, p. 376.
70. See also, Bultmann, *John*, p. 376.
71. S. Schultz, *Komposition und Herkunft der johannesichen Reden* (Stuttgart: Kohlhammer, 1960), pp. 90–131, thinks that the parables of the shepherd and the vine are unique in the Johannine discourses inasmuch as they alone are polemics against the redeemer-figures of Hellenistic gnosis. (The other discourses in John seek to demonstrate that Jesus is the fulfilment of Old Testament and late Judaistic salvific hopes.)
72. Barrett, *John*, p. 308.
73. A. Kragerud, *Der Lieblingsjünger im Johannesevangelium* (Hamburg: Grossohaus Wegner, 1959), pp. 74–81, wishes to identify the Beloved Disciple as the "other disciple" of 18:15–16 and then draw parallels between 18:15–16 and the parable of the shepherd on the basis of vocabulary (he finds eight key words in common: ἄγειν, ἀκολουθεῖν, αὐλή, γινώσκειν, εἰσελθεῖν, ἐξελθεῖν, θύρα, θυρωρός) and the traditional links which the Passion has with the shepherd motif (Mk. 1:18; 10:32,52). He maintains that the shepherd in 10:11–18 and 26–30 is Jesus but in 1–5 and 7–10 the shepherd is the church leader. This parable of the shepherd illuminates the meaning of 18:15–16: for the Beloved Disciple ". . . als der rechte Hirte, geht durch die θύρα in die αὐλή hinein, er ist dort ein Bekannter, und die θυρωρός öffnet ihm die Tür" (p. 78). The story is in fact a *Parallelgestalt*; there are two shepherds (Peter and the Beloved Disciple) but Peter is only a shepherd through the Beloved Disciple (pp. 79–80). We shall discuss the relationship between the Beloved Disciple and Peter below.
74. It is interesting to note that in *Ego Eimi* E. Schweizer argued that the "I am" sayings were to be explained in terms of a Mandaean background. He has since partially abandoned this thesis (see *Gemeinde und Gemeindeordnung im Neuen Testament* [Zürich: Zwingli-Verlag, 1959], pp. 106f., n. 446; ET: *Church Order in the New Testament* [SBT 32; Naperville: Allenson, 1961], p. 118, n. 446), precisely because of his

reconsideration of the parables of the shepherd and the vine.

75. Bultmann, *John*, p. 530.
76. Brown, *The Gospel According to John*, p. 674.
77. Barrett, *John*, p. 393.
78. Bauer, *Lexicon*, p. 237.
79. The word παράκλητος is peculiar to the Fourth Gospel and I John. It occurs four times in the Gospel (14:15–17; 14:26; 15:26–27; 16:7–11) and once in I John (2:1). Many scholars believe that the traditional Christian identification of the Paraclete with the Holy Spirit obscures the fact that originally the Paraclete was an independent salvific figure. It is also maintained by some that the Paraclete references are secondary. Such views arise from the consideration of such fundamental questions as: Why is the title παράκλητος unique to the Johannine corpus? To what (or to whom) does the title refer: the third person of the Trinity? Some impersonal God-given force? Jesus' alter-ego? Answers to these questions would be easier if the etymology of the word παράκλητος could be ascertained with some certainty. Unfortunately, it cannot. The word does not seem to derive from an Aramaic or Hebrew original and therefore the meaning of the term has to be deduced from Greek cognates. R. E. Brown has summarized four possible alternatives. ("The Paraclete in the Fourth Gospel," *NTS* 13 (1967), pp. 113–132. See also *John*, pp. 1135–1143). First, παράκλητος is possibly a passive from the Greek παρακαλέω. Thus it would mean "one called alongside to help" (so frequently rendered "advocate"). Such an interpretation is supported by such texts as Mt 10:20 and Acts 6:10. Unfortunately, as Brown points out, this interpretation is not supported by the *Johannine* texts on the Paraclete, and neither does it "do justice to his [the Paraclete's] role as teacher" ("The Paraclete," p. 117). Second, παράκλητος could be taken in an active sense from ("intercede," "appeal to")—thus, "intercessor," "mediator." This interpretation is supported by I John 2:1, but not by the Gospel texts. Other attempts to render παράκλητος as "helper" may also be deemed unsuccessful. (See Bauer, *Johannesevangelium* on 14:16; Bultmann, *John*, pp. 566–572; and the criticisms of W. Michaelis, "Zur Herkunft des johanneischen Paraklet-Titels," *Coniectanea Neotestamentica* XI (Upsaliense; Lund: C.W.K. Gleerup, 1947), pp. 147–162. Third, possibly the word παράκλητος reflects the meaning of "to comfort"— thus, "comforter," "consoler." Although the idea of consolation appears in the Last Discourse, it does not appear in the specific passages on the Paraclete. Fourth, perhaps the word relates to the Greek word παράκλησις ("exhortation"). C. K. Barrett, "The Holy Spirit in the Fourth Gospel," *JTS* 1 (1950), p. 14, claims that "the Paraclete is the Spirit of Christian paraclesis." But this seems to be a rather restrictive and exclusive under-

standing of παράκλητος, for an examination of the texts suggests that the title is meant to evoke more than this single meaning from the reader. J. Behm, *TWNT*, p. 813, n. 99, thinks that the attempt of Barrett "to ignore derivation from the religious world around and to find the background of the Johannine use of παράκλητος simply in apostolic proclamation is not very convincing in view of the wealth of comparative material available."

Having discussed these four possibilities, Brown makes four further points which he believes will help us to understand the paraclete in the Fourth Gospel. First, he speaks of the "tandem relationship," i.e., "a principal figure dies and leaves another to take his place, carry on his work and interpret his message" ("The Paraclete," p. 120). Thus in the Fourth Gospel the Paraclete carries on the work and interprets the message of Jesus. Second, there is "the concept of the Spirit of God coming upon the prophets that they might speak the words of God to men" (*Ibid.*). In the Fourth Gospel the Paraclete inspires Christians to speak. Third, a study of late Jewish angelology supplies parallels to the teaching function of the Paraclete. Fourth, a study of Jewish angelology is also instructive in revealing the forensic aspect of the Paraclete's work. Thus, an examination of the Jewish background is not uninstructive inasmuch as there we do find the same basic elements as appear in the Johannine description of the Paraclete. Ultimately, however, an examination of the texts themselves is most rewarding in revealing the function of the Paraclete in the Johannine redaction.

80. There are two possible translations of v. 16: he will give (a) "another Paraclete" or (b) "another person to be a Paraclete" (i.e., "another, a Paraclete"). The context suggests strongly the continuity of the offices of Jesus and the Paraclete and there seems little justification for rejecting the sense of (a) which is more in accord with Johannine style.

81. Here the Paraclete is identified with the Holy Spirit. It is, however, quite likely that the original reading should simply be "the holy one," and some later Christian scribe transcribed instead "Holy Spirit." Thus simply to equate the Paraclete with the third person of the Trinity on the basis of this verse glosses over the fact that probably that was not its original sense. This Paraclete does, however, come in Jesus' name i.e., he acts in his place and with his authority. R. Spitta, *Das Johannes-Evangelium als Quelle der Geschichte Jesu* (Göttingen: Vandenhoeck & Ruprect, 1910), pp. 316ff., 358, believes that a redactor made the identification of the Paraclete with the Holy Spirit and that only the following verses are original: 16:7 f.; 16:12–14; 14:14, 16a–b. See also H. Delafosse, *La quatrième Evangile. Traduction nouvelle avec introduction, notes et commentaire* (Paris: Rieder, 1925), pp. 105ff.; O. Betz, *Der Paraklet*

Fürsprecher im häretischen Spätjudentum, Johannes-Evangelium und im neu gefundenen gnostischen Schriften (Leiden/Köln: E. J. Brill, 1963). H. Sasse, "Der Paraklet im Johannes-Evangelium," *ZNW* 24 (1925), 260–277, says that in the Fourth Gospel there are two groups of statements about the Paraclete. One group (15:26–27 and 16:7–11) belongs to an earlier tradition—here a human personality filled with the Spirit and a creator of tradition is meant. This personality Sasse identifies as the Evangelist himself (the Beloved Disciple). (A. Kragerud, *Der Lieblingsjünger im Johannesevangelium*, also makes this identification.) The later tradition (14:15–17, 26) identifies the Paraclete with the Holy Spirit.

    82. Brown, *John.*, p. 712.

    83. Brown, "The Paraclete," p. 128.

    84. The argument of the following pages is that the Beloved Disciple is of central importance in the Johannine redaction, in stark contrast to the thesis of R. Mahoney, *Two Disciples at the Tomb: The Background and Message of John 20.1–10* (Frankfurt: Peter Lang, 1974). Mahoney maintains that the anonymity of this disciple indicates that the Evangelist wished to "keep him a secondary figure, in the background" (n. 103, p. 90). It is, says Mahoney, a "misunderstanding" to see this mysterious disciple as of "central importance to the Evangelist's message as a whole" (p. 304).

    85. Brown, *John*, p. 582.

    86. Bultmann, *John*, pp. 457–637.

    87. J. H. Bernard, *A Critical Commentary on The Gospel According to St.John*, 2 Vols. Ed. A. L. McNeil (Edinburgh: T&T Clark, 1928), pp. xxxiv–xxxvii.

    88. See the extended note of Bultmann, *John*, pp. 469f., n. 2. One of the best arguments for a sacramental interpretation is that of M. -E. Boismard, "Le lavement des pieds (Jn xiii 1–17)," *RB* 71 (1964). A forceful argument against is presented by G. Richter, *Die Fusswaschung im Johannesevangelium: Geschichte ihrer Deutung* (Regensburg: Pustet, 1967).

    89. Bultmann, *John*, p. 479.

    90. Brown, *John*, p. 587.

    91. Bultmann, *John*, p. 486.

    92. Brown, *John*, pp. 858f.

    93. The traditional view is that he was John the son of Zebedee. Irenaeus and Polycrates make this identification (Eusebius, *Ecc. Hist.*, V, 8, 4; V, 24, 3). For further second-century witnesses, see J. Coulson, *L'énigme du Disciple que Jesus aimait* (Theologie Historique 10; Paris: Beauchesne, 1969), pp. 29–63. The most impressive argument for this identification is still in B. F. Wescott, *The Gospel According to St. John* (rev. ed., 1908), pp. xxi–xxv. Others who make this identification include:

J. D. Michaelis, *Introduction to the New Testament* (London: F. & C. Rivington, 1802), III, p. 318; W. Sanday, *The Criticism of the Fourth Gospel* (New York: C. Scribner's Sons, 1905), p. 252; F. -M. Braun, *Jean le Theologien*, pp. 396f.; D. Guthrie, *New Testament Introduction: The Gospels and Acts* (London: Tyndale, 1965), p. 224; H. Rigg, "Was Lazarus 'the Beloved Disciple'?" *ExT* 33 (1921–1922), pp. 232–234; D. G. Rogers, "Who was the Beloved Disciple?" *ExT* 77 (1966), p. 214; B. Silva Santos, "A autoria do Quarto Evangello," *Revista Biblica Brasileira* 5 (1988), pp. 157–181; R. Schnackenburg, *John* pp. 97–104, cautiously identified the Beloved Disciple with John, but has subsequently changed his mind—see "On the Origin of the Fourth Gospel" and "Der Jünger, den Jesus liebte." The traditional evidence in favor of the identification is in fact very suspect (see Kümmel, *Introduction*, pp. 165–174). Moreover, many arguments adduced in favour of the identification center around a comparison with the Synoptics, which does raise certain difficult hermeneutical questions. That is, it seems incumbent upon any commentator who wishes to adduce parallels to first explain precisely how he sees the relationship between John and the Synoptics—for if they both conceive of history in a different way, or have different historical concerns, comparisons can be (at the very least) misleading, and possibly even invalid. In his commentary on John, pp. lxxxvii–cii, R. E. Brown accepted that "John's historical tradition is somewhat of a challenge to the general tradition shared by the Synoptics," but argued that the authority behind the Gospel (to be identified with the Beloved Disciple) was likely to be a real authority in the Church—"a man of status not unlike Peter's"—i.e., John the son of Zebedee. He also relied heavily on arguments which can only be substantiated by a comparison with the Synoptics. He argued that the Beloved Disciple must be identified with one of the Twelve (because of his presence at the Last Supper); that he was probably one of the "inner three" who in the Synoptics are closest to Jesus; moreover, in the Synoptics John often appears with Peter; and in Acts, Peter and John are companions in Jerusalem (Acts 3–4) and on the mission to Samaria (8:14), a fact of significance when one notes a Samaritan mission in the Fourth Gospel. He went on to identify the Beloved Disciple with John the Son of Zebedee (*John*, pp. xcviff.). He subsequently changed his mind, however—see *The Community of the Beloved Disciple*, pp. 33f.: "I am inclined to change my mind . . . from the position that I took in the first volume of my AB commentary identifying the Beloved Disciple as one of the Twelve, viz., John the son of Zebedee. I insisted there on a combination of external evidence and internal evidence which made this the strongest hypothesis. I now recognize that the external and internal evidence is probably not to be harmonized." In the Fourth Gospel *itself* there is no mention of an "inner three," and it is not stated that only the Twelve were at the Last Supper. Indeed, the evidence of the Gospel itself militates against the identification of John the son of Zebedee with the Beloved Disciple—see P. Parker, "John the Son of Zebedee and the Fourth Gospel," *JBL* 81 (1962), pp. 33–43.

The Beloved Disciple has been identified with Lazarus by R. Eisler, *The Enigma of the Fourth Gospel* (London: Methuen, 1938); J. N. Sanders, "Those Whom Jesus Loved (John XI, 5)," *NTS* 1 (1954–1955), pp. 29–41; "Who was the Disciple whom Jesus loved?," in *Studies in the Fourth Gospel*, ed. F. L. Cross (London: A. R. Mowbray, 1957), pp. 72–82; F. V. Filson, "Who was the Beloved Disciple?" *JBL* 68 (1949), pp. 83–88; P. Nepper-Christensen, "Hvem var den discipel, som Jesus elskede?" *Dansk Teol Tids* 53 (1990), pp. 81–105; K. A. Eckhardt, *Der Tod des Johannes als Schlüssel zum Verständnis der johanneischen Schriften* (Studien zur Rechts-und Religionsgeschichte 3, Berlin: De Gruyter, 1961). Eckhardt also wishes to identify Lazarus with John the son of Zebedee.

Others wish to identify the Beloved Disciple with John Mark: L. Johnson, "Who Was the Beloved Disciple?" *ExT* 77 (1966), pp. 157–158; responded to by J. R. Porter, "Who was the Beloved Disciple?" *ExT* 77 (1966) pp. 213–214 and D. G. Rodgers, "Who was the Beloved Disciple?" *ExT* 77 (1966), p. 214.; Johnson replied in *ExT* 77 (1966), p. 380.

There have been yet other suggestions. E. L. Titus, "The Identity of the Beloved Disciple," *JBL* 69 (1950), pp. 323–328, argues for Matthias. M. Hengel, *The Johannine Question* (London, 1989), suggests he is John the Elder mentioned by Papias; B. W. Bacon, *The Fourth Gospel in Research and Debate* (London: T. Fisher Unwin, 1910), pp. 301–331, thinks he is Paul. Lindars, *John*, p. 33, regards this particular suggestion as "grotesque," although Bultmann, *John*, p. 484, n. 5, who still regards the suggestion as "impossible" is more sympathetic: "If one had to posit an actual historical figure who represented [this] free Christendom for the Evangelist, Bacon's view that Paul is intended is best as regards the subject matter."

94. The previous note indicates the difficulties of identifying the Beloved Disciple with John the son of Zebedee. The identification of the Beloved Disciple with Lazarus begins with the assumption that somewhere the Evangelist would indicate the identity of the Beloved Disciple. Given this premise, Lazarus becomes the most likely candidate in view of the fact that the Gospel does state that Jesus "loved" Lazarus (11:5). However, this argument *still* leaves the difficulty of why the Beloved Disciple is not named in chs. 13, 19, and 20. (The particular argument that 11:1–44 and 12:9–11 were added later to the work at a time when the

Evangelist had decided to abandon the anonymity of the disciple is no answer, for it fails to take into account that his identity is still concealed in the postscript.) The proponents of this view have the merit of seeking a solution based in the text itself. However, what they seem unable to accept is the fact that the Evangelist simply does not tell us (for whatever reason) who the Beloved Disciple is. The argument that the Beloved Disciple is John Mark rests on very slender external evidence and unfortunately has no basis in the text. The idea that he is Titus or Paul need not even be considered.

95. Bultmann asserts that there is no accounting for the fact that the Beloved Disciple is never spoken of by name unless he is a symbolic figure. He thinks we must begin with John 19:26f.: "If the scene has symbolic significance, which can scarcely be doubted, it can only be that the mother, professing loyalty to the crucified, and remaining at the cross to the end, stands for Jewish Christendom. And the Beloved Disciple therefore represents Gentile Christendom—not of course with regard to its ethnic character, but insofar as it is the authentic Christendom which has achieved its own true self-understanding. The self-awareness of this Christendom, emancipated from the ties of Judaism, shows itself in the two scenes 13.21–30 and 20.2–10, where the Beloved Disciple appears beside Peter, the representative of Jewish Christendom. It is he and not Peter who reclines in Jesus' bosom, and can mediate Jesus' thought. And the relation between Jewish and Gentile Christendom is portrayed in a characteristic fashion in 20.2–10, where each in his own way, by using the term in two senses, can claim to be 'in front of' the other" (*John*, p. 484). Bultmann leaves out of account in such an interpretation 19:35 and chapter 21, because he regards the former as a redactional gloss and the latter as a redactional appendix. (He freely concedes the point that in chapter 21 "the term beloved disciple stands for a particular historical figure, clearly an authoritative one for the circle which edits the Gospel and one whose authority is placed side by side with that of Peter"—*Ibid.*, p. 483.)

Käsemann proffers the following opinion in "Ketzer und Zeuge. Zum johanneischen Verfasserproblem," *ZTK* 48 (1951), p. 180.: "If, together with the whole of critical research [*sic*], one rejects the historicity of this figure, seeing in him rather the embodiment of the ideal witness, one may even more precisely designate him as a projection of the author and his community into the Gospel history."

The most thorough-going and detailed argument for the interpretation of the Beloved Disciple as a symbolic figure is offered, however, by A. Kragerud, *Der Lieblingsjünger im Johannesevangelium* (Oslo: Osloer Universitätus Verlag; Hamburg: Grossohaus Wegner, 1959). In his work, Kragerud considers that besides the three places in the Fourth Gospel where the Beloved Disciple is explicitly mentioned (13:23, 19:26, and 20:2), two other passages refer to him: 18:18f. and 1:35–40; (he also of course appears in ch. 21). Kragerud considers that the material in these passages is freely invented and cannot be understood unless the Beloved Disciple is a symbolic figure. He considers it self-evident that the Beloved Disciple is of great significance in the interpretation of the Fourth Gospel, and finds the key to such interpretation in this disciple's relationship to Peter. Accordingly, he devotes much of his work to examining the meaning of the Beloved Disciple and Peter Gestalten. The Beloved Disciple represents a Christian "pneumatic" circle: "So ist L als der Representant eines kirchlichen Dienstes, und zwar eines 'pneumatishen' aufzufassen" (p. 82). Peter represents the ecclesiastical office, but the rivalry represented by Peter and the Beloved Disciple is not a matter of teaching but of practice. That is, the apostolic itinerant prophets represented by the Beloved Disciple considered themselves to be the "intellectual" leaders of the communities and conceded their authority to the ecclesiastical office holders in "external matters."

This monograph does have the merit of seeking to locate the historical horizon of the Johannine community. (In particular, it is worth noting that he seeks to relate the Johannine community to the Johannine letters, and often concurs with Käsemann, e.g., "Dass Diotrephes kein anderer als eine Amtsperson in der Gemeinde sein kann, sollte eigentlich selbstverständlich sein," p. 107.) The monograph, however, is open to rather serious difficulties. In particular, not only does he have difficulty with his exegesis of 1:35–42 (see A. Dauer, "Das Wort des Gekreuzigten an seine Mutter und 'der Jünger, den er liebte'," *BZ* 12 [1968], p. 89), but his collective interpretation of 21:24 is untenable (see R. Schnackenburg's review of the book in *BZ* 4 [1960], pp. 302–307, esp. 304f.).

96. One difficulty with purely symbolic interpretations is that they fail to come to terms with the fact that the figures with whom the Beloved Disciple is associated—Peter, Mary, and Jesus himself—are historical (even if a symbolic dimension is attributed to them). It seems to be somewhat incoherent to propose an interpretation in which a purely symbolic figure is juxtaposed with historical ones.

97. This is also the position of the following scholars: T. Lorenzen, *Der Lieblingsjünger im Johannesevangelium* (Stuttgarter Bibel Studien 55; Stuttgart: KBW Verlag, 1971), who says: "For it ought not to be maintained that the Beloved Disciple is no more than an historical figure [*Gestalt*]. Certainly he also has ideal and symbolic traits, but just these traits reflect his important position in the history of the Johannine community, his significant role for the typically Johannine theology, and also the theological situation of the community itself" (pp. 80f.). R. Schnack-

146 THE JOHANNINE WORLD

enburg, "Zur Herkunft des Johannes evangelium," *BZ* 14 (1970) ("On the Origin of the Fourth Gospel," *Jesus and Man's Hope,* ed. P. G. Buttrick) p. 234: "I would say, therefore, that we must settle the controversy in favour of a historical person, but without depriving him of paradigmatic significance." Brown, *John,* p. xcv: "That the BD has a figurative dimension is patent. In many ways he is the exemplary Christian, for in the NT 'beloved' is a form of address for fellow Christians. Yet this symbolic dimension does not mean that the BD is nothing but a symbol." W. Grundmann, *Zeugnis und Gestalt des Johannesevangeliums. Eine Studie zur denkerischen und gestalterischen Leistung des vierten Evangelisten* (Arbeiten zur Theologie 7; Stuttgart: Calwer Verlag, 1961), pp. 71f.: "He is the bearer of revelation and as such a witness and characterization of the historicity of Jesus; he has his position in a charismatic group of the last phase of early Christianity. The Son is the revealer of the Father, the Beloved Disciple of the Son . . . The Beloved Disciple is both individual and type; he dies as individual, he lives on as type." M. Dibelius seems to equivocate: in "John 15, 13: Eine Studie zum Traditionsproblem des Johannesevangeliums," in *Festgabe für Adolf Deismann zum 60. Geburtstag 7. November 1926* (Tübingen: Mohr, 1927), p. 180, he sees the Beloved Disciple as "the man of belief," the representative of "*the* disciple"; however, in *Die Formgeschichte des Evangeliums,* ET: *From Tradition to Gospel* (London: Ivor Nicholson & Watson Ltd., 1934), p. 216, n. 2, he concedes that he is a historical figure who probably belongs to a priestly family in Jerusalem.

98. Schnackenburg, "On the Origin of the Fourth Gospel," p. 235: "There is no possibility that this is an historical scene in the strict sense."

99. Schnackenburg, "On the Origin of the Fourth Gospel," p. 235: the Beloved Disciple is thus presented to the readers "as the disciple closest to Jesus, as his confidant"; Barrett, *John,* p. 372: "The specially favoured disciple is represented as standing in the same relationship to Christ as Christ to the Father"; (Lorenzen, *Der Lieblingsjünger im Johannesevangelium,* pp. 83f., takes exception to this formulation by Barrett—only a *similar* relationship is meant, and one may not speak of it as the *same*).

100. It has been argued that Peter could not speak out aloud because the meal was modelled on that of either the Essene or Qumran community. At such meals one could only speak in due order—IQS 6:10. See especially K. G. Kuhn, "The Lord's Supper and the communal meal at Qumran," in *The Scrolls and the New Testament,* ed. K. Stendahl (New York: Harper, 1969), p. 69. This interpretation suggests, however, that this is meant to be a historical scene rather than an ideal one.

101. It is true that Jesus does not specifically *name* Judas to the

Beloved Disciple, but to assume that the Beloved Disciple did not understand the reply of Jesus (v. 26) is to assume that he was rather dim-witted, which hardly squares with the general picture we are given of him.

102. So Kragerud, *Der Lieblingsjünger im Johannesevangelium*, p. 22.

103. Contrary to, for example, Arthur A. Maynard, *Understanding The Gospel of John* (Lewiston: Edwin Mellen Press, 1991), who sees a deliberate attempt to denigrate Peter here. He says, "In the Synoptic Gospels Peter is clearly the leader of the disciples, but when one turns to the Fourth Gospel, there is an obvious depreciation of his importance . . . while the disciples are still in the upper room, Peter is further depreciated, first by his position at the table, and second by having him fail to understand the statement of Jesus that he is going where they cannot follow . . . In view of the prominent role played by Peter in the Synoptics and in the early chapters of Acts, one is forced to ask, why this depreciation of Peter and exaltation of the beloved disciple which is carried so consistently through the book? If the symbolism of the beloved disciple as the charismatic church leadership is accepted, one does not have far to look for the answer, for Peter was very early associated with Rome, and the Roman church very early based its authority on Peter. Could it not be that through this gospel the leader of the Johannine community of churches is saying (1) that Peter (i.e., Rome) needed a lesson in humility, (2) that Peter (i.e., Rome) was not superior to, but subservient to, the the total church, (3) that Mary (i.e., the whole church) was responsible for carrying on his work, and that (4) no one section of the church could claim priority for the faith?" (pp. 57ff.)

104. Bultmann, *John*, p. 673.

105. So E. Meyer, "Sinn und Tendenz der Schlusszene am Kreuz im Johannesevangelium (Joh 19, 25–27)," *Sitzungsberichte der Preussischen Akademie der Wissenschaften. Philosophisch-Historische Klasse* (1924), pp. 157–162.

106. A. Dauer, "Das Wort des Gekreuzigten an seine Mutter und 'der Jünger, den er liebte,'" *BZ* 11 (1967), pp. 222–239 and 12 (1968), pp. 80–93. Brown, *John*, p. 904, criticizes this position.

107. Cf. Brown, *John*, p. 925: "The episode at the foot of the cross has these details in common with the Cana scene: the two scenes are the only places in the Gospel that the mother of Jesus appears; in each she is addressed as "Woman"; at Cana her intervention is rejected on the grounds that Jesus' hour has not yet come, but here we are in the context of Jesus' hour . . . In becoming the mother of the Beloved Disciple (the Christian), Mary is symbolically evocative of Lady Zion who, after the birth pangs, brings forth a new people in joy (John xvi 21; Isa xlix 20–22, liv1, lxvi 7–11)."

108. Dauer, "Das Wort des Gekreuzigten," p. 81.

109. K. Quast, *Peter and the Beloved Disciple: Figures for a Community in Crisis* (Sheffield: Sheffield Academic Press, 1989), p. 120: "No contrast is intended between the faith of the Beloved Disciple and apparent lack of faith on Peter's part. Rather, the faith of the Beloved Disciple is emphasized for the purpose of encouraging the readers to respond in a similar act of faith."

110. Bultmann, *John*, p. 684.

111. *Ibid.*, p. 685.

112. Contrary to Mahoney, *Two Disciples at the Tomb*, who argues that there is no significance to the relationship of Peter and the Beloved Disciple. Mahoney claims that a careful reading of 20:1–10 shows that "the touted race was not intended as a race at all, but represents the evangelist's device to bring the two disciples separately onto the same scene for related but independent assignments. Peter's assignment, as the best known human bond between later believers and the historical Jesus of Nazareth, was to notarize the precisely recounted details of the tomb's interior. The details leave no doubt that this is Jesus' tomb, where the preceding pericope had seen him laid, and that the body cannot have been hastily removed by any third party, whether friend or foe. The assignment of the other disciple is one that Peter or another of the historical disciples could not so easily have filled without involving the continuing narrative with consequences they wanted to avoid; in other words, his assignment is functionally like those he carried out in chapters 13 and 19. His mission is, faced with the details Peter had notarized for all of us, to see and believe, thus illustrating that the empty tomb can work analogously to a sign in prodding faith, in being the means by which God can draw the reader of the Gospel to believe" (p. 307). In treating the narrative in this way Mahoney destroys its structural and thematic integrity.

113. He initiates the electing of the successor of Judas (Acts 1:15–22); he speaks on the day of Pentecost (2:14–41); he is the first Apostle to perform a miracle in the name of Jesus (3:1–10); he is the spokesman before the Sanhedrin (4:1–21); it is he who pronounced judgement on Ananias and Sapphira (5:1–11). It is true, however, that James appears to take over Peter's position in Jerusalem at an early date—quite possibly after Peter accepts the principle of the Gentile mission by admitting Cornelius to the Church (10:1–11, 18).

114. Peter is, of course, a key figure in Matthew—G. Bornkamm, "The Authority to 'Bind' and 'Loose' in Matthew's Gospel: The Problem of Sources in Matthew's Gospel," *Perspective* II (1970), p. 48: "The congregation which acts in Matthew 18:15–18 knows itself as founded on the teaching of Jesus as guaranteed through Peter."

115. Cf. Eusebius, *Ecc. Hist.*, III, iii, 6.

116. This is, of course, a thorny issue. Ignatius (Rom. 4:2) seems to suggest that Peter and Paul were persons of special authority in Rome, and Irenaeus (*Adv. Haer.*, III, i, 2; III, iii, 1) explicitly says that they founded the Church in Rome. Eusebius (*Ecc. Hist.*, II, xxv, 5–8) cites both Gaius of Rome and Dionysius of Corinth as substantiating this tradition.

117. So, similarly, Quast, *Peter and the Beloved Disciple*, pp. 122f.: "A move toward bringing the Apostolic and Johannine Christians together is discernible throughout the Gospel of John, and it finds its culmination in the final chapter of the Gospel. The passages which bring Peter and the Beloved Disciple together may reflect a later stage in the composition of the Gospel, but this is not to suggest that they are contrary to the Johannine tradition. At least a part of the Johannine community eventually followed the lead of the Gospel and entered in to a 'partnership' with the Apostolic stream. This is indicated by the presence of the Johannine literature in the New Testament canon."

118. M. Pamment, "The Fourth Gospel's Beloved Disciple," *ExT* 94 (1983), p. 367, interprets the reference to the death of the Beloved Disciple as a symbolic reference to the possible death of Gentile Christianity. She follows Bultmann in seeing Peter as the representative of Jewish Christianity and the Beloved Disciple as the representative of Gentile Christianity. Citing 21:22 she declares, "The saying would naturally give rise to the belief that Gentile Christianity or Gentile Christians would not die before the final transformation of the world . . . the saying in Jn 21:23 tries to obviate these difficulties . . . in other words, the saying is open-ended. The fate of Gentile Christianity is uncertain."

119. It is sometimes maintained that "these things" refer only to the contents of chapter 21. Years ago T. Zahn, *Einleitung in das Neue Testament* (Leipzig: A. Deichert, 1897–1899); ET: *Introduction to the New Testament*, III, (Edinburgh: T&T Clark, 1909), p. 237, made a point which is still valid: "If it was necessary to assure the readers that chap. 21 was written by the Beloved Disciple of Jesus, it was even more important to make clear to them who wrote chaps. i–xx."

120. Bultmann, *John*, p. 718, n. 1.

121. In 1:35–42 two disciples of John the Baptist follow Jesus. One of the two, Andrew, next brings Simon Peter (his brother) to Jesus. If the reading πρῶτος (1:41) be accepted, then the unnamed disciple would be one of a pair of brothers, i.e., James or John. However, the reading πρῶτον is probably preferred (so also Barrett, *John*, pp. 151f.) and this reading does not allow such an inference. To assume that the reader is supposed to identify the Beloved Disciple with the unnamed disciple is

entirely unwarranted by the text (so also Lorenzen, *op. cit.*, pp. 37–46). In the other pericope (18:15–17), "another disciple," known to the High Priest, brings Peter into the High Priest's courtyard. The fact that this disciple is not named and is associated with Peter has led many to speculate that he is the Beloved Disciple. But again, this is unwarranted by the text, which simply does not support the identification (see Bultmann, *John*, n. 4, p. 645).

122. W. Sanday, *The Criticism of the Fourth Gospel* (New York: C. Scribner's Sons, 1905), pp. 75f.

123. J. Roloff, "Der johanneische 'Lieblingsjünger' und der Lehrer der Gerechtigkeit," *NTS* 15 (1968), pp. 129–151.

124. Lorenzen, *Ibid.*, p. 105.

125. R. E. Brown, *The Community of the Beloved Disciple*, p. 116.

126. In what follows I am indebted to J. Painter, *John: Witness and Theologian*, pp. 115–127.

127. This history is recounted in chart form in Chart One in *The Community of the Beloved Disciple*, pp. 166–7.

128. Brown, *The Community of the Beloved Disciple*, p. 112.

129. *Ibid.*, p. 117.

130. Cf. J. O'Grady, "The Role of the Beloved Disciple," *Biblical Theology Bulletin* 9 (1979), p. 64: "In any reading of the gospel or epistles there appears a sectarian consciousness, a sense of exclusivity. This sensibility is sharper in I Jn (2.15–17) but it is also present in the gospel (3.16–17; 12.47; 17.9–14, 21, 23) . . . *The sectarianism is without dispute*" (emphases added).

131. W. Meeks, "The Man From Heaven in Johannine Sectarianism," *JBL* 9 (1972), pp. 44–72.

132. *Ibid.*, p. 71.

133. J. H. Neyrey, *An Ideology of Revolt: John's Christology in Social Science Perspective*, (Philadelphia: Fortress Press, 1988).

134. Neyrey, p. 209.

135. Two other scholars who have taken a line similar to Meeks and Neyrey are Bruce Malina and Mark Stibbe. Malina concludes that the language of the Fourth Gospel is an anti-language, the language of an antisocial group. He claims that the Johannine community is a "counter-society" which is typical of a "social collectivity that is set up within a larger society as a conscious alternative to it" (B. Malina, "The Gospel of John in Socio-Linguistic Perspective" *48th. Colloquy of the Centre for Hermeneutical Studies*, ed. H. Waetjen (Berkeley: Centre for Hermeneutical Studies, 1985), p. 11. Stibbe believes that the "future of redaction criticism of John's Gospel depends upon its moving away from the hypothetical reconstructions of Martyn and Brown and moving towards the

more sociological approaches of Wayne Meeks and Bruce Malina" (*John as Storyteller: Narrative Criticism and the Fourth Gospel* [Cambridge: C.U.P., 1992], p. 61.) Stibbe's own effort seeks to "highlight the relationship between narrative and social identity in John's story" and to show how the narrative recreates "the sense of family and home in a people faced with the crisis of metaphorical and actual homelessness" (p. 166). Norman R. Petersen, *The Gospel of John and the Sociology of Light: Language and Characterization in the Fourth Gospel* (Valley Forge, Pennsylvania: Trinity Press International, 1993), also, like Malina, speaks of an "anti-language." The Fourth Evangelist has a "special language" which is the "anti-language of the anti-society. The Johannine community is anti-society because it understands itself as other to the dominant society that has made it other. The very identity of his [the Evangelist's] people is dependent upon their being other, and this is evident in their special use of the everyday language of the society that has rejected them" (p. 89). Thus for Petersen the Fourth Evangelist's use of special "anti-language," which gives the community its sectarian character, arises out of opposition to the language of a Jewish community that had persecuted it.

136. Neyrey, p. 209.

137. E. F. Scott, *The Varieties of New Testament Religion* (New York: C. Scribner's Sons, 1944), p. 15.

CHAPTER 3. UNDERSTANDING THE MODERN CONTEXT

1. For an excellent discussion of this term see Ched Myers, *Binding the Strong Man: A Political Reading of Mark's Story of Jesus* (Maryknoll: Orbis Books, 1988), pp. 3–38.

2. George Grant, *Technology and Justice* (Toronto: Anansi, 1986).

3. See E. Layton, "Conditions of Technological Development," in *Science, Technology and Society: A Cross-Disciplinary Approach*, eds. I. Spiegel-Roesing and D. De Solla Price (London and Beverley Hills: Sage Publications, 1977), pp. 208ff. See also John M. Staudenmaier, *Technology's Storytellers: Reweaving the Human Fabric* (Cambridge, Mass.: MIT, 1985), pp. 95–103.

4. J. Salomon, *Science and Politics*, (London: Macmillan, 1973).

5. J. R. Ravetz, "Criticisms of Science," in *Science, Technology and Society*, p. 80.

6. See R. MacLeod, "Changing Perspectives in the Social History of Science," in *Science, Technology and Society*, pp. 151–59.

7. R. Ruerup, "Historians and Modern Technology: Reflections on the Development and Current Problems of the History of Technol-

ogy," *Technology and Culture* 15 (1974), p. 162. Quoted by Staudenmaier, *Technology's Storytellers*, p. 134.

8. In the capitalist world efficiency has become equated with profitablity. A technology is deemed efficient only if it is profitable.

9. Jaques Ellul, *The Technological Society*, trans. John Wilkinson, (New York: Knopf, 1964). See also *Le Systeme technicien* (Paris: Calmann-Levy, 1977). ET: *The Technological System*, trans. J. Neugroschel (New York: Continuum, 1980). A good summary of Ellul's views appears in his article "The Technological Order," *Technology and Culture* 3 (1962), pp. 394–421.

10. Ellul, "From Jacques Ellul," *Katallagete* 2 (1970), p. 5: "Since 1935, I have been convinced that on the sociological plane, technique was by far the most important phenomenon, and that it was necessary to start from there to understand everything else." As Paul Thompson, "Ellul and Technology," *Cross Currents* 34 (1984), p. 133, remarks, studies of Ellul have been "plagued by the opacity of 'technique'." Thompson continues: "In early translations, the French 'technique' was translated as English 'technique'; but Ellul's use of the term . . . was a substantial deviation from common English speech. In *The Technological System* Ellul explains that his use of the French 'technique' was intended to appeal to French colloquial designation of the processes of constructing and exploiting machines, as distinct from the science of these processes, for which he uses the French 'technologie'. It turns out that 'technique' is technology, while 'technologie' is engineering."

11. Ellul, *Technological Society*, p. xxv.

12. *Ibid.*, p. 5.

13. "Henceforth, there will be no conflict between contending forces among which technique is the only one. The victory of technique has already been secured. It is too late to set limits to it or put it in doubt. The fatal flaw in all systems designed to counterbalance the power of technique is that they come too late" *Ibid.*, p. 130.

14. See *ibid.*, p. 80: "[Man] is a device for recording effects and results obtained by various techniques. He does not make a choice of complex, and, in some way, human motives." Also, p. 135: "Man is reduced to the level of a catalyst. Better still, he resembles a slug inserted into a slot machine, he starts the operation without participating in it."

15. *Ibid.*, p. 141.

16. *Ibid.*, p. 58. See also his, *Metamorphose du Bourgeois* (Paris: Calmann-Levy, 1967), pp. 255ff.

17. Ellul, *Metamorphose du Bourgeois*, pp. 218ff.

18. As Langdon Winner, *Autonomous Technology: Technics-out-*

of-control as a theme in Political Thought (Cambridge, Mass.: MIT Press, 1977), p. 348. n. 46.

19. Ellul, "La Technique et les Premiers Chapitres de la Genesis," *Foi et Vie* 59 (1960), pp. 112f.

20. Ellul, "A little Debate About Technology," *Christian Century* 90 (1973), p. 707.

21. Ellul, *Hope in Time of Abandonment*, trans. C. E. Hopkin (New York: Seabury Press, 1973), p. 212.

22. Ellul, *The Meaning of the City*, trans. Dennis Pardee (Grand Rapids, Mich.: Wm. B. Eerdmanns, 1970), p. 21.

23. Ellul, "La Technique," pp. 110f.

24. Ellul, *The Betrayal of the West*, trans. Matthew J. O'Connell (New York: Seabury, 1978), p. 137.

25. Katharine C. Temple, *The Task of Jacques Ellul: A Proclamation of Biblical Faith as Requisite for Understanding the Modern Project* (unpublished Ph.D. dissertation, McMaster University, 1976), p. 440.

26. Ellul, "From Jacques Ellul," *Katallagete* 2 (1970), p. 5.

27. Ellul, "'The World' in the Gospels," *Katallagete* 6 (1974), p. 19.

28. "Notes Préliminaires" p. 4.

29. Jerry Mander, *Four Arguments for the Elimination of Television* (New York: William Morrow and Company, Inc., 1978), p. 44.

30. This is how the blurb describes Clara G. Livsey's *The Marriage Maintenance Manual: How to Get into It and How to Keep It Going* (New York: Dial Press, 1977).

31. See Langdon Winner, *Autonomous Technology* (Cambridge, Mass.: MIT Press, 1977) and *The Whale and the Reactor: A Search for Limits in an Age of High Technology* (Chicago: University of Chicago Press, 1986).

32. See George P. Grant, "The Computer Does Not Impose on Us the Ways It Should Be Used" in *Beyond Industrial Growth*, ed. A. Rotstein (Toronto: University of Toronto Press, 1976), pp. 117–31. The title is, of course, used ironically. For a view different from that of Grant, see R. D. Schwartz, "Where is Silicon Culture?" *Canadian Journal of Sociology* 11 (1986), pp. 57–68.

33. Arthur Koestler, *The Heel of Achilles: Essays 1968–1974* (London: Hutchinson, 1974).

34. Desmond Morris, *The Naked Ape: A Zoologist's Study of the Human Animal* (New York: McGraw-Hill, 1967), p. 14, and K. Lorenz, *On Aggression* (New York: Harcourt, Brace and World Inc., 1963), esp. pp. 192ff.

35. George Grant, "The University Curriculum," in *Technology and*

Empire (Toronto: House of Anansi, 1969), pp. 113–33.

36. *Ibid.*, p. 119.

37. *Ibid.*, pp. 119f.

38. Cf. Ellul, "The Technological Order," pp. 414f.: "The further we advance into the technological society, the more convinced we become that, in any sphere whatever, there are nothing but technical problems. We conceive all problems in their technical aspect, and think that solutions to them can only appear by means of further perfecting techniques. In a certain sense we are right; it is true that Technique permits us to solve the majority of the problems we encounter. But we are compelled to note (perhaps not often enough) that each technical evolution raises new problems, and that, as a consequence, there is never one technique which solves one problem. The technological movement is more complicated; one technique solves one problem, but at the same time creates others."

39. See George Grant, *Technology and Empire*, p. 114, n. 3: liberalism is " a set of beliefs which proceed from the central assumption that man's essence is his freedom and that therefore what chiefly concerns man in this life is to shape the world as he wants it."

One of the many ironies of liberalism is that not only does it discard limits imposed by traditional teaching, but it also ignores the implications of such thinkers as Darwin. In Darwin's thought the human being is no longer the apogee of creation but shares the same "brute origin" as other creatures. Liberalism, however, exalts human beings above other creatures by endowing them with the freedom to control nature for their own purposes (See R. Gruner, "Science, Nature and Christianity," *JTS* 26 [1975], pp. 77f.) Technology is concerned with the control of nature, but if human beings are part of nature then technology and human freedom are ultimately opposed to each other. Thus here we have an inherent contradiction in liberalism. It is interesting that much of science fiction is more consistent than liberalism in this regard and displaces humans from their central position in the world—see, for example, Carl Sagan, *Contact*; Arthur C. Clarke, *Rendezvous with Rama*; and the film *Star Trek IV: The Voyage Home*.

40. The *locus classicus* is, of course, Lk 10:42: Μαριὰμ γὰρ τὴν ἀγαθὴν μερίδα ἐξελέξατο. Cf. Dom Cuthbert Butler, *Western Mysticism: The Teaching of Augustine, Gregory and Bernard on Contemplation and the Contemplative Life*, (London: Constable, 1967), p. 160: "St. Augustine has no hesitation in affirming the superiority of the contemplative life over the active. This judgement he, in common with the rest of theologians, bases in the story of Martha and Mary, which forms the theme of his discourses in various of the *Sermons*." See also Butler, p. 174: "St. Gregory follows closely St. Augustine in the teaching that though the active life is more productive than the contemplative, the contemplative is

better and greater than the active." On Origen, see *Dictionnaire de Spiritualité*, Vol. 2, cols. 1769–70. For Cassian, see cols. 1921–22. Note also Julianus Pomerius, *The Contemplative Life*, (*Ancient Christian Writers*, 4; 1947), pp. 31f.: "The active life is the journeying; the contemplative is the summit." I am grateful to my colleague David N. Bell for drawing these references to my attention.

41. F. Bacon, "The Great Instauration" in *The English Philosophers from Bacon to Mill*, ed. Edwin A. Burtt, (New York: The Modern Library, 1967), p. 13; see also *Novum Organum*, I, iii.

42. F. Bacon, *The Advancement of Learning*, Book I, ed. H. G. Dick (New York: Random House, 1955), p. 193.

43. F. Nietzsche, *The Joyful Wisdom*, trans. Walter Kaufmann in *The Portable Nietzsche* (New York: Viking Press, 1968), pp. 95f. See also my book *Christ and Modernity: Christian Self-Understanding in a Technological Age* (Studies in Religion Supplement Series 17; Waterloo: Wilfrid Laurier University Press, 1985), esp. pp. 75ff.

44. It was Feuerbach who later said "compassion is before thought."

45. B. F. Skinner, *Walden Two* (Boston: Beacon, 1964), p. 262.

CHAPTER 4. THE POLITICS OF ETERNITY: JOHANNINE THEOLOGY TODAY

1. See Käsemann's *Jesus Means Freedom* (London: SCM, 1969).

2. *Der Glaubende und die Feindliche Welt. Beobachtungen zum gnostichen Dualismus und seiner Bedeutung für Paulus und das Johannesevangelium* (Neukirchener-Vluyn: Neukirchener Verlag, 1970).

3. B. F. Meyer, *The Church in Three Tenses* (Garden City, New York: Doubleday and Co., 1971), p. 140.

4. Dorothy A. Lee, *The Symbolic Narratives of the Fourth Gospel: The Interplay of Form and Meaning* (Sheffield: JSOT Press, 1994), pp. 233f.

5. Grant, *Technology and Empire*, p. 114, n.3.

6. Gad Horowitz, "Red Tory" in *Canada: A Guide to the Peaceable Kingdom*, ed. William Kilbourn (Toronto: Macmillan, 1970), p. 257.

7. See my *Christ and Modernity*, p. 78.

8. See E. M. Sidebottom, *The Christ of the Fourth Gospel in the Light of First Century Thought* (London: S.P.C.K., 1961).

9. Sidebottom, *The Christ of the Fourth Gospel*, pp. 97f.

10. See Neyrey, p. 107.

11. G. Tinder, *The Political Meaning of Christianity: An Interpretation* (Baton Rouge: Louisiana State University Press, 1989).

BIBLIOGRAPHY

COMMENTARIES ON THE GOSPEL OF JOHN

Barrett, C. K. 1955, 1978. *The Gospel according to St. John: An Introduction with Commentary and Notes on the Greek Text.* London: S.P.C.K.

Bauer, W. 1912, 1933, 1925. *Das Johannesevangelium Erklärt.* Handbuch zum NT 6. Tübingen: J. C. B. Mohr.

——— . 1934, 1965. *Rechtgläubigkeit und Ketzerei im ältesten Christentum.* Tübingen: Mohr/Siebeck. ET: R. A. Kraft and G. Krodel, 1971. *Orthodoxy and Heresy in Earliest Christianity,* Philadelphia: Fortress Press.

Beasley-Murray, G. R. 1987. *John.* Waco, Texas: Word Publishing.

Bernard, J. H. 1929. *The Gospel according to St. John,* 2 vols. New York: C. Scribner's Sons.

Brown, R. E. 1966. *The Gospel according to John (i–xii)* Anchor Bible 29. Garden City, New York: Doubleday.

——— . 1971. *The Gospel according to John (xiii–xxi)* Anchor Bible 29a. Garden City, New York: Doubleday.

Bultmann, R. 1941, 1966. *Das Evangelium des Johannes.* With the supplement. Göttingen: Vandenhoeck & Ruprecht. ET: 1971. *The Gospel of John.* Oxford: Blackwell.

Dodd, C. H. 1963. *The Interpretation of the Fourth Gospel.* Cambridge: CUP.

Ellis, P. F. 1984. *The Genius of John: A Composition—Critical Commentary on the Fourth Gospel.* Collegeville: Liturgical Press.

Haenchen, E. 1980. *Das Johannesevangelium.* Ed. U. Busse, Tübingen: J. B. C. Mohr. ET: 1984. *A Commentary on the Gospel of John.* 2 vols. Philadelphia: Fortress Press.

Hirsch, E. 1936. *Das vierte Evangelium in seiner ursprünglichen Gestalt verdeutscht und erklärt.* Tübingen: J.B.C. Mohr.

Hoskyns, E. C. 1940, 1947. *The Fourth Gospel.* Ed. F. N. Davey, London: Faber and Faber.

Lightfoot, R. H. 1956. *St. John's Gospel: A Commentary.* Oxford: Clarendon.

Lindars, B. 1972. *The Gospel of John.* New Century Bible. London: Oliphants.

Loisy, A. 1903. *Le Quatrième Évangile.* Paris: A. Picard et Fils.

Odeberg, H. 1929. *The Fourth Gospel: Interpreted in Its Relation to Contemporaneous Religious Currents in Palestine and the Hellenistic-Oriental World.* Uppsala: Almqvist & Wiksells.

Schlatter, A. 1930, 1975. *Der Evangelist Johannes: Wie Er Spricht, Denkt und Glaubt: Ein Kommentar.* Stuttgart: Calwer Vereinsbuchhandlung.

Schnackenburg, R. 1965. *Das Johannesevangelium.* Vol. I. Freiburg: Herder. ET: 1968. *The Gospel according to St. John.* Vol. I. Trans. Kevin Smyth, New York: Herder & Herder; London: Burns & Oates Ltd.

———. 1970. *Das Johannesevangelium.* Vol. II., Freiburg: Herder. ET: 1980. *The Gospel according to St. John.* Vol. II. Trans. Cecily Hastings, Francis McDonagh, David Smith, Richard Foley. New York: Seabury Press.

———. 1975. *Das Johannesevangelium.* Vol. III., Freiburg: Herder. ET: 1982. *The Gospel according to St. John.* Vol. III. Trans. David Smith and G. A. Kon. New York: Crossroad.

Wellhausen, J. 1908. *Das Evangelium Johannes.* Berlin: Georg Reimer.

Westcott, B. F. 1880, 1882. *The Gospel according to St. John.* London: James Clarke & Co. Ltd.

BOOKS AND ARTICLES ON THE GOSPEL OF JOHN, EARLY CHRISTIANITY, AND BIBLICAL THEOLOGY

Ashton, J., ed. 1986. *The Interpretation of John.* London: Fortress Press.

Bacon, B. W. 1910, 1918. *The Fourth Gospel in Research and Debate.* New York: Moffat, Yard and Co.

Baldensperger, W. 1898. *Der Prolog des vierten Evangeliums: Sein polemisch-apologetischer Zweck.* Freiburg im Breisgau.

Barrett, C. K. 1947. "The Old Testament in the Fourth Gospel," *JTS* 48:155–169.

———. 1950. "The Holy Spirit in the Fourth Gospel," *JTS* 1:1–15.

———. 1971. *The Prologue of St. John's Gospel.* London: Athlone Press.

———. 1971. "Review of R. T. Fortna, *The Gospel of Signs,*" *JTS* 22:570–74.

———. 1973, 1974. "John and the Synoptic Gospels," *ExT* 85:228–33.

———. 1975. *The Gospel of John and Judaism.* London: S.P.C.K.

———. 1982. "Christocentric or Theocentric? Observations on the Theological Method of the Fourth Gospel," in *Essays on John*. London: S.P.C.K.: 1–18.

Baur, F. C. 1847. *Handbuch zum Neuen Testament 6. Kritische Untersuchungen über die kanonischen Evangelien: Ihr Verhältnis zu einander, ihren Charakter und Ursprung*. Handbuch zum Neuen Testament 6. Tübingen: L. F. Fues.

Becker, H. 1956. *Die Reden des Johannesevangeliums und der Stil der gnostischen Offenbarungsreden*. Ed. R. Bultmann. FRLANT 50. Göttingen: Vandenhoeck & Ruprecht.

Behm, J. Παράκλετος in *TWNT*.

Betz, H. -D. 1965. "Orthodoxy and Heresy in Primitive Christianity: Some Critical Remarks on Georg Strecker's Republication of Walter Bauer's *Rechtgläubigkeit und Ketzerei im Ältesten Christentum*," *Interpretation* 19:299–311.

Betz, O. 1963. *Der Paraklet. Fürsprecher im häretischen Spätjudentum, im Johannesevangelium und in neu gefundenen gnostischen Schriften* (Arbeiten zur Geschichte des Spätjudentums und Urchristentums II). Leiden/Köln: E. J. Brill.

Bishop, E. F. 1960. "The Door of the Sheep in John 10:7–9," *ExT* 71:307–309.

Blank, J. 1963. "Der johanneische Wahrheits-Begriff," *BZ* 7:164–73.

Blinzler, J. 1965. *Johannes und die Synoptiker: Ein Forschungsbericht*. Stuttgart: KBW Verlag.

Boff, L. and C. Boff 1988. *Introducing Liberation Theology*. Trans. Paul Burns. Maryknoll: Orbis.

Boismard, M. -E. 1947. "Le chapitre xxi de Saint Jean: essai de critique littéraire," *RB* 54:473–501.

———. 1957. *St. John's Prologue*. Westminster: Newman.

———. 1964. "Le lavement des pieds (Jn xiii 1–17)," *RB* 71:5–24.

Borgen, P. 1965. *Bread from Heaven: An Exegetical Study of the Concept of Manna in the Gospel of John and the Writings of Philo*. Leiden: E. J. Brill.

Borig, R. 1967. *Der Wahre Weinstock*. Münich: Kösel.

Boring, M. E. 1978/9. "The Influence of Christian Prophecy on the Johannine Portrayal of the Paraclete and Jesus," *NTS* 25:113–23.

Bornkamm, G. 1968. "Zur Interpretation des Johannes-Evangeliums: Eine Auseinandersetzung mit Käsemanns Schrift 'Jesu letzter Wille nach Johannes 17," *EvTh* 28:8–25. ET: 1986. "Towards the Interpretation of John's Gospel: A Discussion of *The Testament of Jesus* by Ernst Käsemann," in *The Interpretation of John*. Ed. J. Ashton. Philadelphia: Fortress Press: 79–96.

———. Πρέσβυς in *TWNT*.

Bousset, W. 1909. "Ist das vierte Evangelium eine literarische Einheit?" *TrU* 12:1–12; 39–64.

———. 1912. "Johannesevangelium," *RGG* cols: 608–36.

Bowen, Clayton R. 1930. "The Fourth Gospel as Drama," *JBL* 49:292–305.

Bowman, J. 1957, 1958. "Samaritan Studies I: The Fourth Gospel and the Samaritans," *BJRL* 40:298–327.

Braun, F. -M. 1959. *Jean le théologien et son évangile dans l'Eglise anciene.* Vol. I. Paris: Gabalda.

———. 1964. *Jean le théologien.* Vol. II. Les grandes traditions d'Israel et l'accord des Ecritures selon le quatrième Evangile. Paris: Gabalda.

———. 1966. *Jean le théologien.* Vol. III. *Sa théologie. Le Mystère de Jésus-Christ.* Paris: Gabalda.

Brown, R. E. 1955. "The Qumran Scrolls and the Johannine Gospel and Epistles," *CBQ* 17:403–19; 559–74.

———. 1965. *The Gospel of John and the Johannine Epistles.* Collegeville: Liturgical Press.

———. 1967. "The Kerygma of the Gospel according to John," *Interpretation* 21:387–400.

———. 1967. "The Paraclete in the Fourth Gospel," *NTS* 13:113–132.

———. 1977. "Johannine Ecclesiology — The Community's Origins," *Interpretation* 31:379–93.

———. 1978. "Other Sheep Not of This Fold: The Johannine Perspective on Christian Diversity in the Late First Century," *JBL* 97:5–22.

———. 1979. *The Community of the Beloved Disciple: The Life, Loves and Hates of an Individual Church in New Testament Times.* New York/London: Paulist Press.

Brown, S. 1990. "The Beloved Disciple: A Jungian View" in R. T. Fortna and B. R. Gaventa, eds. *The Conversation Continues: Studies in John and Paul in Honor of J. L. Martyn.* Nashville: Abingdon Press: 366–77.

Brownson, J. 1988. "The Odes of Solomon and the Johannine Tradition," *JSP* 2:49–69.

Bruns, J. E. 1983. "Ananda: The Fourth Evangelist's Model for 'The Disciple Whom Jesus Loved'?" *Studies in Religion/Sciences Religieuses* 3: 236–43.

Büchsel, F. 1911. *Der Begriff der Wahrheit in dem Evangelium und in den Briefen des Johannes.* Gütersloh: Bertelsmann.

———. 1928. *Johannes und der hellenistische Syncretismus.* Gütersloh: Bertelsmann.

Bultmann, R. 1925. "Der religionsgeschichtliche Hintergrund des Prologs zum Johannesevangelium," *EYXAPISTHPION, Festschrift für H.*

Gunkel. Göttingen: Vandenhoeck & Ruprecht: 3–26. A slightly abbreviated version of this article may be found in *The Interpretation of John*: 18–35.

———. 1925. "Die Bedeutung der neuerschlossenen mandäischen und manichäischen Quellen für das Verständnis des Johannesevangeliums," *ZNW* 24:100–146.

———. 1928, 1930. "Untersuchungen zum Johannesevangelium," *ZNW* 27:113–63; 29:169–92.

———. 1931. *Die Geschichte der Synoptischen Tradition.* 2 neub. Aufl. Göttingen: Vandenhoeck & Ruprecht. ET: 1963, 1972. *The History of the Synoptic Tradtion.* Trans. John Marsh. New York: Harper & Row.

———. 1934. *Jesus and The Word.* New York: Charles Scribner's Sons.

———. 1957. *History and Eschatology.* Edinburgh: Edinburgh University Press.

———. 1958. *Jesus Christ and Mythology.* New York: Charles Scribner's Sons.

———. 1958. *Theologie des Neuen Testaments.* Tübingen: J. C. B. Mohr. ET: 1951–1955. *Theology of the New Testament.* 2 vols. New York: Charles Scribner's Sons.

———. 1959. "Johannesevangelium," *RGG* cols: 840–50.

———. 1960. *Primitive Christianity in Its Contemporary Setting.* Trans. R. H. Fuller. London: Collins.

———. 1964. "Das Verhältnis der urchristlichen Christusbotschaft zum historischen Jesus," *Exegetica*: 445–69. ET: "The Primitive Christian Kerygma and the Historical Jesus" in *The Historical Jesus and the Kerygmatic Christ.* Ed. C. E. Braaten and F. A. Harrisville. Nashville: Abingdon: 15–42.

———. 1968. *The History of The Synoptic Tradition.* Oxford: Blackwell.

———. 1969. *Faith and Understanding: Collected Essays.* London: SCM.

———. 1969. "The Eschatology of the Gospel of John" in *Faith and Understanding.* London: SCM: 165–83.

———. Ἀλήθεια in *TWNT.*

Carroll, K. L. 1957, 1958. "The Fourth Gospel and the Exclusion of Christians from Synagogues," *BJRL* 40:19–32.

Chapman, C. C. 1970. "Some Theological Reflections on Walter Bauer's *Rechtgläubigkeit und Ketzerei im ältesten Christentum*: A Review Article," *Journal of Eccumenical Studies* 7:564–74.

Charles, R. H., ed. 1913. *The Apocrypha and Pseudepigrapha of the Old Testament in English.* Vol. II. *The Pseudepigrapha.* Oxford: Clarendon Press.

———, ed. 1897. *The Assumption of Moses.* London: A & C Black.

Charlesworth, J. H., ed. 1972. *John and Qumran*. London: Geoffrey Chapman Pub.

————, ed. 1990. *John and The Dead Sea Scrolls*. New York: Crossroad Pub. Co.

Colwell, E. C. 1936. *John Defends the Gospel*. New York: Willett, Clark & Co.

Connick, C. M. 1953. "The Dramatic Character of the Fourth Gospel," *ExT* 65:173–76.

Coulson, J. 1969. "L'enigme du Disciple que Jesus aimait," *Theologie Historique* 10:29–63.

Cox, Harvey. 1988. *The Silencing of Leonardo Boff: The Vatican and the Future of World Christianity*. Oak Park, Ill.: Meyer-Stone.

Cullmann, O. 1976. *The Johannine Circle: Its Place in Judaism, among the Disciples of Jesus and in Early Christianity: A Study in the Origin of the Gospel of John*. London: SCM.

Culpepper, R. A. 1975. *The Johannine School: An Evaluation of the Johannine-School Hypothesis Based on an Investigation of the Nature of Ancient Schools*. Missoula: Scholars Press.

————. 1983. *The Anatomy of the Fourth Gospel: A Study in Literary Design*. Philadelphia: Fortress Press.

Dauer, A. 1967–1968. "Das Wort des Gekreuzigten an seine Mutter und 'der Jünger, den er liebte,'" *BZ* 11:222–39; *BZ* 12:80–93.

Davies, J. G. 1953. "The Primary Meaning of ΠΑΡΑΚΛΗΤΟΣ," *JTS*, n.s. 4:35–38.

Davis, G. H. 1981. *Technology — Humanism or Nihilism*. Washington: University of America Press.

Deeks, D. 1968. "The Structure of the Fourth Gospel," *NTS* 15:107–29.

Dibelius, M. 1927. "Joh 15, 13: Eine Studie zum Traditionsproblem des Johannesevangeliums" in *Festagabe für Adolf Deissmann zum 60. Geburtstag 7. November, 1926*. Tübingen: J. C. B. Mohr: 168–86.

————. 1934. *Die Formgeschichte des Evangeliums*. ET: *From Tradition to Gospel*. Trans. Bertram Lee Woolf. London: Ivor Nicholson and Watson

Dodd, C. H. 1936. *The Apostolic Preaching and Its Developments*. London: Hodder & Stoughton.

————. 1946. *The Johannine Epistles*. The Moffatt Commentary. London: Hodder & Stoughton.

————. 1953. *The Interpretation of the Fourth Gospel*. Cambridge: CUP.

————. 1963. *Historical Tradition in the Fourth Gospel*. Cambridge: CUP.

————. 1968. *More New Testament Studies*. Manchester: Manchester University Press.

Duke, P. D. 1985. *Irony in the Fourth Gospel*. Atlanta: J. Knox.

Eckhardt, K. A. 1961. *Der Tod des Johannes als Schlüssel zum Verständnis der johanneischen Schriften*. Studien zur Rechts-und Religionsgeschischte. Berlin: De Gruyter.

Ehrhardt, A. A. T. 1962. "Christianity before the Apostles' Creed," *HTR* 55:73–119. Reprinted in *The Framework of the New Testament Stories*. Manchester: University Press, 1964: 151–99.

Eisler, R. 1938. *The Enigma of the Fourth Gospel*. London: Methuen.

Ellis, P. 1984. *The Genius of John: A Composition-Critical Commentary on the Fourth Gospel*. Minnesota: Liturgical Press.

Enz, J. J. 1957. "The Book of Exodus as a Literary Type for the Gospel of John," *JBL* 76:208–15.

Eusebius, Bishop of Caesarea. *The Ecclesiastical Hisory and the Martyrs of Palestine*. Trans. H. L. Lawlor and J. E. L. Oulton. New York and Toronto: McMillan, Vol. I, 1927, Vol. II, 1928.

Evans, C. F. 1956. "The Kerygma," *JTS.*, n.s. 7:25–41.

Filson, F. V. 1949. "Who Was the Beloved Disciple?" *JBL* 68:83–88.

Fortna, R. T. 1970. *The Gospel of Signs: A Reconstruction of the Narrative Source Underlying the Fourth Gospel*. Cambridge: CUP.

———. 1970. "Source and Redaction in the Fourth Gospel's Portrayal of Jesus' Signs," *JBL* 89:151–66.

———. 1974, 1975. "Christology in the Fourth Gospel: Redaction-Critical Perspectives," *NTS* 21:489–504.

———. 1988. *The Fourth Gospel and Its Predecessor: From Narrative Source to Present Gospel*. Edinburgh: T & T Clark.

Fowler, R. M. 1981. *Loaves and Fishes: The Function of the Feeding Stories in the Gospel of Mark*. Chico, California: Scholars' Press.

Freed, E. D. 1965. *Old Testament Quotations in the Gospel of John*. Leiden: Brill.

Gardner-Smith, P. 1938. *Saint John and the Synoptic Gospels*. Cambridge: CUP.

Giblet, J. 1973. "Aspects of Truth in the New Testament" in *Truth and Certainty*. Eds. E. Schillebeeckx and Bas van Iersel. New York: Herder & Herder: 35–42.

Glasson, T. F. 1945–1946. "Inaccurate Repetitions in the Fourth Gospel," *ExT* 57:111–112.

———. 1963. *Moses in the Fourth Gospel*. London: SCM.

Goodwin, C. 1954. "How Did John Treat his Sources?" *JBL* 73:61–75.

Grassi, J. A. 1992. *The Secret Identity of the Beloved Disciple*. Mahwah: Paulist Press.

Grayston, K. 1967. "Jesus and the Church in St. John's Gospel," *LondQuartHolR* 36:106–15.

Guilding, A. 1960. *The Fourth Gospel and Jewish Worship. A Study of the Relation of John's Gospel to the Ancient Jewish Lectionary System.* Oxford: Clarendon.

Haenchen, E. 1959. "Johanneische Probleme," *ZTK* 56:19–54.

———. 1960. "Neuere Literatur zu den Johannesbriefen," *ThR* 26:1–43; 267–291.

———. 1966. *Der Weg Jesu. Eine Erklärung des Marcus-Evangeliums und der kanonischen Parallelen.* Berlin: Töpelmann.

Hanson, R. P. C. 1981. *The Continuity of Christian Doctrine.* New York: Seabury.

Harner, P. B. 1970. *The 'I Am' of the Fourth Gospel: A Study in Johannine Usage and Thought.* Philadelphia: Fortress Press.

Hartin, P. J. 1990. "The Role of Peter in the Fourth Gospel," *Neotestamentica* 24: 49–61.

Hartman, G. 1960. "Marie-Madéleine et les disciples au tombeau selon Joh. 20, 1–18" in *Judentum, Urchristentum und Kirche: Festschrift für J. Jeremias.* Beihefte zur *ZNW* 26. Berlin: Töpelmann: 141–152.

Harvey, A. E. 1976. *Jesus on Trial: A Study in the Fourth Gospel.* London: S.P.C.K.

Hawkin, D. J. 1975. "Orthodoxy and Heresy in John 10:1–27 and 15:1–17," *Evangelical Quarterly* 47:208–13.

———. 1976. "A Reflective Look at the Recent Debate on Orthodoxy and Heresy in Earliest Christianity," *Eglise et Théologie* 7:367–78.

———. 1977. "The Function of the Beloved Disciple Motif in the Johannine Redaction," *Laval Théologique et Philosophique* 33:135–50.

———. 1980. "Johannine Theology and the Johannine Transposition," *Laval Théologique et Philosophique* 36:89–98.

———. 1985. "Thirty Years Later: A Retrospective on H. E. W. Turner's *The Pattern of Christian Truth*," *Churchman* (England) 99:51–56.

———. 1987. "The Johannine Concept of Truth and its Implications for a Technological Society," *Evangelical Quarterly* 59:3–13.

———. 1990. "Ideological Commitment and Johannine Theology," *ExT* 102:74–77.

——— and T. Robinson 1990. *Self-Definition and Self-Discovery in Early Christianity: A Study in Changing Horizons.* Lewiston/Queenston/Lampeter: The Edwin Mellen Press.

Hengel, M. 1989. *The Johannine Question.* London: SCM.

Hendrick, Charles W. and Robert Hodgson, Jr., eds. 1986. *Nag Hammadi, Gnosticism, and Early Christianity.* Peabody: Hendrickson Pub. Inc.

Herzog, F. 1972. *Liberation Theology: Liberation in the Light of the Fourth Gospel.* New York: Seabury.

Hoare, F. R. 1944. *The Original Order and Chapters of St. John's Gospel*. London: Burns, Oats & Washbourne.

Hollenbach, P. 1989. "The Historical Jesus Question in North America Today," *Biblical Theology Bulletin* 19:11–22.

Horbury, W. 1982. "The Benediction of the *Minim* and Early Jewish-Christian Controversy," *JTS* 33:19–61.

Hoskyns, E. C. 1920. "Genesis i–iii and St. John's Gospel," *JTS* 21:210–18.

Howard, W. F. 1931. *The Fourth Gospel in Recent Criticism and Interpretation*. London: Epworth.

––––––. 1947. *The Fourth Gospel*. Ed. F. N. Davey. London: Faber & Faber.

Jeremias, J. 1941. "Johanneische Literarkritik," *Theologische Blätter* 20:33–46.

Johansson, N. 1940. *Parakletoi: Vorstellungen von Fürsprechern für die Menschen vor Gott in der altestestamentlichen Religion, im Spätjudentum und Urchristentum*. Lund: Hakan Ohlssons Boktryckeri.

Johnson, L.1960. "Who Was the Beloved Disciple?" *ExT* 77:157–158.

––––––. 1966. "Who Was the Beloved Disciple?" *ExT* 77:380.

Johnston, G. 1970. *The Spirit-Paraclete in the Gospel of John*. Cambridge: CUP

Jonge, M. de. 1977. *Jesus: Stranger from Heaven and Son of God*. Missoula: Scholars Press.

Käsemann, E. 1942–1946. "Rudolf Bultmann, Das Evangelium des Johannes" in *Verkündigung und Forschung, Theologischer Jahresbericht*: 182–201.

––––––. 1951. "Ketzer und Zeuge. Zum johanneischen Verfasserproblem," *ZTK* 48:292–311.

––––––. 1957. "Aufbau und Anliegen des johanneischen Prologs" in *Libertas Christiana, Festschrift für F. Delekat*. München: C. Kaiser Verlag: 75–99. ET: 1969. "The Structure and Purpose of the Prologue to John's Gospel" in *New Testament Questions of Today*. London: SCM: 138–67.

––––––. 1960. "Begründet der neutestamentliche Kanon die Einheit der Kirche?" in *Exegetische Versuche und Besinnungen* I. Göttingen: Vandenhoeck und Ruprecht: 214–25. ET: 1965. "The Canon of the New Testament and the Unity of the Church" in *Essays on New Testament Themes*. STB 41. London: SCM: 95–107.

––––––. 1965. "The Problem of the Historical Jesus" in *Essays on New Testament Themes*: 15–47.

––––––. 1966, 1971. *Jesu Letzter Wille nach Johannes 17*. Tübingen: Mohr/Siebeck. ET: 1968. *The Testament of Jesus: A Study of the*

Gospel of John in the Light of Chapter 17. London: SCM.

——. 1969. *New Testament Questions of Today*. London: SCM.

——. 1969. "The Beginnings of Christian Theology" in *New Testament Questions of Today*: 82–107.

——. 1969. "Blind Alleys in the 'Jesus of History' Controversy" in *New Testament Questions of Today*: 23–65.

——. 1969. "On the Subject of Primitive Christian Apocalyptic" in *New Testament Questions of Today*: 108–37.

——. 1969. "The Structure and Purpose of the Prologue to John's Gospel" in *New Testament Questions of Today*: 138–67.

——. 1970. *Exegetische Versuche und Besinnungen*. 2 vols. Göttingen: Vandenhoeck & Ruprecht.

——. 1988. "What I Have Unlearned in 50 Years as a German Theologian," *Currents in Theology and Mission* 15:325–35.

Kaufman, Philip S. 1991. *The Beloved Disciple. Witness Against Anti-Semitism*. Collegeville: Liturgical Press.

Klauck, Hans-Josef. 1988. "Internal Opponents: The Treatment of the Secessionists in the First Epistle," *Concilium* 200:55–65.

Koester, C. R. 1991. "R. E. Brown and J. L. Martyn: Johannine Studies in Retrospect," *BibTheol* 21:51–55.

Koester, J. 1964. "Häretiker im Urchristentum als Theologisches Problem" in *Zeit und Geschichte, Dankesgabe an Rudolf Bultmann zum 80. Geburtstag, im Aufträge der Alten Marburger und in Zusammenarbeit mit Hartwig Thyen*. Ed. E. Dinkler. Tübingen: Mohr/Siebeck: 61–76. ET: 1971. "The Theological Aspects of Primitive Christian Heresy" in *The Future of Our Religious Past*. Ed. J. M. Robinson. New York, Evanston, San Francisco, and London: Harper & Row: 65–83.

——. 1965. "GNOMAI DIAPHORAI: The Origin and Nature of Diversification in Early Christianity," *HarvThR* 58:279–318.

——. 1971. "One Jesus and Four Primitive Gospels" in *Trajectories through Early Christianity*. Eds. J. M. Robinson and H. Koester. Philadelphia: Fortress Press: 158–204.

——. 1971. "The Structure and Criteria of Early Christian Beliefs" in *Trajectories through Early Christianity*: 205–31.

Kragerud, A. 1959. *Der Lieblingsjünger im Johannesevangelium*. Oslo: Osloer Universitäts Verlag; Hamburg: Grossohaus Wegner.

Kuhn, K. G. 1969. "The Lords Supper and the Communal Meal at Qumran" in *The Scrolls and the New Testament*. Ed. K. Stendahl. New York: Harper: 65–93.

Kümmel, W. G. 1973. *The New Testament: The History of the Investigation of Its Problems*. London: SCM.

————. 1974. *The Theology of the New Testament*. London: SCM.

Kurz, W. S. 1989. "The Beloved Disciple and Implied Readers," *BibTheolBull* 19/3:100–107.

Kysar, R. 1970. *The Maverick Gospel*. Atlanta: John Knox Press.

————. 1973. "The Source Analysis of the Fourth Gospel: A Growing Consensus?" *NovT* 15:134–52.

————. 1975. *The Fourth Evangelist and His Gospel*. Minneapolis: Augsburg Publishing House.

Lee, Dorothy A. 1994. *The Symbolic Narratives of the Fourth Gospel: The Interplay of Form and Meaning*. Sheffield: JSOT Press.

Leroy, H. 1968. *Rätsel und Misverständnis: Ein Beitrag zur Formgeschichte des Johannesevangeliums*. Bonn: P. Hanstein.

Lieu, J. M. 1991. *The Theology of The Johannine Epistles*. Cambridge: Cambridge University Press.

Lightfoot, R. H. 1935. *History and Interpretation in the Gospels*. London: Hodder & Stoughton.

————. 1950. *The Gospel Message of St. Mark*. Oxford: Clarendon.

Lindars, B. 1971. *Behind the Fourth Gospel*. London: S.P.C.K.

————. 1972. *The Gospel of John*. New Century Bible. London: Oliphants.

Loader, W. 1989. *The Christology of the Fourth Gospel: Structure and Issues*. Beiträge zur biblischen Exegese und Theologie 23. Frankfurt: Lang.

von Loewenich, W. 1932. *Das Johannes-Verständnis im zweiten Jahrhundert*. Berlin: Töpelmann.

Lofthouse, W. F. 1936. *The Disciple Whom Jesus Loved*. London: Epworth.

Lorenzen, T. 1971. *Der Lieblingsjünger im Johannevangelium*. Stuttgarter Bibel Studien 55. Stuttgart: KBW Verlag.

————. 1969. *Die Bedeutung des Lieblingsjungers fur die johanneische Theologie*. Stuttgart: Ruschlikon.

MacGregor, G. H. C. 1923/24. "A Suggested Rearrangement of the Johannine Text (Jn 3, 14–36; 12, 30–36)," *ExT* 35:476–7.

———— and A. Q. Morton. 1961. *The Structure of the Fourth Gospel*. London: Oliver & Boyd.

MacRae, G. 1970. "The Fourth Gospel and *Religionsgeschichte*," *CBQ* 32:13–24.

Mahoney, Robert K. 1975. *Two Disciples at the Tomb*. Frankfurt: Peter Lang.

Martyn, J. L. 1968, 1979. *History and Theology in the Fourth Gospel*. New York and Evanston: Harper & Row; Reprinted Nashville: Abingdon.

———. 1979. *The Gospel of John in Christian History*. New York: Paulist Press.

———. 1986. "Source Criticism and *Religionsgeschichte* in the Fourth Gospel" in *The Interpretation of John*. Ed. J. Ashton: 99–121.

Marxsen, W. 1959. *Der Evangelist Markus*. Göttingen: Vandenhoeck & Ruprecht.

Maynard, A. H. 1991. *Understanding The Gospel of John*. Lewiston: Edwin Mellen Press.

McGann, D. 1988. *Journeying Within Transcendence: A Jungian Perspective on the Fourth Gospel*. New York: Paulist Press.

Meeks, W. A. 1966. "Galilee and Judaea in the Fourth Gospel," *JBL* 85:159–69.

———. 1967. *The Prophet-King: Moses Traditions and the Johannine Christology*. Leiden: Brill.

———. 1972. "The Man from Heaven in Johannine Sectarianism," *JBL* 91:44–72.

Meyer, E. 1924. "Sinn und Tendenz der Schlussene am Kreuz im Johannesevangelium (Joh 19, 25–27)" in *Sitzungsberichte der Preussischen Akademie der Wissenschaften. Philosophisch-Historische Klasse*. Berlin: Verlag der Akademie der Wissenschaften: 157–62.

Meyer, Ben F. 1970. *The Man for Others*. New York: Bruce Publishing Co.

———. 1971. *The Church in Three Tenses*. Garden City, New York: Doubleday & Co.

———. 1979. *The Aims of Jesus*. London: SCM.

———. 1989. *Critical Realism and The New Testament*. Princeton Theological Series 17. Allison Park, Pa.: Pickwick Publications.

Michaelis, W. 1947. "Zur Herkunft des johanneischen Paraklet-Titels," *Coniectanea Neotestamentica. Im honorem Antonii Fridriechsen sexagenarii edenda curavit Seminarium Neotestamentium*. Upsaliense, Lund: C. W. K. Gleerup: 147–162.

Minear, Paul S. 1977. "The Beloved Disciple in the Gospel of John: Some Clues and Conjectures," *Novum Testamentum* 19:105–23.

Miranda, J. P. 1977. *Being and The Messiah: The Message of St. John*, Maryknoll: Orbis.

Moloney, F. J. 1976. *The Johannine Son of Man*. Rome: LAS.

Moore, Stephen D. 1989. *Literary Criticism and The Gospels: The Theoretical Challenge*. New Haven: Yale University Press.

Moore, G. F. 1927–30. *Judaism in the First Centuries of the Christian Era*. 3 vols. Cambridge, Mass.: Harvard University Press.

Morgan, R, Ed. 1973. *The Nature of New Testament Theology*. London: SCM.

Mowinckel, S. 1933. "Die Vorstellung des Spätjudentums vom heiligen Geist als Fürsprecher und der johanneische Paraklet," *ZNW* 32:97–130.

Myers, C. 1988. *Binding the Strong Man: A Political Reading of Mark's Story of Jesus*. Maryknoll, New York: Orbis Books.

Neill, S. 1964, 1988. *The Interpretation of the New Testament*, London: SCM; Oxford: Oxford University Press.

Neufeld, V. H. 1963. *The Earliest Christian Confessions*. Leiden: E. J. Brill.

Newman, J. H. 1878, 1960. *An Essay on the Development of Christian Doctrine*. Reprinted. London: Sheed & Ward.

Nicholson, G. C. 1983. *Death as Departure*. Chico, California: Scholars Press.

Nock, A. D. 1964. "Gnosticism," *HTR* 57:255–79.

Norden, E. 1913. *Agnostos Theos: Untersuchungen zur Formgeschichte religiöser Rede*. Leipzig/Berlin: B.G. Teubner.

Norman, E. 1979. *Christianity and The World Order*. Oxford: O.U.P.

O'Day, G. M. 1986. *Revelation in the Fourth Gospel*. Philadelphia: Fortress Press.

O'Grady, J. 1979. "The Role of the Beloved Disciple," *BibTheolBull* 9:58–65.

Pamment, M. 1992. *Rhetoric and Reference in the Gospel of John*. Sheffield: Sheffield Academic Press.

———. 1983, "The Fourth Gospel's Beloved Disciple," *ExT* 94:363–367.

Pancaro, S. 1975. *The Law in the Fourth Gospel: The Torah and the Gospel, Moses and Jesus, Judaism and Christianity according to John*. Leiden: Brill.

Parker, P. 1956. "Two Editions of John," *JBL* 75:303–14.

———. 1962. "John the Son of Zebedee and the Fourth Gospel," *JBL* 81:33–42.

Perrin, N. 1969. *What is Redaction Criticism?* Philadelphia: Fortress Press.

Petersen, Norman R. 1993. *The Gospel of John and the Sociology of Light: Language and Characterization in the Fourth Gospel*. Valley Forge, Pennsylvania: Trinity Press International.

Porter, J. R. 1966. "Who Was the Beloved Disciple?" *ExT* 77:213–14.

Potter, B. 1962. "The Disciple Whom Jesus Loved," in *Life of the Spirit* 16:293–97.

de la Potterie, I. 1959. "L'arrière-fond du thème johannique de vérité," *Studia Evangelica* I:277–94.

———. 1959. "οἶδα et γινώσκω les deux modes de la connaissance dans le quatrieme Evangile," *Bib* 40:709–25.

————. 1963. "La Verità in San Giovanni," *RivBib* 11:3–24.

————. 1966. "'Je suis la Voie, la vérité et la Vie' (Joh 14:6)," *NRT* 88:907–42.

———— and S. Lyonnet. 1971. *The Christian Lives by the Spirit.* New York: Alba House.

————. 1977. *La Vérité dans Saint Jean, i. Le Christ et la vérité. L'Esprit et la vérité: Le croyant et la vérité.* Vol. 2. Rome: Biblical Institute Press.

————. 1986. "The Truth in St. John" in *The Interpretation of John.* Ed. J. Ashton: 53–66.

Purvis, J. D. 1975. "The Fourth Gospel and the Samaritans," *NT* 17:161–98.

Quast, K. 1989. *Peter and the Beloved Disciple: Figures for a Community in Crisis.* Sheffield: Sheffield Academic Press.

————. 1988. "Internal Opponents: The Treatment of the Secessionists in the First Epistle of John," *Concilium* 200: 55–65.

Rensberger, D. 1988. *Johannine Faith and Liberating Community.* Philadelphia: Westminster Press.

Richard, E. 1985. "Expressions of Double Meaning and Their Function in the Gospel of John," *NTS* 31:96–112.

Richter, G. 1967. *Die Fusswaschung im Johannesevangelium: Geschichte ihrer Deutung.* Regensburg: Pustet.

————. 1967. "Review of R. Schnackenburg, *Das Johannesevangelium*," *MünchTheolZeit* 18:247–50.

————. 1970. "Blut und Wasser aus der durchbohrten Seit Jesu (Joh. 19, 34b)," *MünchTheolZeit* 21:1–21.

————. 1977. *Studien zum Johannesevangelium.* Ed. J. Hainz. Regensburg: F. Pustet.

Riesenfeld, H. 1965. "Zu den johanneischen *hina*-Sätzen," *StudTheol* 19:213–20.

Rigg, H. 1921–1922. "Was Lazarus 'the Beloved Disciple'?" *ET* 33:232–34.

Robinson, J. A. T. 1957, 1962. "The Baptism of John and the Qumran Community," *HTR* 50:175–191. Reprinted in *Twelve New Testament Studies.* London: SCM: 11–27.

————. 1970. "The Destination and Purpose of St. John's Gospel" in *New Testament Issues.* Ed. R. Batey. London: SCM: 191–209.

————. 1976. *Redating the New Testament.* London: SCM

————. 1985. *The Priority of John.* London: SCM

Robinson, J. M. 1956–1957. "Review of R. Bultmann, *Theology of the New Testament II*," *Theology Today* 13:261–69.

————. 1962. "Basic Shifts in German Theology," *Interpretation* 16:76–97.

————. 1971. "The Johannine Trajectory" in *Trajectories through Early*

Christianity. Ed. J. M. Robinson and H. Koester: 232–68.

———. 1971. "*Logoi Sophon:* On the *Gattung* of Mark (and John)" in *The Future of Our Religious Past:* 84–130.

———. 1978. "Gnosticism and the New Testament" in *Gnosis: Festschrift für Hans Jonas, in Verbindung mit U. Bianchi et al.* Ed. B. Aland. Göttingen: Vandenhoeck & Ruprecht: 125–43.

——— and Koester, H, Eds. 1971. *Trajectories through Early Christianity.* Philadelphia: Fortress Press.

Rogers, D. G. 1966. "Who Was the Beloved Disciple?" *ExT* 77:214.

Rowland, C. 1988. *Radical Christianity: A Reading of Recovery.* Maryknoll, New York: Orbis Books.

Rowland, C. and M. Corner, 1989. *Liberating Exegesis: The Challenge of Liberation Theology to Biblical Studies.* Louisville: Westminster/John Knox Press.

Roloff, J. 1968. "Der johanneische 'Lieblingsjünger' und der Lehrer der Gerechtigkeit," *NTS* 15:129–151.

Ruckstuhl, E. 1951. *Die literarische Einheit des Johannesevangelium.* Ed. E. Paul. Freiburg in der Schweiz: Paulusverlag.

Sanday, W. 1905. *The Criticism of the Fourth Gospel.* New York: C. Scribner's Sons.

Sanders, J. N. 1943. *The Fourth Gospel in the Early Church.* Cambridge: CUP.

———. 1954–1955. "Those Whom Jesus Loved (John XI, 5)," *NTS* 1:29–41.

———. 1957. "Who Was the Disciple Whom Jesus Loved?" in *Studies in the Fourth Gospel.* Ed. F. L. Cross. London: A.R. Mowbray: 72–82.

Sanders, J. T. 1971. *The New Testament and Christological Hymns.* Cambridge: CUP.

Sasse, H. 1925. "Der Paraklet im Johannes-Evangelium," *ZNW* 24:260–77.

Schencke, H. M. "The Function and Background of the Beloved Disciple in the Gospel of John," in C. H. Hendrick and R. Hodgson, eds. *Nag Hammadi, Gnosticism and Early Christianity.* Peabody: Hendrickson.

Shepherd, J. J. 1970. "Norman Wisdom?" *ExT* 90:262–64.

Schmithals, W. 1967. *Die Theologie Rudolf Bultmanns, Eine Einführung* Tübingen: Mohr/Siebeck. ET: 1968. *The Theology of Rudolf Bultmann.* London: SCM.

Schnackenburg, R. 1957. "Logos-Hymnus und johanneischer Prolog," *BZ*:69–109.

———. 1960. "Review of A. Kragerud, *Der Lieblingsjünger im Johannesevangelium,*" *BZ* 4:302–7.

———. 1970. "Der Jünger, den Jesus liebte" in *Evangelisch-Katholischer Kommentar zum Neuen Testament: Vorarbeiten.* Neukirchen-Vluyn:

Neukirchener-Verlag; Einsiedeln: Benziger, Heft. 2, ed. J. Gnilka, *et al.*: 97–117.

———. 1970. "Zur Herkunft des Johannesevangelium," *BZ* 14:1–23. ET: "On the Origin of the Fourth Gospel" in *Jesus and Man's Hope* I. Ed. D. G. Buttrick: 223–46.

Schottroff, L. 1969. "Heil als Innerweltliche Entweltlichung," *NovT* 11:294–311.

———. 1969. "Joh. iv 5–15 und die Konsequenz des johanneischen Dualismus," *ZNW* 60:199–214.

———. 1970. *Der Glaubende und die feindliche Welt: Beobachtungen zum gnostischen Dualismus und seiner Bedeutung für Paulus und das Johannesevangelium.* Neukirchen-Vluyn: Neukirchener Verlag.

Schultz, S. 1960. *Komposition und Herkunft der johanneischen Reden.* Stuttgart: Kohlhammer.

Schweitzer, A. 1910, 1954. *The Quest of the Historical Jesus.* London: A & C Black.

Schweizer, E. 1939, 1965. *Ego Eimi. Die Religionsgeschichliche Herkunft und Theologische Bedeutung der johanneische Bildreden, zugleich ein Beitrag zur Quellenfrage des vierten Evangeliums.* Göttingen: Vandenhoeck & Ruprecht.

———. 1957. "Zu den Reden der Apostelgeschichte," *TZ* 13:1–11.

———. 1959. *Gemeinde und Gemeindeordnung im Neuen Testament.* Zurich: Zwingli-Verlag. ET: 1961. *Church Order in the New Testament.* Naperville: Allenson.

———. 1962. "Two New Testament Creeds Compared" in *Current Issues in New Testament Interpretation: Essays in Honor of Otto A. Piper.* Ed. W. Klassen and G. W. Snyder. New York: Harper & Row: 166–77.

———. 1966. "Zum religionsgeschichtlichen Hintergrund der 'Sendungsformel': Gal. 4, 4 f.; Rm. 8, 3 f.; Joh. 3, 16 f.; I Joh 4, 9," *ZNW* 57:199–210.

Sidebottom, E. M. 1961. *The Christ of the Fourth Gospel in the Light of First Century Thought.* London: S.P.C.K.

Sinclair, S. G. 1994. *The Road and the Truth: The Editing of John's Gospel.* Vallejo: BIBAL.

Smalley, S. S. 1970–1971. "Diversity and Development in John," *NTS* 17:276–92.

Smith, D. M. 1963–1964. "The Sources of the Gospel of John. An Assessment of the State of the Problem," *NTS* 10:336–51.

———. 1965. *The Composition and Order of the Fourth Gospel.* New Haven: Yale University Press.

———. 1984. *Johannine Chrisitianity: Essays on Its Setting, Sources, and Theology.* South Carolina: University of South Carolina Press.

Snaith, N. 1945. "The Meaning of the 'Paraclete,'" *ExT* 57:47–50.

Spitta, F. 1910. *Das Johannes-Evangelium als Quelle der Geschichte Jesu.* Göttingen: Vandenhoeck & Ruprecht.

Staley, J. L. 1988. *The Print's First Kiss: A Rhetorical Investigation of the Implied Reader in the Fourth Gospel.* Atlanta, Ga.: Scholars Press.

Stein, R. H. 1969. "What is *Redaktionsgeschichte?*" *JBL* 88:45–56.

Stibbe, M. W. G. 1993. *The Gospel of John as Literature: An Anthology of Twentieth-Century Perspectives.* Leiden: Brill.

———. 1995. *John as Storyteller. Narrative Criticism and the Fourth Gospel.* New York: Cambridge University Press.

Strack, H. L., and Billerbeck, P. 1978. *Commentar zum Neuen Testament aus Talmud und Midrasch.* 6 vols. Munich: Beck.

Strauss, D. F. 1835–1836, 1840, 1860, 1970. *Leben Jesu, The Life of Jesus Critically Examined.* Trans. from the fourth edition by Marion Evans. New York: Calvin Blanchard; Michigan: Scholarly Press.

Strecker, G. 1965. "Report on the New Edition of Walter Bauer's *Rechtgläubigkeit und Ketzerei in ältesten Christentum,*" *Journal of Bible and Religion* 33:53–56.

Streeter, B. H. 1924, 1936. *The Four Gospels: A Study in Origins.* London: McMillan.

Sykes, S. W., and J. P. Clayton, eds. 1972. *Christ, Faith and History.* Cambridge: CUP

Teeple, H. M. 1960. "Qumran and the Origin of the Fourth Gospel," *NT* 4:6–25.

———. 1961. "Methodology in Source Analysis of the Fourth Gospel," *JBL* 80:220–32.

Thompson, M. M. 1988. *The Humanity of Jesus in the Fourth Gospel.* Philadelphia: Fortress Press.

Thyen, H. "Entwicklungen innerhalb der johanneischen Theologie und Kirche im Spiegel von Joh 21 und der Lieblingsjüngertexte des Evangeliums" in *L'Évangile de Jean.* Ed. M. de Jonge: 259–99.

———. 1987. "Johannesbriefe," *Theologische Realenzyklopaedie* 17:186–200.

Thornecroft, K. 1987. "The Redactor and the 'Beloved' in John," *ExT* 98:135–39.

———. 1980. "Das Heil kommt von den Juden" in *Kirche: Festschrift für Gunther Bornkamm zum 75. Geburtstag,* Tübingen: Vandenhoeck & Ruprecht: 163–184.

van Tilborg, S. 1993. *Imaginative Love in John.* Cologne: Brill.

Titus, E. L. 1950. "The Identity of the Beloved Disciple," *JBL* 69:323–28.

Turner, H. E. W. 1954. *The Pattern of Christian Truth: A Study in the Relations between Orthodoxy and Heresy in the Early Church.* Bampton Lectures. London: Mowbray.

——. 1972. "Orthodoxy and the Church Today," *The Churchman* 86:166–173.

Wahlde, U. C. von. 1982. "The Johannine Jews: A Critical Survey," *NTS* 28:33–60.

Wead, D. W. 1970. *The Literary Devices in the Fourth Gospel.* Basle: Fredrich Reinhardt Kommissionsverlag.

White, H. 1973. *Metahistory: The Historical Imagination in Nineteenth-Century Europe.* Baltimore/London: Johns Hopkins University Press.

——. 1978. *Tropics of Discourse.* Baltimore/London: Johns Hopkins University Press.

Whiteacre, R. 1982. *Johannine Polemic.* Chico: Scholars.

Wiles, M. F. 1960. *The Spiritual Gospel: The Interpretation of the Fourth Gospel in the Early Church.* Cambridge: CUP.

Wilkens, W. 1958. *Die Entstehungsgeschichte des vierten Evangeliums.* Zollikon-Zürich: Evang Verlag.

Wilson, R. McL. 1968. *Gnosis and the New Testament.* Oxford: Blackwell.

Wilson, W. G. 1949. "The Original Text of the Fourth Gospel: Some Objective Evidence Against the Theory of Page Displacements," *JTS* 50:59–60.

Windisch, H. 1927. "Die fünf johanneische Parakletsprüche" in *Festgabe für Adolf Jülicher zum 70. Geburtstag.* Tübingen: Mohr/Siebeck: 110–37. ET: 1968. *The Spirit-Paraclete in the Fourth Gospel.* Trans. J. W. Cox. Philadelphia: Fortress Press.

——. 1933. "Jesus und der Geist im Johannes-Evangelium" in *Amicitiae Corolla: Essays Presented to James Rendel Harris.* Ed. H. G. Wood. London: 303–18.

Woll, D. B. 1981. *Johannine Christianity in Conflict.* Ann Arbor: Scholars Press.

Wrede, W. 1901. *Das Messiageheimnis in den Evangelien.* Göttingen: Vandenhoeck & Ruprecht. ET: 1971. *The Messianic Secret.* Trans. J. C. G. Greig. Cambridge/London: J. Clarke.

Wright, N. T. 1986. "'Constraints' and the Jesus of History," *Scottish Journal of Theology* 39:190.

BOOKS AND ARTICLES ON THE TECHNOLOGICAL SOCIETY

Berger, P. L., *et. al.* 1973. *The Homeless Mind: Modernization and Consciousness.* New York: Random House.

Broad, W. 1985. *Star Warriors. A Penetrating Look into the Lives of the Young Scientists Behind Our Space Age Weaponry*. New York: Simon & Schuster.

Burtt, Edwin A., ed. 1967. Francis Bacon, *The Great Insaturation* and *Novum Organum* in *The English Philosophers from Bacon to Mill*. New York: Modern Library.

Coulson, C. A. 1955. *Science and Christian Belief*. Oxford: O.U.P.

———. 1960. *Science, Technology and the Christian*. London: Epworth.

———. 1971. *Faith and Technology*. Nashville: The Upper Room.

Davis, G. H. 1981. *Technology — Humanism or Nihilism*. Washington: University of America Press.

Dick, H. G., ed. 1955. Francis Bacon, *The Advancement of Learning*. New York: Random House.

Douglas, Jack D. 1970. *Freedom and Tyranny: Social Problems in a Technological Society*. New York: Knopf.

Durbin, P. T., ed. 1980. *A Guide to the Culture of Science, Technology, and Medicine*. New York: The Free Press.

Ellul, J. 1960. "La Technique et les Premiers Chapitres de la Genesis," *Foi et Vie* 59:97–113.

———. 1962. "The Technological Order," *Technology and Culture* 3:394–421.

———. 1964, 1977. *The Technological Society*. New York: Knopf. Updated version: *Le Système technicien*. Paris: Calmann-Levy. Trans. (1980) *The Technological System*. New York: Continuum.

———. 1967. *Metamorphose du Bourgeoisie*. Paris: Calmann-Levy.

———. 1970. *The Meaning of the City*. Grand Rapids: Eerdmanns.

———. 1973. *Hope in Time of Abandonment*. New York: Seabury Press.

———. 1978. *The Betrayal of the West*. New York: Seabury Press.

———. 1980. "Nature, Technique and Artificiality," *Research in Philosophy and Technology* 3:263–83.

———. 1990. *The Technological Bluff*. Grand Rapids: Eerdmans.

Ferkiss, V. 1993. *Nature, Technology, and Society. Cultural Roots of the Current Environmental Crisis*. New York: New York University Press.

Forbes, R. J. 1958. *Man the Maker: A History of Technology and Engineering*. London: Constable and Co. Ltd.

Franklin, U. 1992. *The Real World of Technology*. Concord, Ont.: Anansi.

Gendron, B. 1977. *Technology and the Human Condition*. New York: St. Martin's Press.

Gilder, G. 1989. *Microcosm. The Quantum Revolution in Economics and Technology*. New York: Simon & Schuster.

Grant, G. P. 1966. *Philosophy in the Mass Age*. Toronto: Copp Clark.

———. 1969. *Technology and Empire*. Toronto: House of Anansi.

———. 1974, 1985. *English-Speaking Justice*, Toronto: House of Anansi.

———. 1976. "The Computer Does Not Impose on Us the Ways It Should Be Used" in *Beyond Industrial Growth*. Ed. A. Rotstein. Toronto: University of Toronto Press: 117–31.

———. 1986. *Technology and Justice*. Toronto: House of Anansi.

Hawkin, D. J. 1985. *Christ and Modernity: Christian Self-Understanding in a Technological Age*. Waterloo: Wilfrid Laurier University Press.

——— and Eileen Hawkin. 1989. *The Word of Science: The Religious and Social Thought of C. A. Coulson*. London: Epworth.

Heidegger, M. 1977. *The Question Concerning Technology and Other Essays*. New York: Haper & Row.

Idhe, D. 1979. *Technics and Praxis*. Boston: Reidel.

Jones, J. W. 1984. *The Redemption of Matter*. Washington: University Press of America.

Juenger, F. G. 1956. *The Failure of Technology*. Chicago: Henry Regnery.

Kass, L. 1974. "The New Biology: What Price Relieving Man's Estate?" in *Science, Technology and Freedom*. Eds. Willis H. Truitt and T. W. Graham Solomons. Boston: Houghton Mifflin Co.

Kaufmann, W. 1968. *The Portable Nietzche*. New York: Viking Press.

Kohák, E. 1984. *The Embers and the Stars: A Philosophic Inquiry into the Moral Sense of Nature*. Chicago: University Press.

Landes, D. S. 1969. *The Unbound Prometheus*. Cambridge, Mass.: Harvard University Press.

Leiss, W. 1972. *The Domination of Nature*. New York: George Braziller.

Lewis, C. S. 1943. *The Abolition of Man*. Oxford: O.U.P.

Lonergan, B. J. F. 1957. *Insight: A Study in Human Understanding*. London: Darton, Longman & Todd.

———. 1972. *Method in Theology*. London: Darton, Longman & Todd.

Mesthene, E. 1967. *The Myth of the Machine: Technics and Human Development*. Secker and Warburg.

———. 1970. *Technological Change*. Cambridge, Mass.: Harvard University Press.

Mitcham, C., and Mackey, R. 1972, 1983. *Philosophy and Technology: Readings in the Philosophical Problems of Technology*. New York: The Free Press.

——— and Jim Grote. 1984. *Theology and Technology: Essays in Christian Analysis and Exegesis*. Washington: University Press of America.

Monsma, S. V., ed. 1986. *Responsible Technology: A Christian Perspective*. Grand Rapids: Eerdmanns.

Muller. H. J. 1970. *The Children of Frankenstein*. Bloomington and London: Indiana University Press.

Mumford, L. 1934. *Technics and Civilization*. London: George Routledge and Sons Ltd.
Newton-Smith, W. H. 1981. *The Rationality of Science*. London: Routledge & Kegan Paul.
Polkinghorne, J. 1986. *One World*. London: S.P.C.K.
———. 1988. *Science and Creation*. London: S.P.C.K.
Rapp, F. 1974. *Contributions to a Philosophy of Technology*. Boston: Reidel.
Rhodes, R. 1986. *The Making of the Atomic Bomb*. New York: Simon & Schuster.
Rothenberg, D. 1993. *Hand's End: Technology and the Limits of Nature*. Berkeley: University of California Press.
Salomon, J. 1973. *Science and Politics*. London: Macmillan.
Schwartz, R. D. 1986. "Where is Silicon Culture?" *Canadian Journal of Sociology* 11:57–68.
Staudenmaier, J. M. 1985. *Technology's Storytellers: Reweaving the Human Fabric*. Cambridge, Mass.: MIT Press.
Strauss, L. 1975. "The Three Waves of Modernity" in *Political Philosophy: Six Essays*. Ed. Hilail Gildin. New York: Pegasus: 81–98.
Street, J. 1992. *Politics and Technology*. London: MacMillan.
Teich, A. H., ed. 1972. *Technology and Man's Future*. New York: St. Martin's Press.
Temple, K. 1980. "No Nukes is Not Enough," *Research in Philosophy and Technology* 3:223–81.
———. 1983. "Doubts about the Religious Origins of Technological Civilization," *Research in Philosophy and Technology* 6:227–40.
Thompson, P. 1984. "Ellul and Technology," *Cross Currents* 34:132–136.
Tinder, G. E. 1989. *The Political Meaning of Christianity: An Interpretation*. Baton Rouge: Louisiana State University Press.
Vahanian, G. 1977. *God and Utopia: On Church and Technique*. New York: Orbis.
Vanderburg, W. 1985. *Technique and Culture*. Vol. I, *The Growth of Minds and Cultures: A Unified Theory of the Stucture of Human Experience*. Toronto: University of Toronto Press.
Weizenbaum, J. 1976. *Computer Power and Human Reason: From Judgement to Calculation*. San Francisco: W. H. Freeman and Co.
White, L. 1976. *Virgin and Dynamo Reconsidered*. Cambridge, Mass.: MIT Press.
———. 1978. *Medieval Religion and Technology*. Berkley: University of California Press.
Wiener, N. 1964. *God and Golem: A Comment on Certain Points Where*

Cybernetics Impinges on Religion. Cambridge, Mass.: MIT Press.

Winner, L. 1977. *Autonomous Technology.* Cambridge, Mass.: MIT Press.

———. 1986. *The Whale and the Reactor: The Search for Limits in an Age of High Technology.* Chicago: University of Chicago Press.

Zuboff, S. 1988. *In the Age of the Smart Machine: The Future of Work and Power.* New York: Basic Books.

INDEX